Critical Pragmatics

Critical Pragmatics develops three ideas: language is a way of doing things with words; meanings of phrases and contents of utterances derive ultimately from human intentions; and language combines with other factors to allow humans to achieve communicative goals. In this book, Kepa Korta and John Perry explain why critical pragmatics provides a coherent picture of how parts of language study fit together within the broader picture of human thought and action. They focus on issues about singular reference, that is, talk about particular things, places, or people, which have played a central role in the philosophy of language for more than a century. They argue that attention to the 'reflexive' or 'utterance-bound' contents of utterances shed new light on these old problems. Their important study proposes a new approach to pragmatics and should be of wide interest to philosophers of language and linguists.

KEPA KORTA is Senior Lecturer in Philosophy at the University of the Basque Country. He is the co-author (with John Perry) of articles in *Mind and Language*, *Synthèse*, *Philosophy and Phenomenological Research*, and *The Stanford Encyclopedia of Philosophy*.

JOHN PERRY is Distinguished Professor of Philosophy at the University of California, Riverside and Emeritus Professor of Philosophy at Stanford University. He is the author of *The Problem of the Essential Indexical* (1993; 2000), *Reference and Reflexivity* (2001), *Knowledge, Possibility and Consciousness* (2001), and *Identity, Personal Identity and the Self* (2002), and co-author (with Jon Barwise) of *Situations and Attitudes* (1983).

T0370769

Critical Pragmatics

An Inquiry into Reference and Communication

Kepa Korta and John Perry

CAMBRIDGE
UNIVERSITY PRESS

Shaftesbury Road, Cambridge CB2 8EA, United Kingdom

One Liberty Plaza, 20th Floor, New York, NY 10006, USA

477 Williamstown Road, Port Melbourne, VIC 3207, Australia

314–321, 3rd Floor, Plot 3, Splendor Forum, Jasola District Centre, New Delhi – 110025, India

103 Penang Road, #05–06/07, Visioncrest Commercial, Singapore 238467

Cambridge University Press is part of Cambridge University Press & Assessment, a department of the University of Cambridge.

We share the University's mission to contribute to society through the pursuit of education, learning and research at the highest international levels of excellence.

www.cambridge.org
Information on this title: www.cambridge.org/9780521748674

First published 2011

A catalogue record for this publication is available from the British Library

Library of Congress Cataloging-in-Publication data
Korta, Kepa.
    Critical pragmatics: an inquiry into reference and
    communication / Kepa Korta and John Perry.
        p.   cm.
    Includes bibliographical references and index.
    ISBN 978-0-521-76497-1 (hardback)
    1. Language and languages–Philosophy.   2. Semantics.   3. Communication.
    4. Reference (Linguistics)   I. Perry, John, 1943-   II. Title.
    P107.K723 2011
    401´.45–dc22
    2011009934

ISBN   978-0-521-76497-1   Hardback
ISBN   978-0-521-74867-4   Paperback

For our beloved siblings
Mikel Korta
Susan Perry

Contents

Preface   *page* xi
Acknowledgments   xiii

1   Introduction   1
    1.1   A conversation at Hondarribia airport   1
    1.2   Three ideas   3
    1.3   The anatomy of an utterance   8
    1.4   Singular reference   12
    1.5   The plan   14

2   A short history of reference   15
    2.1   Introduction   15
    2.2   One hundred-plus years of reference   15
    2.3   The problem of cognitive significance   21
    2.4   From Kaplan to utterances   22

3   Acts, roles, and singular reference   25
    3.1   Introduction   25
    3.2   Acts and actions   25
    3.3   Roles   28
    3.4   Signs and information   30
    3.5   Gricean reference   31

4   Elements of reference   37
    4.1   Introduction   37
    4.2   Cognition and information: an analogy   37
    4.3   A modest theory of ideas   38
    4.4   Paradigm referential plans   40
    4.5   Examples   43

5   Demonstratives   46
    5.1   Introduction   46
    5.2   The professor and the portrait   47
    5.3   Forensics   48
    5.4   Walking through Donostia   51
    5.5   Truth-conditions   53
    5.6   Demonstratives and the problems of cognitive
          significance   55

vii

6   Context sensitivity and indexicals   59
    6.1   Role-contexts   59
    6.2   Indexicals   60
    6.3   Using 'I'   63
    6.4   Indexicals, dates, and time   69
    6.5   Technology and indexicals   71

7   Names   74
    7.1   Introduction   74
    7.2   Names and nambiguity   74
    7.3   Networks and reference   76
    7.4   Names and roles   82
    7.5   Names as role-coordination devices: examples   83
    7.6   Names and cognitive significance   85
    7.7   The no-reference problem   88

8   Definite descriptions   90
    8.1   Introduction   90
    8.2   Incomplete descriptions   92
    8.3   Designational truth-conditions and referring*   94
    8.4   Inaccurate descriptions   96
    8.5   Conclusion   100

9   Implicit reference and unarticulated constituents   102
    9.1   Introduction   102
    9.2   Unarticulated constituents and the supplemental nature of language 102
    9.3   Three kinds of unarticulated constituents   104
    9.4   Whence unarticulated constituents?   109
    9.5   Are unarticulated constituents a myth?   111

10 Locutionary content and speech acts   114
    10.1 Introduction   114
    10.2 Locutionary content versus what is said   114
    10.3 Locutionary acts and locutionary content   116
    10.4 Locuted but not said: some examples   118
    10.5 Locutionary versus propositional content   120
    10.6 Conclusion   124

11 Reference and implicature   125
    11.1 Introduction   125
    11.2 Grice and what is said   126
    11.3 Eros' thirst   128
    11.4 Identity, implicature, and cognitive significance   130
    11.5 The man who has run out of petrol   132
    11.6 The maxim of manner of reference   134
    11.7 Conclusion   138

12 Semantics, pragmatics, and Critical Pragmatics   139
    12.1 Introduction   139
    12.2 Situating semantics   140

	12.3	Semantic content, raw and refined	142
	12.4	Minimalism, contextualism, and Critical Pragmatics	143
	12.5	Grice's circle	147
13	**Harnessing information**		**150**
	13.1	Introduction	150
	13.2	Content	150
	13.3	Propositions and the structure of action	158
	13.4	Coding and classification	160
	13.5	Back to Hondarribia	163
14	**Examples**		**166**
Bibliography			170
Index			175

Preface

How do a professor of philosophy from Stanford and Riverside universities in California and a senior lecturer from the University of the Basque Country at Donostia (San Sebastian) end up writing a book on the pragmatics of reference together?

The connection between Stanford and Donostia started through an encounter of two members of, at the moment, a tiny set of people: the set of Basque (including Basque-American) logicians. In the 1980s, Jesus Mari Larrazabal and John Etchemendy met at a logic colloquium in England and a friendship was born; a friendship that caused an interesting exchange: various logicians and philosophers – mostly young researchers during their PhD studies, including Korta – had the opportunity to visit the philosophy department and the Center for the Study of Language and Information (CSLI) at Stanford during the 1990s. Several logicians, computer scientists, psychologists, and philosophers – including Perry – took part in workshops and conferences in Donostia in more or less the same period. The research atmosphere of Stanford and, especially, the interdisciplinary approach of CSLI inspired the most determined people in Donostia to create the Institute for Logic, Cognition, Language and Information (ILCLI). In 2002, proposed by the Institute, the University of the Basque Country conferred on Perry the honorary degree of Doctor Honoris Causa.

In 2001, CSLI had not much space available, so Perry was kind enough that summer to share his office with Korta, who at the time was working on the semantics/pragmatics divide and the pragmatically determined elements of what is said – along with some boring stuff for a promotion that never happened. John handed a copy, still warm, of the first edition of *Reference and Reflexivity* to Kepa. It was not only less boring but also very relevant to many phenomena at the border of semantics and pragmatics, or that's what Kepa thought. We didn't talk seriously about it until later that year, when we met again at the semantics, pragmatics, and rhetoric workshop (SPR-01) in Donostia.

There, listening to some of the best specialists in semantic and pragmatics, we convinced ourselves that something was missing in the received framework of pragmatics. The picture of language as action wasn't fully accepted and exploited for the analysis of the role that conventions, the minds of the

speaker-hearers, and the conversational situation play in linguistic communication. We thought some of the ideas from *Reference and Reflexivity* would
allow us to make something between a major repair and a minor revolution in
the foundations of pragmatics.

speaker-hearers, and the conversational situation play in linguistic communication. We thought some of the ideas from *Reference and Reflexivity* would
allow us to make something between a major repair and a minor revolution in
the foundations of pragmatics.

We met several times to think, read, and write about pragmatics both in
California and the Basque Country, but it was thanks to the Diamond XX
Philosophy Institute (that is, Perry's doublewide trailer in the Sierra foothills)
that we were able to spend August of 2004 together and write our first paper:
'Three Demonstrations and a Funeral.' In that article early versions of many
of the ideas developed in this book and in our other articles can be found.
Although Austin's and Grice's pragmatics caused the fall of the code model
of communication, stressing the basic idea that language is action and that our
intentions and beliefs are critical for the right account, we remained convinced
that pragmatic theories were not adequately grounded in a theory of action.
Just to give an example, while in action theory it is common to distinguish
a plurality of contents for an act – that is, *things that are done* – depending
on several factors that can be taken as given, in pragmatics utterances were
still considered by most authors to have a single truth-conditional content –
thing that is said. We saw this 'mono-propositionalism' as a remnant of the
code model, that would be naturally overcome in our approach to utterances as
intentional acts with an interlocking structure of planned results.

With the publication of Recanati's *Literal Meaning* [Recanati, 2004] and
Cappelen and Lepore's *Insensitive Semantics* [Cappelen and Lepore, 2005] the
debate between minimalists and contextualists arrived at its height, and like
many others we felt obliged to define our view in this framework.[1] In our
approach, a level of content with no pragmatic 'intrusion' came naturally as the
minimal utterance-bound content of the utterance. This wouldn't correspond
to what is said, but it's truth-conditionally complete and apt as the 'input'
for pragmatic reasoning, giving a natural way to get out of a vicious circle
that threatens Gricean pragmatics theories and which Levinson (2000) dubbed
'Grice's circle.'

We thought that our ideas on pragmatics could also allow us to shed new light
on a classic topic that has occupied philosophers of language for a hundred-
plus years: the nature of singular reference. By studying the pragmatics of
reference, old issues could be seen in new ways. Hence the ideas for this book
were worked out.

---

[1] See [Korta and Perry, 2007b,c] in which we see ourselves as both minimalists in semantics,
certainly more radical than Cappelen and Lepore (2005) and even Borg (2004), and as moderate contextualists in pragmatics. Other positions include 'indexicalism' [Stanley, 2000] and
'situationalism' [Corazza and Dokic, 2007]; the latter seems closer to our view.

Acknowledgments

After writing this book, and using 'I' in many of our examples, we have some difficulty in telling our own individual thoughts about the issues apart. Something similar happens with our acknowledgments. We share most of our friends and colleagues, and workplaces such as the Diamond XX Philosophy Institute, so we share our feelings of gratitude to the members of the Pragmatics Project at CSLI and the Language and Communication Seminar at ILCLI, including Xabier Arrazola, Eros Corazza, Joana Garmendia, Jesus Mari Larrazabal, María Ponte, and Larraitz Zubeldia. We are also thankful to the students of our graduate seminar on the philosophy of language at Stanford in 2009. Perry's discussions with Robin Jeshion and their students in a pragmatics seminar at the University of California at Riverside were very helpful, and special thanks are due to Megan Stotts from that seminar, who gave us detailed comments on an earlier draft of this book. Our friends Jérôme Dokic and Stefano Predelli also gave us very helpful comments.

Hilary Gaskin, Joanna Garbutt, and Gillian Dadd from Cambridge University Press deserve special thanks for their infinite patience.

We can still tell our institutions and governments apart, so Kepa acknowledges the support of ILCLI, the Basque Government (IT323-10), and the Spanish Ministry of Science and Innovation (HUM2006-11663/FISO; FFI2009-08574). John wishes to thank the departments of philosophy at Stanford and UC Riverside, and CSLI at Stanford, for their support.

1 Introduction

1.1 A conversation at Hondarribia airport

Arriving at Hondarribia airport, John guesses that the pair of students approaching him are in charge of taking him to the pragmatics conference in Donostia. He tells them: "/ninaizdjon/." Joana, a philosopher, has heard that John is very fond of both identity statements and jokes, so she takes him to have uttered the English sentence:

(1.1) Nina is John.

Although she thinks she has identified the English sentence used, Joana is puzzled about what John could be saying. She expects he is referring to himself with his use of 'John'.[1] But then to whom is he referring with the typically feminine name 'Nina'? And why is he saying that he is Nina? What is he trying to do? She suspects John is trying to convey something funny connected with identity sentences and what philosophers say about them, but she can't figure out what this hypothetical joke might be.

Joana's friend, Larraitz, a Basque philologist, was not required to learn much about issues of reference and identity, and doesn't know much about John. This gives her an advantage in understanding what he is saying. She correctly takes John's utterance to be a use of a Basque sentence,

(1.2) Ni naiz John,

a rather literal if clumsy equivalent of 'I am John.' Her only doubts concern the proper way to greet him: shaking hands, the American way, or giving a kiss on each cheek, the usual way in this part of Europe. She decides that she should first respond to John by telling him who she is, using a more appropriate Basque word order than he had:

(1.3) Ni Larraitz naiz [I-Larraitz-am].

---

[1] We will use single quotation marks for mentioning and as 'scare' quotes. We will reserve double quotation marks for utterances, when we don't number them.

Both Joana and Larraitz wondered what John had said, and they came to different conclusions. Intuitively, there is a real issue here, with a right and wrong answer; Joana got it wrong, and Larraitz got it right. The issue isn't settled by the sounds that came out of John's mouth. And neither the fact that Basque is the language spoken in the region where the conversation takes place, nor the fact that John's native language is English, settles it either. The answer seems to be provided in large part by what John was *trying* to do, what his intentions were in making the sounds he did. In trying to figure out what John said, a large part of what Joana and Larraitz were trying to do was discover his intentions: what he meant to say. Humans engage in a lot of intentional action, and humans are rather good, given the complexity of the matter, at figuring out why other humans do what they do – at *intention discovery*. Our example suggests that human language and its understanding are an instance of this. Speaking is an intentional activity, and understanding centrally involves intention discovery.

If Larraitz were to try to explicitly reconstruct John's practical reasoning in this case, she would attribute something like the following intentions to him:

  (i) to produce a grammatical sentence of Basque by speaking;
 (ii) to use the sounds appropriate to produce the sentence '[Ni]$_{NP}$ [[naiz]$_V$ [John]$_{NP}$]$_{VP}$';
(iii) to use the indexical 'Ni' to refer to himself;
 (iv) to use the name 'John' to refer to himself;
  (v) to state that *he* is John;
 (vi) to imply that he is ready to trust them to be driven to wherever he is supposed to stay during the conference;
(vii) to please them by showing that he has learned some Basque.

Intentions do not occur on their own, but with beliefs, and one can have no reasonable hypothesis about intentions without at the same time having a hypothesis about beliefs. In John's case:

(a) beliefs about the pronunciation and grammar of some Basque expressions, phrases, and sentences;
(b) beliefs about what these expressions and phrases mean;
(c) beliefs about his own name;
(d) beliefs about the correct intonation for assertions in Basque;
(e) beliefs about what his audience would naturally infer from his assertion and the goal of the conversation;
(f) beliefs about how Basque speakers are usually very pleased to see a foreigner trying to speak their language.

In order for John to do, by speaking, what he intends to do, his beliefs need to be true or nearly so. If he is wrong about (a) and (b), he may not produce a meaningful Basque phrase at all. If, for some mysterious reason, he is wrong about his own name, he misleads. If he is wrong about (e) and (f) he won't have the effect on his listeners that he intends, even if he manages to say what he means.

1.2 Three ideas

Pragmatics is the study of how we use language to communicate, and to do the other things we use language to do. Pragmatics involves the formation of intentions on the part of speakers (including, unless noted, writers, typers, and signers) and the discovery of intentions on the part of hearers (including, unless noted, readers and sign interpreters). Pragmatics is but one of the major divisions of the study of language, but it is the one that makes sense of the others. If we look at John's plan, we see it involves knowledge of phonology, syntax, and semantics as well as intentions and beliefs about what he wants to accomplish. That is, John exercises his limited knowledge about what sounds can carry meaning in Basque, how they can be put together into phrases, and what they mean. All of this activity of John's, however, makes sense to us only when we see what he is doing or trying to do; what he wants to say, and to achieve by saying it.

Our approach to pragmatics emphasizes three ideas – we like to think of them as insights – that we think together can provide an approach to the subject that gives a coherent picture of how the parts of language study fit together within a larger picture of human thought and action.

Language as action. The first idea, that we see ourselves getting from Austin, is that language use is a way of doing things with words. Acts of using language, or *utterances*, have a basic structure that is an instance of the general structure of actions: an agent, by moving her body and its parts in various ways, in various circumstances, accomplishes things. By moving my forefinger, in the circumstance in which my hands are poised over a keyboard, I depress the 'j' key;[2] by doing that, in the circumstance in which the keyboard is suitably attached to a computer and monitor, I make a 'j' appear on the screen. As the example suggests, the circumstances and accomplishments are *nested*; wider and wider circumstances give rise to more and more remote accomplishments. By depressing the 'Return' key, in suitable circumstances, I may send an email that angers a friend, or seals a deal, or precipitates a family or departmental crisis. In our example, John makes noises in circumstances where they count as words of Basque – the circumstances being his intentions and the phonological conventions of Basque – and thereby says something, and thereby, if all goes

---

[2] Although the book is co-authored, and there really is no referent for 'I,' we find the first-person singular too effective for presenting examples to give it up.

according to plan, ensures a ride to the conference and pleases the students. As Austin said, by making noises, John performs a locutionary act (saying that he is John), an illocutionary act (introducing himself), and a couple of perlocutionary acts – pleasing Larraitz and puzzling Joana.

Communicative intentions.   The second idea, that we see coming from Grice, connects language as action to language as a possessor of content. John said *that he was John*; he conveyed *that he was happy to see the students.* We classify and describe utterances with the same devices, in particular that-clauses of the sort italicized, that we use to describe beliefs, desires, and other mental states. In a wide range of cases, these that-clauses tell us the conditions under which the belief or utterance is true, in others, the conditions under which a desire or request will be satisfied.

Grice's idea was that the meanings of phrases and contents of utterances derive ultimately from human *intentions*, and in particular a special sort of intentions, communicative intentions.[3] Communicative intentions have a feature that is characteristic of, but not limited to, the use of language. A communicative intention has its own recognition as one of its goals. John intended to get Larraitz and Joana to believe that he was John, and he intended that an early step in their coming to believe that was to recognize his intention to get them to so believe. From that, together with a bit of common sense and trust, they should conclude that the man speaking to them was indeed John.

Intentions are typically parts of plans. A plan is based on the structure of acts: one does one thing by doing another in certain circumstances. A plan combines a structure of intentions to do one thing *by* doing another with relevant beliefs about the circumstances that support each link. Of course plans can go awry, if the beliefs on which they are based are incorrect. So there are two important structures involved in utterances (and in all intentional action). There is the actual structure: what movements the agent makes, and what results are brought about, given the wider and wider circumstances in which these occur. And there is the structure of the speaker's plan: what movements he intends to make, how he takes the circumstances to be, and so what he intends to accomplish, by moving the way he does, in those circumstances.

Grice's theory of meaning is related to his famous theory of implicatures, which we discuss in Chapter 11, but there is also a certain tension between the two. The tension can be seen by reference to the 'code model' of language. The idea is that the speaker codes up his ideas according to the rules of some language in a linguistic token; the hearer perceives the token, decodes it, and thus comprehends the speaker. Semantics, especially in its more formal versions, can be seen as the key to the code. But the model falls short as an account of

---

[3] He used the term 'M[eaning]-intention' [Grice, 1969a].

all human linguistic communication, for it cannot deal with common linguistic phenomena such as ambiguity, indexicality, and illocutionary force in any straightforward way.

An original motive of Grice's theory of implicatures seemed to be to preserve an important and central place in the theory of language for the coding model and formal semantics. We use the coding model to arrive at what is said; then intention discovery takes over. But Grice's theory of meaning also seems capable of supporting a more radical critique of the code picture. Speaking is a matter of acting on a complex intention; comprehension is discovering the intention; something like coding and decoding may be peripherally involved, but it is not central. We agree with Sperber and Wilson's claim [Sperber and Wilson, 1986] that Grice's picture of meaning and communication can be interpreted either way. We are also sympathetic to their own view that treats intention formation and discovery as central, and decoding as relatively peripheral, at least for understanding ordinary communication in natural language. We return to the issue of coding in the final chapter.

If we combine Austin's and Grice's ideas, we get two results. First, that the *speaker's plan* – what the speaker intends to say and do by making the sounds he does – should be a basic unit of study in pragmatics. It is this that the hearer has to grasp to understand the utterance; it is this that we have to understand, in a way that makes clear how hearers can grasp it, in order to develop our account of pragmatics.

The second result is that what language provides, what all the conventions of Basque and English and the other languages that are recorded in dictionaries and taught to children come to, and what semantics systematically treats, are *ways of acting* and in particular *ways of disclosing one's intentions* to others. Learning language is basically a matter of learning how to do things with words, and in particular how to convey one's own intentions with the help of words, and thereby impart beliefs, desires, suspicions, and all sorts of other things.

Reflexive versus referential truth-conditions. The third idea comes from Perry [Perry, 2000, 2001b]; he thinks of it as ultimately coming from Hume, by way of Perry's work with Jon Barwise on situation semantics [Barwise and Perry, 1983] and with David Israel on information, and Israel and Syun Tutiya on action [Israel and Perry, 1990, 1991; Israel, Perry, and Tutiya, 1993]. This is the distinction between reflexive and referential truth-conditions, and more generally, the idea that utterances and other information-carrying events have different levels of truth-conditions or contents, depending on what one takes as fixed and what one allows to vary. Suppose Elwood falls off his bike, injures his arm, and goes to the emergency room to find out how bad things are. They take an x-ray of his arm, call it **F**. **F** exhibits a certain pattern ψ that shows a break. We might ordinarily say:

(1.4)   **F** shows that the person of whose arm it was taken has a broken arm.

or

(1.5)   **F** shows that Elwood has a broken arm.

Hume pointed out that nothing shows anything about the rest of the world, except given some patterns of (more or less) constant conjunction between types of events or situations. He was worried, of course, about how we could legitimately extend such patterns into the future, since our evidence for them holding was based on past observations. We're not worried about that, at least not for the purposes of this book. But we adopt and adapt the idea of (more or less) constant conjunctions as the basis for knowledge gained by observation. Following Barwise and Perry we'll call them 'constraints'; they require that if one type of situation occurs, so does another.

The basic idea is that what an event or a state of a thing – like that pattern on Elwood's x-ray – shows is relative to a constraint. It shows what the rest of the world has to be like, for the event to have occurred, or the thing to be in that state, given the constraint. This conception of the information carried by an event (what is shown by an event; the informational content of an event), makes sense of (1.4), given the constraint:

(1.6)   If an x-ray y of a human arm exhibits pattern ψ, then *the person of whose arm y was taken* has a broken arm.

When we instantiate this to **F** and discharge the antecedent, we get (1.4).

This doesn't yet make sense of (1.5), however. Elwood isn't part of the constraint. Most x-rays that exhibit ψ do not show that Elwood has a broken arm, fortunately. Elwood's relevance is that he plays the role, relative to **F**, identified by the antecedent of (1.5). We can say that (1.5) gets at what the rest of the world must be like given first, the constraint (1.6), and, second, the fact,

(1.7)   Elwood is the person of whose arm **F** was taken.

Now consider the propositions

(1.8)   That the person of whose arm **F** was taken has a broken arm.

(1.9)   That Elwood has a broken arm.

Notice that (1.8) is a proposition that is ultimately about **F** *itself*. For this reason Israel and Perry call (1.8) the *reflexive* information carried by **F**, or, more correctly, carried by the event or fact that **F** exhibits pattern ψ.[4] In the terminology of this book, we could call it the *x-ray-bound* information. Suppose

---

[4] They also sometimes call it the 'pure' information, for reasons lost in the fog of history.

a nurse found the x-ray on the floor, with no indication of whose arm had been x-rayed. She would know that the person it was of had a broken arm, but she would have no way of identifying that person except as the person of whom it was taken; her knowledge is *bound*, in that sense, to the x-ray **F**.

(1.9) on the other hand is not about **F** but about Elwood. It could be true even if **F** were never taken; Israel and Perry call (1.9) the *incremental* information carried by **F**, by which they meant that it gets at what the rest of the world must be like, for the x-ray to turn out as it did, given not only the constraint (1.6) but also, in addition, the 'connecting fact' (1.7).

In *Reference and Reflexivity* and elsewhere, Perry argues that basically the same distinction needs to be made, in the philosophy of language, with respect to the truth-conditions or content of utterances. The idea is that we can consider under what conditions an utterance might be true – or more precisely, what the rest of the world has to be like for the utterance to occur and be true – simply given the constraints on truth-conditions provided by the meanings of words as fixed by the conventions of language, or, taking in addition, further facts about the utterance, such as the speaker, time, place, and objects referred to with the use of names and demonstratives. Suppose Elwood says

(1.10) I have a broken arm.

Call his utterance **u**.

The rules of English tell us that

(1.11) Any English utterance **u** of the form 'I have a broken arm' is true if and only if the speaker of **u** has a broken arm.

If we instantiate **u** and discharge the antecedent, we get, as the truth-conditions of **u**:

(1.12) That the speaker of **u** has a broken arm.

That's what Perry calls the 'reflexive truth-conditions' of **u**, as we do in this book, but we also call it the 'utterance-bound' truth-conditions. If, in addition, we are given that fact,

(1.13) Elwood is the speaker of **u**

then we get (1.9) as the truth-conditions of **u**. Perry calls this the 'referential' truth-conditions, or content, of **u**, as do we in this book.

Given the complexity of language, and especially the different sorts of roles that the rules of language establish, the simple distinction between utterance-bound and referential truth-conditions gives way to a more complex scheme, as we shall see in the ensuing chapters.

1.3   The anatomy of an utterance

Now let's return to John's utterance. John's act is in a sense rather simple; he simply produces the sound '/ninaizdjon/.' And yet by doing this he manages to do something rather complex; there is a lot of structure in his plan of action. He intends to make certain sounds, and thereby produce certain phonemes of Basque, and thereby say something, and thereby have various effects on his listeners. The sound '/ninaizdjon/' makes only an incremental contribution to accomplishing all of this; John relies on a lot of structure that is already in place. He relies on the conventions of Basque, on the structure of the particular situation, in which the students will see him as using language to say something to them, and he relies on the structure of human psychology and Basque culture. John's utterance is hardly a very dramatic example; wars have been started, discoveries promulgated, lives saved, and philosophical positions refuted by pronouncing a few suitable syllables in the right situations.

John realizes that the effects he wants to have on Joana and Larraitz will not be produced merely by their hearing the sounds '/ninaizdjon/.' He wants them to know that he is John; they will do this by recognizing that he is saying he is John (and trusting that he is sincere and knows who he is). They will recognize what he is saying by recognizing what he is trying to say. If John's pronunciation is too terrible, or his syntax too garbled, he might try to say that he was John and not manage to say it. And yet Larraitz might still have figured out what he was trying to say, and that's what would have been important in her coming to believe that he was John. But of course, usually the best way to convey to people what you are trying to say is to successfully say it.

John also wants to convey to Joana and Larraitz that he is happy to put the next leg of his journey in their hands. This fact does not follow from the fact that he is John. Indeed, he might have made his pleasure and relief clear without using language at all, simply by looking pleased and entrusting his luggage to them to carry to the car. His communication, though not involving language, still fits the Gricean model; his intention is not simply to get help with his bag, but to let them know he is pleased to be in their hands, by their recognizing that he intends to convey this.

Finally, John wanted to please Joana and Larraitz by his efforts to learn a little Basque. Just saying that he is John won't get this effect. He has to say it in a certain way – in Basque, not in English, and in good enough Basque to suggest he has made some effort. Here the intention is not Gricean. John wants to please them, but not necessarily by recognition of his intention to do so. He wants to please them because they are impressed with the quality of his Basque and the effort that must have gone into learning even that much of this notoriously difficult language. This is what Austin calls a perlocutionary effect, a result of one's saying what one does, but a further effect, not something one does *in* saying it.

Joana's and Larraitz's task is then, in a sense, quite formidable. Their challenge is to infer, from the few sounds they hear, the complex of intentions, the plan of action, that animates John. Just as John could not hope to accomplish what he plans without relying on pre-existing structures, they have no hope of discovering his intentions without building on a lot of structure: the conversational situation, the larger situation involving the conference, human psychology, John's psychology, and the conventions of language. Larraitz meets the challenge, while Joana does not.

Joana's problems began with a wrong hypothesis about John's overall purpose in speaking – what he was trying to do by saying what he did. This is what we call *far-side pragmatics*, that is, pragmatic reasoning about why the speaker says what he does, what he is trying to communicate or accomplish by saying it. This mistake of Joana's led to a mistake about *near-side pragmatics*, that is, pragmatic reasoning about what the speaker is trying to say by producing the sounds he does. If she hadn't suspected that John was trying to be funny, then when she saw that the apparent English sentence, (1.1), made no sense, she might have questioned her assumption that he was speaking English, and recognized his less than fluent Basque for what it was.

The near-side and far-side terminology suggests that there is a central aspect of an utterance that marks an important divide. Historically, this aspect has been identified with 'saying something,' and we'll stick with that terminology for now, although in time we'll use Austin's concept of a *locutionary act* to explicate it. The picture is that a speaker produces sounds *in order to say something*, and says something *in order to accomplish further results* – to communicate further information, or to perform various speech acts. The sorts of knowledge and planning that the speaker has to bring to bear on the near side to get something said have largely to do with the conventions of language. He needs to know that certain sounds are ways of producing certain phonemes in a given language; that producing a certain string of phonemes is a way of producing a certain sentence in that language; and that in that language and in the context he is in, producing that sentence is a way of saying what he has chosen to say. His reasoning on the far side, about what he will accomplish in or by saying what he does, has mostly to do with people, context, and culture rather than the conventions of the language he uses. John drew on his meager knowledge of the conventions of Basque to say that he was John; he drew on his slightly more extensive knowledge of Basques to realize that by saying this, he would communicate his pleasure in having the students take charge of his journey, and please them with his efforts to speak their language.

1.3.1   Far-side traditions

Both Austin and Grice focus on what speakers try to do beyond saying what they do; Grice on their further communicative intentions, Austin on the speech acts they intend to perform in or by saying it. From the 1960s until the mid 1980s, with some important exceptions, such issues of far-side pragmatics dominated the field of pragmatics.

Grice was concerned with making a distinction among the contents conveyed by an utterance – within the 'utterance meaning,' in his terminology. He distinguished between what a speaker *says* and what she *implicates* in uttering a sentence. He convincingly showed that there always are contents that a speaker communicates without saying. The speaker does not codify them in sentences, so they are not there for the hearer to decode. The hearer has to infer them, attending to pragmatic principles and contextual information aimed at recognizing the speaker's intentions, because the speaker's communicative intentions are intended to be recognized by the addressee. Grice thus showed that there is much more to human communication than using semantics of language to code up one's thoughts in language, and decode the utterances of others. Pragmatic reasoning is also critical for a theory of human linguistic communication. This was particularly clear for the case of implicatures. In our example, intentions (i–v) and beliefs (a–d) would be the relevant ones for determining what John said; the remaining ones would affect what he implicated by his saying it and other perlocutionary aspects of his utterance.

Austin was concerned with the difference between what a person said and other 'speech acts' that he performs, and, in this latter class, between those things he does *in* saying what he does (the 'illocutionary acts') and those things he does *by* saying what he does (the 'perlocutionary acts'). So he made a threefold distinction among the different levels of a speech act, so that intentions (i–iv) and beliefs (a–c) would correspond to the *locutionary* act performed, all those plus intention (v) and belief (d) would determine the illocutionary act performed, and the remaining one would be relevant to the (intended) *perlocutionary effects* of the speech act. Austin's threefold distinction and Grice's twofold distinction are not competitors, but complement one another. In their broad lines, at least, most philosophers and linguists accept both sets of distinctions.

Hence both Grice and Austin saw a major theoretical break between what is said (or the locutionary act) and the further things accomplished in speaking. Study of that latter is the sort of pragmatics we call 'far-side pragmatics.' If this line is identified with the border between semantics and pragmatics, far-side pragmatics is all there is to the discipline.

1.3.2   Near-side debates

But as our example makes clear, far-side pragmatics does not exhaust pragmatics. That is, intention and intention-discovery are involved on the near side, when the speaker figures out what he needs to say and how he needs to say it in order to do what he wants to do, and when the hearer figures out what the speaker intended to say. This is what we call 'near-side pragmatics': that part of pragmatics concerned with the formation and discovery of intentions that are relevant to determining what is said.

The importance of near-side pragmatics is particularly clear from the hearer's point of view. Larraitz and Joana are presented with the sound '/ninaizdjon/.' This sound constrains what John might be saying, but does not determine it, as the different hypotheses of Joana and Larraitz show. They need to figure out what language John intends to be speaking and what words he intends to be using.

At first glance, it might seem that the approach to intention discovery developed in the service of far-side pragmatics cannot be employed with near-side pragmatics: we face an apparent circle. Far-side pragmatics is based on looking for the reasons the speaker might have had for *saying* what he did. As Grice put it:

He has said that p; there is no reason to suppose that he is not observing the maxims, or at least the C[onversational] P[rinciple]; he could not be doing this unless he thought that q; he knows (and knows that I know that he knows) that I can see that the supposition that he thinks that q is required; he has done nothing to stop me thinking that q; he intends me to think, or is at least willing to allow me to think, that q; and so he has implicated that q. [Grice, 1967a; here 1989, p. 31]

But we cannot very well use *what the speaker said* as evidence to work out what language he used, and what words he intended to employ, and with which of their meanings. All of these things must be grasped, before we can figure out what he said. We seem to be involved in what Levinson called 'Grice's circle':

Grice's account makes implicature dependent on a prior determination of 'the said.' The said in turn depends on disambiguation, indexical resolution, reference fixing, not to mention ellipsis unpacking and generality narrowing. But each of these processes, which are prerequisites to determining the proposition expressed, may themselves depend crucially on processes that look indistinguishable from implicatures. Thus what is said seems both to determine and to be determined by implicature. [Levinson, 2000, p. 186]

The way out of this circle, and one of the major themes of this book, is illustrated by our example. Theories in the philosophy of language are often shaped by an assumption, often implicit, that intention formation and discovery are *linear* processes. One recognizes the language and the words; one selects among the possible meanings based partly on context; one determines the content – what is said, the proposition expressed – with further appeals to context; then, one employs Gricean reasoning to figure out why the speaker said what he did – what additional (or alternative) information he intended to convey, and what speech act he is trying to perform – and finally, perhaps, one figures out what acts he actually performed, perhaps quite unintentionally. Each 'level' determines, possibly with the help of appropriate contextual information, the next.

Joana and Larraitz clearly did not limit themselves to linear reasoning. Each of them tries to come up with a coherent account of a number of aspects of John's act: what language he was using, what words he was using, what he was saying, why he was saying it. These aspects need to fit together; each aspect constrains the others. Coming up with a theory that works is not a matter of successively computing functions, going from sounds to phones to meanings to contents. Rather, like most reasoning, it is a matter of coming up with a theory, or more modestly an account, of what is going on that satisfies a number of constraints.

Giving up the linear picture does not require giving up the idea that what is said, or the locutionary act, is a major divide in understanding an utterance. But Joana and Larraitz need not be able to *express* what John said to start their reasoning; it suffices that they have a *description* of what is said. They can identify what John said as 'what John said, in the utterance I just heard.' They then look for an account that makes sense of all of their evidence; that is, one that is constrained by the sounds they heard, the rules of the languages he might have been speaking, the meanings of the words he might have been using, and the further intentions he might have had in speaking, and the beliefs he might have had about the situation he is in.

As we said above, the key concept of our theory is that of a *speaker's plan*. We regard the distinction between semantics and pragmatics as one to be made within the context of the speaker's intentions, having to do with the tools he intends to use to accomplish his goals. Semantics basically provides an understanding of how the conventions of language permit us to use certain sounds to refer to various objects, predicate certain properties, and express emotions, moods, and intentions. Pragmatics deals with the overall intentions one has in using language, the ways in which these intentions can be conveyed using conventional and non-conventional resources, and the strategies for intention discovery.

1.4   Singular reference

While we hope and plan to extend our pragmatic theory to a large number of topics, in this book we focus on the pragmatics of singular reference. Reference occurs when a speaker intends to impart to the hearer a belief about a particular object, that it has a certain property (broadly speaking), or of several objects, that they stand in a certain relation (broadly speaking), and does so by referring to that object and predicating something of it, or referring to those objects, and predicating something of them. Names, personal pronouns, demonstratives, and demonstrative phrases are widely thought to refer to things; and definite descriptions, like 'the largest state east of the Mississippi', are thought by some to refer, while others deny this.

In contemporary philosophy, utterances involving singular reference are widely, if not universally, understood as expressing propositions that are about particular objects. A proposition is an abstract object that encodes the truth-conditions of an utterance – of an assertive utterance of a declarative sentence – which are usually taken to be paradigmatic. For example, a proposition might be conceived as, or modeled as, a set of possible worlds or counterfactual situations. The proposition usually taken to be expressed by an utterance of 'Obama lives in Washington, D.C.' would be conceived as the set of worlds in which a particular person, Barack Obama, lives in a particular city, Washington, D.C. Obama wouldn't have to be named 'Obama' in all of these worlds, and Washington, D.C. wouldn't necessarily have that name, either. The city wouldn't have to be the capital of the United States, and Obama wouldn't have to be a politician, or be married to Michelle Obama. There are of course philosophical disagreements about what makes a person in various possible worlds Obama, or a given city Washington D.C.; the issue of singular reference is, so to speak, philosophically downstream from those decisions. One philosopher might think that Obama has to have certain genetic material to exist, another might disagree. One philosopher might think it makes sense for a city like Washington, D.C. to have been founded in a different way, or in a different place, than it actually was, while another might think those are not possibilities. They could agree, nevertheless, that an utterance of 'Obama lives in Washington, D.C.' expresses a proposition about Obama and the city, and is true in worlds in which he lives in the city.

The topic of singular reference – that is, proper names, definite descriptions, demonstratives, indexicals, and other sorts of pronoun – has been a central topic in the philosophy of language for more than one hundred years, at least since the seminal works of Frege and Russell. Usually discussions of singular reference are regarded as squarely in semantics; nevertheless, since the early works of Frege and Russell, considerable attention has been paid to the 'problem of cognitive significance.' This problem is closely connected with pragmatics. Even if 'Tully,' 'Cicero,' 'the greatest Roman philosopher,' and 'that man' should all refer to the same person – perhaps in a situation in which he has been a topic of conversation – the differences in the singular terms will make a difference in the situations in which they are used. Whether a speaker uses one of the names, the description, or the demonstrative phrase will depend on his communicative intentions. It is this that we hope to understand and seek to explain. And because of the close connection between the problem of cognitive significance and the pragmatics of singular reference, we believe our account can both build on and contribute to the rich tradition of discussion of singular reference in the philosophy of language.

1.5   The plan

In Chapter 2 we briefly review the history of singular reference in the philosophy of language of the twentieth and early twenty-first centuries, from Frege and Russell to Kaplan and Kripke. We end with a discussion of Kaplan's theory of indexicals, which we believe, in spite of Kaplan's own aims, provides a good starting point for a theory of utterances.

In Chapter 3 we introduce concepts from the philosophy of action, and explain our way of looking at reference as an example of Gricean meaning, and explain the important concept of *role-management*. We claim that the importance of roles is at the heart of Kaplan's approach to indexicals, although this is only apparent when one re-interprets his ideas, as providing a basis for a theory of utterances. In Chapter 4 we explain our theory of reference, explaining the important distinction between utterance-bound and utterance-independent conditions of reference and truth. In Chapters 5–9 we apply our theory to major categories of singular terms: demonstratives, indexicals, names, and definite descriptions. In Chapter 9 we consider unarticulated constituents. In Chapters 10–12 we discuss major topics in pragmatics in the light of our theory: speech-act theory, Grices's theory of implicatures, and the semantics/pragmatics interface. In the concluding chapter, we connect our picture to larger issues about content and communication.

2   A short history of reference

2.1   Introduction

The topic of this book is certain kinds of utterances, those in which the speaker *refers* to an object or objects, and *predicates* properties of it, or a relation among them. We are interested in how the differences among the ways we have of referring to things connect to the different effects that such utterances have on those who hear them, and how this is reflected in the intentions of those who use them. Whatever intrinsic interest the topic may have is augmented by the central role singular reference played in the philosophy of language throughout the twentieth century, and continues to play. If we understand singular reference, we should be able to explain its pragmatics.

Our main aim in this chapter is to sketch some main developments in thinking about reference, from Frege to Kaplan, and then to suggest how we see ourselves fitting, and not fitting, into this tradition.

2.2   One hundred-plus years of reference

The issue of singular reference was intensely investigated by philosophers during the twentieth century, and lively interest in the topic continues. The inquiry is usually regarded as a matter of semantics, the theory of meaning and truth. The key question is usually taken to be what contribution referring expressions make to the truth-conditions of the statements of which they are a part, and not how they fit into the speaker's plan to convey implicatures and perform speech acts. Nonetheless, we believe our investigations into the pragmatics of singular reference shed considerable light on issues of semantics.

2.2.1   *From Frege and Russell to the new theory of reference*

The topic of reference has been dominated, since the beginning of the last century at least, by two paradigms, naming and describing. Imagine you own a small used-car lot. At any given time you have a dozen or so cars. You need to refer to these cars for several purposes. You have a log book in which you keep track of when and where you obtained each car, and what you paid for it, and when and to whom you sold it, and for how much. You have a couple of employees, and you need to refer to the cars to get them washed, repaired, moved, and the like. It seems like there are two methods you could use. You could put a tag on each car, with a symbol written on it, say a capital letter. Then you use tokens of that same symbol to refer to the car. You write in your log "C was bought on December 12 for $500," and so forth. You say things like "Wash C, and move it to the front of the lot." Here you are creating new conventions for referring to the cars. The symbols you use had no meaning, at least in the context of your used-car lot, before you assigned them. Underlying the assignment is a practice, tagging: directly associating a token of a certain type with an object, and then using other tokens of that type to refer to that object. Such tagging is a way of setting up a system of names. The assignment is the important thing; the tags are aids to memory.

The other method you could use is denoting. The language you and your employees already share has words with the resources to pick out the cars. The words 'blue two-door Ford with a dent in the side' may be true of only one car on your lot. If so, you can record information about this car, and give orders to your staff about the car, by using the definite description, 'The blue two-door Ford with a dent in the side.' You don't need any new conventions. As both Frege and Russell noted [Frege, 1892; Russell, 1905], sentences involving different descriptions of the same thing can have different meanings, so we can explain why one can learn something from, say, 'The car that has the flat tire I want you to fix is the blue Ford with the dented right fender,' even though both descriptions pick out the same car. And a sentence using a description can be meaningful, even if the description doesn't pick out a unique object, like

(2.1)   The present king of France is a Catholic,

or

(2.2)   The senator from Utah is a Mormon.

(Russell thought such sentences were straightforwardly false; Frege had a more nuanced view.)

Frege and Russell both wanted to extend these same virtues to proper names as ordinarily used for people, places, and things we talk about in daily life. Otherwise, how are we to explain the difference in 'cognitive significance' between (2.3) and (2.4)?

(2.3)   Hesperus is Hesperus.

(2.4)   Hesperus is Phosphorus.

Or the fact that

(2.5)   Nessie lives in Loch Ness

makes sense, even though (perhaps) there is no monster in the loch? They
thought that ordinary proper names are not, as Mill thought, simply tags for
objects, but instead or in addition incorporated something like abbreviations
for descriptions. (At a deeper level, Russell thought that naming was basic,
but what gets tagged, or named by 'logically proper names,' are not ordinary
objects, but the universals exemplified in our experience, our sense data, and,
possibly, our selves, the only things that, in his terminology, are known by
acquaintance. The things we ordinarily refer to with the subject terms of our
sentences are usually things we know only by description, and these we cannot
simply tag, but must describe.)

On this issue of how reference worked, there was a sort of consensus
throughout the first half of the twentieth century. Definite descriptions refer
by describing objects; ordinary names refer by abbreviating or being associated with descriptions. The consensus began to fall apart in the 1950s and 1960s,
and a set of ideas Howard Wettstein dubbed 'the New Theory of Reference'
became widely accepted [Wettstein, 1991].

The new theory of reference developed from pressures on the old consensus theory from two rather different directions, and from two rather different
schools in the philosophy of language – although the term 'school' is not too
apt for the very fluid situation in analytical philosophy of language after World
War II. Oxford 'ordinary language philosophers' of the 1950s and 1960s, including Austin, J. O. Urmson, and P. F. Strawson, were worried that the logic that
developed from Frege and Russell did not provide a good picture of ordinary
language, and that the latter had virtues that philosophers missed. Strawson in
particular thought the subject–predicate structure of ordinary language, which
Russell mostly abhorred, was deeply tied to the way humans experience and
think about the world, as structured mainly by individuals with properties,
including relational properties, spread out in space. Strawson thought that Aristotle's logic had some ideas worth salvaging. Strawson's work was a main
impetus to the rediscovery of a robust concept of reference [Strawson, 1950,
1964].

Keith Donnellan's work on definite descriptions and proper names
[Donnellan, 1966, 1970, 1974] was influenced by Strawson. In 'Proper Names
and Identifying Descriptions,' Donnellan was critical of both Strawson and Russell. Although he defended Russell against some of Strawson's criticisms, in
the end he advocated a more radical departure from Russell than Strawson had.
In terms we explain in the next section, Strawson's main point was about the
contribution of referring expressions rather than the *mechanism* behind them;

he thought that both descriptions and names are used to refer, to make 'statements' that are about particular objects, and could have been made by other means that referred to the same objects; but he assumed that the mechanism by which these devices picked out the objects to which they referred were basically descriptive. Donnellan argued that definite descriptions, used referentially, can refer to objects that do not fit the description, and that proper names do not need a backing of descriptions to pick out the object they refer to. Donnellan's ideas emphasized the role of the speaker's intentions in securing reference.[1]

The second stream came from more formally minded philosophers, including Ruth Marcus [Marcus, 1946, 1961], Dagfinn Føllesdal [Føllesdal, 2004], Saul Kripke [Kripke, 1980], and David Kaplan [Kaplan, 1989a]. These philosophers were all involved in the development of modal and intensional logic and semantics, developing Carnap's ideas, particularly in *Meaning and Necessity* [Carnap, 1956], and were motivated in part by Quine's criticisms of that whole enterprise [Quine, 1953]. The issue of quantifying into modal and intensional context was crucial. In her early systems and discussion of quantified modal logic, Marcus advocated the necessity of identity, and Mill's idea that names be regarded as tags. In his dissertation and articles based on it, Føllesdal argued for the necessity of such logics, and explored the idea of getting around Quine's worries by countenancing what he called 'genuine singular terms,' which, like variables, contributed the objects they stood for, and not any descriptive material, to the semantics of the larger sentences formed by adding modal operators. Genuine singular terms were, in Kripke's later terminology, rigid designators. But Føllesdal did not claim that ordinary proper names were genuine singular terms, and did not contemplate a causal theory of reference, which would allow abandoning the idea that names were hidden descriptions. A causal theory of names had been developed by Peter Geach, a seminal thinker who does not fit squarely in either of these traditions [Geach, 1969]. Kaplan, in 'Quantifying In' [Kaplan, 1969], explored the underpinnings of quantified modal and intensional logic and Quine's objections to them. He developed the idea of standard names and vivid names.

The key work in this tradition was clearly Saul Kripke's *Naming and Necessity* [Kripke, 1980]. Kripke had already developed Kripke-structures, a semantics for modal logic that permitted crucial and illuminating model theoretic results about the completeness of and differences between various systems and has been the basis for developments in a wide variety of areas of logic and computer science [Kripke, 1963]. Kripke argued that ordinary proper names

---

[1] As Perry remembers of Donnellan's seminars at Cornell in the mid 1960s, and seminars and conversations with Grice, who visited there during that time. Donnellan was intrigued by the possibility of applying Grice's intentional theory of meaning to issues of reference, but Grice himself was not so enthusiastic. See Grice's 'Vacuous Names' [Grice, 1969b]. However, this is a leading idea behind the present work.

were rigid designators; that they expressed propositions about particular objects, and that the mechanism of reference was causal, and did not require a backing of descriptions. Thus on the issue of names, Donnellan and Kripke ended up with very similar views, which form the core of contemporary referentialism.[2]

2.2.2 Two questions

As Genoveva Martí has pointed out, the classics of the new theory of reference – which we'll just call 'referentialism' – grappled with two issues about reference, without always clearly distinguishing them, the mechanism of reference and the contribution of reference [Martí, 1995]. We will say that according to Russell's account of definite descriptions, descriptions *denote* and *describe*. To say they denote is to say that they pick out the object that meets the identifying condition. To say they describe is to say that it is this identifying condition that is contributed to the proposition that statements containing them express.

But according to referentialism about names, names *name* and *refer*. To say they name is to say that they pick out the individual in virtue of an assignment of a type of expression to the individual, rather than an assignment to an identifying condition that in turn picks out the individual. The model is tagging, but the actual process in most cases is more complex; a causal/historical process associates the name with the individual. In saying that names refer, referentialists usually appeal to an intuitive and fairly robust concept of what a person says, or what is said by a person in making a certain statement. In characterizing what is said, by identifying a proposition that captures it, or, what is often considered the same thing, the set of worlds in which it is true, one focusses on the individual, not any identifying condition he meets. Kripke said that proper names were 'rigid designators,' picking out the same thing in every possible world. The idea is that if you want to consider the possible worlds in which a sentence like

(2.6) Cicero was bald

is true, you don't worry about the descriptions the speaker associates with 'Cicero' (which may be incomplete and inaccurate). The sentence is true in any world in which the person Cicero is bald, whether or not he has, in that world, the familiar properties that we associate with his name, like being a Roman orator and philosopher. Donnellan argued that people can associate quite different descriptions with the same name, but nevertheless say the same thing.

---

[2] Arthur Burks is another important figure, who doesn't fit in either tradition, but was inspired by Peirce [Peirce, 1931–36, 1958]. His important work on indexicals [Burks, 1949] is discussed by Perry in *Reference and Reflexivity*.

The theses that names name and refer are connected in that they both deny descriptions or identifying conditions key roles, but the key roles denied are different. To say that names name is to say that their connection with the object named is not via a description; to say that they refer is to say that the object so named is essential to the claim that is made. Thus we have, according to the standard referentialist, the following scheme:

	Name	**Denote**
Refer	Names	
Describe		Descriptions

2.2.3   *Indexicals*

Strawson's criticisms of Russell were tied to a view he had at the time, that ordinary language had no exact logic, and the use of the techniques of formal logic distorted seeing how it works. One of the reasons for this view was the heavy reliance on context in the ordinary use of language, and the associated fact that one can use the same sentence to say different things, in different contexts, and different sentences to say the same thing, in appropriately related contexts. This is particularly clear with indexicals, about which Strawson made some important points. The phenomenon had been noted by Frege in 'The Thought' [Frege, 1918], where he notes that to say the same thing tomorrow that I say today with a sentence like, 'Today it is sunny,' one will have to change the wording to 'Yesterday was sunny.'

David Kaplan, in 'Demonstratives,' demonstrated that the techniques of formal logic, and in particular ideas from modal and intensional logic, could be applied to indexicals with illuminating results. On Kaplan's theory a sentence like 'I am sitting' has a certain sort of meaning, which he calls 'character,' that is modeled as a function from contexts to contents. 'Content' is used by Kaplan as a theoretical term, that gets at the ordinary concept of 'what is said' or 'the proposition expressed.' Following the tradition that came from Carnap and had been developed in modal and intensional logic, Kaplan took propositions to be *intensions*, that is, functions from possible worlds (or pairs of times and worlds – Kaplan's own preference) to truth-values for sentences, and other appropriate values for other expressions. Contexts were sequences of an agent, a time, a location, and a world. So the character of the sentence 'I am tired now', as spoken by a at t gives us the proposition that a is tired at time t. Spoken by b at t', the same sentence with the same character gives us the content that b is tired a t'. The sentence 'It is Saturday today' spoken on Saturday, has the same content as 'It was Saturday yesterday,' spoken on Sunday.

In our terminology, according to Kaplan's theory indexicals-in-context denote and refer. They denote the object that meets the identifying condition provided by the character and the context; e.g., 'I' in a context denotes the agent of that context. They refer, because the object denoted, and not the identifying condition, is contributed to the content. When Obama says "I am happy to be in Oslo," his use of 'I' picks out Obama, in virtue of a property Obama has: being the speaker (or agent). But this identifying condition is not contributed to the proposition Obama expressed, what he says. Obama says the very same thing Michelle Obama would have said, if she had said to him, "You are happy to be in Oslo," and the very same thing the headline says that reads, "Obama is happy to be in Oslo." So now our table looks like this:

	Name	**Denote**
Refer	Names	Indexicals
Describe		Descriptions

2.3 The problem of cognitive significance

Kaplan's work forced abandonment of the idea that reference required a backing of descriptions to pick out the object referred to, without relying on intuitions about proper names of the sort to which Donnellan and Kripke had appealed. When one uses the word 'I' to refer, it is clear that one refers to oneself, however misguided one's view of oneself may be. When one uses 'today,' one refers to the day on which one speaks, even if one is wildly wrong about what day that is – think of Rip Van Winkle, who was asleep for twenty years and woke up thinking that he had slept only for a night.[3]

This result, however, seems to leave referentialism with problems, which the descriptive framework of Frege and Russell seemed to have solved, the problems of co-reference and no-reference. These are problems about the *cognitive significance* of referring expressions. Frege begins his essay 'Über Sinn und Bedeutung' [Frege, 1892] with the problem of co-reference, the differing cognitive significance or 'information value' of "A = A" and "A = B" when 'A' and 'B' stand for the same thing. This is a key motivation for his theory, according to which the two statements express different *Gedanken* or thoughts, thoughts being for Frege basically what are now called propositions, abstract

---

[3] See Perry, 2000.

objects that get at the truth-conditions of beliefs and statements. So in Frege's theory the terms 'A' and 'B' make different contributions to the truth-conditions of the statements, related to the different descriptions or identifying conditions language associates with them, and this explains the difference in cognitive significance. In Frege's view, in truly scientific language there will be no empty singular terms – terms that don't refer to anything. But he acknowledges that these occur in ordinary language. His theory seems capable of handling this problem, the problem of no-reference, as well. A singular term can have a *Sinn*, and a statement using it can express a thought, even if it has no *Bedeutung*, that is, doesn't stand for anything. With his very different theoretical apparatus Russell considers the same problems, and solves them with his theory of descriptions. So for both philosophers, their versions of the descriptive theory handle the problems of cognitive significance.

But how is the referentialist to solve these problems? On the referentialist view of proper names, the statements "Cicero was an orator" and "Tully was an orator" express the same proposition, the singular proposition about the Roman who had both names, the proposition true in just those worlds in which that person was an orator, whatever his name in them. But then what does someone who knows that Cicero was an orator, but doesn't know whether Tully was, learn when he is told that Cicero is Tully, that he wouldn't learn by simply being reminded that Cicero is Cicero, or Tully is Tully?

This problem is especially acute for pragmatics. What we do with words, the speech acts we perform, and the implicatures we convey, and what we manage to inform people about and enable them to do, depends on the singular terms we use to refer to them, as various of our examples have shown. There is some difference between 'Tully' and 'Cicero' that affects which beliefs we can impart with statements containing them, and that speakers need to take account of in using language to do things.

We believe the problems can be solved, without giving up the basic insights of referentialist semantics. The first step is to see how some of Kaplan's ideas can be reformulated within a theory of utterances.

2.4   From Kaplan to utterances

We think Kaplan's investigation of indexicals, and his concept of character, suggest a new paradigm for thinking about singular reference. (Of course, one person's idea of a new paradigm is another person's idea of setting aside hard-won results for fog and mirrors.) They suggest the importance of what we call 'utterance-relative roles.' Our version of the rule for 'I' is a generalization that quantifies over utterances: an utterance of the English word 'I' refers to the speaker of that very utterance, that is, the person who plays the role *speaker of* relative to the utterance. The role provides an identifying condition of the referent, but one that is *utterance-bound*, which is not what classic description theorists had in mind. And even though an utterance of 'I' refers rather than describes, no tag-like direct connection between the expression and the referent is involved. In the case of indexicals, utterance-relative roles are the key to understanding how things work. We think that utterance-relative roles are an important part of the story in *all* cases of reference, and a good bit of this book is devoted to spelling out that idea. This is *not* to say that all kinds of singular terms are indexicals. It is rather to say that something comes out very clearly in the case of indexicals that is also very important, if more difficult to ferret out, in the cases of names, pronouns, and descriptions.

Finding this sort of inspiration in Kaplan's work requires a bit of re-interpretation. Kaplan said he was *not* providing a theory of utterances, but a theory of 'sentences-in-context' [Kaplan, 1989a]. Utterances do not appear at all in his formal theory. But they often are mentioned in the informal remarks that motivate the theory. It seems plausible that the contextual elements of agent, location, time, and world, and the fundamental stipulation that the agent be in the location at the time in the world, are suggested by the utterance-relative roles of speaker, location, time, and world, and the fact that the speaker of an utterance is in the location of the utterance at the time of the utterance. Be that as it may, when he turns to developing a formal theory, Kaplan notes that utterances don't fit well with his goal of developing a logic of indexicals. For one thing, utterances take time, so the premises of a spoken argument won't all occur at the same time, but for the purposes of logic we want them to occur all in the same context. For another, Kaplan wants to consider the content of context-sentence pairs in which no utterance of the sentence by the agent at the time occurs – hence the agent is not dubbed 'the speaker.'

From the point of view of pragmatics, however, utterances do not get in the way; they are central to the project. Gricean intentions are intentions to bring about changes in the hearer; they are intentions to produce concrete utterances, in order to have effects on the hearer. The meanings and contents of the concrete utterance contribute to the effect. At the heart of the conversational transaction is the hearer perceiving a concrete token or event, and reasoning about its cause, that is, about the intentions that led to its production. Properties of meaning and content are relevant to intention discovery, but so are many other properties. Joana went wrong in interpreting John's utterance in Chapter 1 because she took him to be attempting to amuse by telling a philosophical joke rather than impress by saying something quite prosaic in Basque.

The concept of a pair of a Kaplanian context and sentence type makes intuitive sense to us if we think of it as a model for an utterance in which a speaker at a time makes use of a sentence of the type. Much the same is true of other concepts important in the development of referentialism; by our lights, they fit better with a theory of utterances than with a theory of sentences and other formal objects.

The intentions to which Donnellan appealed in his referential–attributive distinction are intentions that lead to particular acts of using expressions. The causal and historical chains appealed to in the referentialist account of proper names are best thought of as connecting utterances and earlier events.

Thus, in what follows we develop an account of the semantics of singular reference within a theory of utterances, based on the concept of utterance-relative roles, and of the pragmatics of singular reference, based on the speaker's need to manage roles to produce the intended effect on his audience.

3 Acts, roles, and singular reference

3.1 Introduction

Our approach to pragmatics emphasizes that utterances are acts and language is action. But of course it is a special kind of action; it paradigmatically involves communication of information. (We use 'information' rather loosely, basically as meaning 'information or misinformation.' When we use it more strictly, as implying accuracy or truth, we'll alert the reader.) Basically, the speaker is the agent, communicating information to the hearer. (We also use 'speaker' and 'hearer' loosely, to include producers and readers of written texts and users of sign languages like ASL.) The hearer is the interpreter. The link between them is the sign, the linguistic token. The speaker intentionally produces it, the hearer perceives and interprets it. In this chapter we say a bit about the picture of actions and signs that underlies our version of the Gricean picture.

3.2 Acts and actions

Acts (particulars) involve agents at times and locations performing mental operations, and moving their bodies, limbs, and other body parts, including vocal cords, in various ways, which they can do at will. Such basic actions we call 'executions.' The basic actions one executes at will have various results, depending on the circumstances in which they occur. The actions have a direct effect on objects that play various roles in the agent's life, like the computer key he is touching, or the person he is talking to, and as a result may have more and more remote effects. All these results we call 'accomplishments,' whether or not they are what the agent had in mind [Israel, Perry, and Tutiya, 1993].

We use the locutions 'by' and 'way of' to get at the various relations between executions and accomplishments, and accomplishments and further accomplishments. To return to an example of the last chapter, moving one's right forefinger downward is an action: it is a type of movement, which we call an *execution*. Making an 'h' appear on the screen is an action, a case of making something happen, that we call an *accomplishment*. One *way of* making an 'h' appear on the screen is moving one's forefinger down in the circumstance in which one's forefinger is perched over the 'h' key of a properly functioning keyboard attached in the right way to a properly functioning computer. That is the way I just used; I made the 'h' appear *by* moving my forefinger.[1] There are other ways of doing the same thing. In different circumstances I could have moved my middle finger, or hit the 'h' key with the end of a pencil, or said "Horatio" into the microphone of my voice-recognition system.

When I type an 'h' in the usual way, by depressing my finger, the 'h' key plays what we will call a *direct pragmatic role* in my life. That is, by executing a movement, in the appropriate circumstances, I have a direct effect on the key. If I hold a pencil in my hand and use it to poke the key, the pencil plays a direct pragmatic role, and the key an *indirect pragmatic role*. The pencil is basically a *tool*; by having an effect on it, in appropriate circumstances, I have an effect on the key.

Tools depend on structure. The pencil is rigid, and the way the world is set up by nature, moving rigid things is a way, in appropriate circumstances, of moving other items those things come into contact with. But of course many structures we rely on are not provided by nature directly, but are the products of human invention. The fact that when the key is depressed the computer is affected in a certain way, which makes an 'h' appear on the screen, is the result of structures provided by humans.

Structures, whether natural or products of human invention, create way-of relations, and so the possibility of accomplishing one thing by accomplishing another. The fact that moving rigid objects move suitably sized objects they contact, if those objects are themselves rigid enough and capable of movement, created the possibility of depressing the key by holding the pencil and moving it. The fact that the computer is constructed and programmed as it is, created the possibility of making an 'h' appear by depressing the key. When the structures are combined, I can make an 'h' appear by moving a pencil; moving a pencil is a *way of* making an 'h' appear.

As I move the pencil around to type, various keys will play the role, vis-à-vis the pencil, of being *the key in contact with it*. The pencil plays a role in my life, being *the object I am holding and moving*. The roles combine: the key is the one I depress, by moving the pencil. The role of being the key in contact with the pencil is *nested* in a more complicated one: being the key in contact with the pencil that I hold in my hand.

Learning to use tools, even tools so simple as a pencil used to type, involves learning that by executing certain actions, one does things with the tool, and that by doing things with the tool, one has various effects on things related to the tool and hence to oneself. This learning is often a matter of know-how and is relatively unconscious; it is a matter of forming certain habits that can then be

---

[1] We remind the reader of our use of the authorial 'I' in giving examples.

unconsciously deployed in appropriate circumstances. In some cases, however, one needs to consciously keep track of what one is doing to achieve the appropriate effects. In the modern world, one can send a fax to a machine thousands of miles away. Which distant fax machine one has an effect on depends on the number one types into the fax, and usually this is done by paying careful attention to something the number is written on as one types.

Typically when one acts, one perceives the object or objects to which one has a direct pragmatic relation. But one perceives them *as* objects that stand in relation, sometimes quite complicated, to other objects, which it is one's goal to have an effect on. Thus those objects play roles in our lives, roles in which the simpler roles the perceived objects play are nested. We think of all the information involved in purposeful, intentional action as residing in a certain kind of idea, or *notion*, the agent has of the direct object or objects of his action, which we call the *agent's buffer*. Buffers are notions that are actively involved in picking up information, or applying information to guide action. As one moves the pencil around the keyboard, one sees it not just as a stick, but as a stick related to keys which are related to a computer, a computer that is or will be related to a printer, or to other computers in distant places; it is the pieces of paper the printer will print, or the screens on which the email will eventually appear, that one aims to affect in certain predictable ways. And of course that's not the end of it; usually one wants to affect the people that read the paper or the email in certain ways, too. Even something so simple as poking a key with a pencil, or with one's finger, can be part of a complicated plan to make someone think one thing rather than another. The agent's buffer is the link between the goal of the activity and the particular means he chooses to carry it out.

If action is purposeful and intelligent, the agent expects that by moving in certain ways, he will, or probably will, or at least may have, certain results on the rest of the world, the results he would like to bring about. He needs to think, at some level, about what the results of his act will be on the rest of the world, given the way things are independently of the act, and the way things work: the *incremental* results. Of course one seldom considers *all* the results of one's acts. One has a plan in mind, conscious or unconscious, about how moving in various ways will bring about the desired results. That is, what results will this act have, given that *this* is how the world is, and *this* is how things work.

When one thinks about how the world is, one typically doesn't take a 'view from nowhere,' but the agent's view, the agent's conception of how the things on which he will have a direct effect are related to the rest of the world, and especially to the objects on which he plans to have an indirect effect. If you are talking on the phone, your plan will be a combination of general knowledge of how phones work and particular knowledge about the phone in question. You know that by speaking into the mouthpiece of a phone you (somehow) will create sounds in whichever phone it is (somehow) connected to, and so experiences of hearing those sounds in the mind of the person holding that phone. In a given case, based on the number you have dialed, you think a particular phone is connected to one being held, say, by your boss. So you tell her why you will be late for work. The job of the agent's buffer is to keep track of the complex nested role that the objects you want to have an indirect effect on (your boss, the distant phone) play in your life, as a result of their connections to the things you will have a direct effect on (your phone) and the way things work, which, of course, you may only dimly understand.

3.3   Roles

We use the word 'role' a lot in this book. We talk about utterance-relative roles, speaker-relative roles, epistemic roles, pragmatic roles, and so forth. So we should say a little bit about roles.[2]

Roles aren't an addition to a metaphysics that recognizes individuals of various sorts, properties, and relations. Rather they are a way of talking about and organizing information about important relations things have to one another. They provide a way of organizing information that comes naturally to humans and is reflected in many ways in language.

Roles are, first of all, important relations. If we ask Elwood, "what role do you play in your son's life?" we expect an answer like, "provider, mentor, friend, disciplinarian." If he said, "my bedroom is down the hall from his," we would expect he was telling us that he played no role worth mentioning in his son's life.

Roles are often significant because they are involved in constraints, the laws, principles, rules, conventions, and other regularities that provide the structure within which we perceive and plan.

Consider the constraint from Chapter 1

(1.6)   If an x-ray y of a human arm exhibits pattern ψ, then *the person of whose arm y was taken* has a broken arm.

The constraint makes the relation, between an x-ray and a person, that the former was taken of the latter's arm something of importance. It means that the x-ray can give us information about the person's arm. And of course (1.6) is simply one of a family of constraints that x-ray technologists learn, telling what kinds of break x-rays mean, for various bones, and much else. Within the practice of using x-rays in medicine, the relation of being the person of whom an x-ray was taken is critical. Similarly with being the speaker-of, in the realm of utterances. In these cases we generalize across roles; it is the health of the patient – that is, the person the x-ray was taken of – that is disclosed by the

---

[2] See also Korta and Perry, 2009.

x-ray. It is the state of mind of the speaker – that is, the speaker *of* the utterances – that is disclosed by its linguistic properties.

A list of key roles can provide a schema for characterizing salient facts about an object. Sometimes when we are dealing with a lot of facts about numerous inter-related objects, one object will take center stage for a period of time, during which we focus on which objects stand in various relations to it, or, as we say, play various roles relative to it. We call this object 'the index'. Elwood is interviewing Angus, asking him a series of one-word questions: Father? Mother? Birthplace? Year of Birth? Angus can give one-word answers or one-phrase answers, specifying the objects that stand in those relations to him, or, as we say, play those roles in his life. Angus could start his answers with words like, 'My father is ...,' and 'My birthplace is ...,' but he really needn't mention himself at all. His place in the facts he is using language to state doesn't have to be indicated linguistically, because it is built into the situation. Angus' system of representation is asymmetrical; the objects that play the key relations to him get named, but he makes it into the propositions he asserts just by his role in the conversation.

As Elwood records the information he may also use an asymmetrical system of representation. Angus' name is written in on the top of a card, perhaps, on which words for the various important roles Elwood is to query him about are printed; Elwood fills them in, in response to Angus' answers. For another example, think of a party invitation. The invitation as a whole represents the party; on the invitation the objects (broadly speaking) that fill various roles relative to the party are linguistically identified: time-of, place-of, hosts-of, purpose-of, and so forth.

Handling relational information with roles is useful when one object is the focus of attention, a participant in all the relational facts being discussed, and where, as a result of the situation, the way information is being obtained, communicated, or used there is no need to re-identify him or her or it. During Angus' interview, he is the one Elwood is asking about. As long as we have one of the realtor's cards in front of us, the house whose area, address, number of rooms, etc. that we are talking about is the one the card stands for. We know that all the information given on the invitation is for the same party, the party the invitation is an invitation for.

A particularly important example of organizing information by roles is our ordinary way of perceiving the world in those uncomplicated cases where neither communication, long-term memory, nor long-term intentions are involved; we'll call this 'the natural stance.' Here the perceiver/agent is the index. We look out on the world and see objects to the left, to the right, above, and below; we hear things to the left and to the right, near at hand, and in the distance; we feel the heft of things we hold in our right or left hands, and the taste of things in our mouth.

Often the occupants of different roles are known to be the same, in virtue of the common index and the architecture of the situation. The stuff I put in my mouth is the stuff I taste in my mouth; the things I hold in front of me are the things I see in front of me. The car I slow by stepping on the brakes is the same one I steer by turning the wheel, and the same one I gather information about by looking through the windshield.

3.4   Signs and information

Humans are blessed with a rich variety of perceptual abilities, which allow them to find out things about objects that stand in certain relations to them; that is, play certain roles in their lives. I can find out the color and shape of the object I am looking at; I can discover the hardness and weight of the object I hold in my hand, and so forth. Such objects, we will say, play *direct epistemic roles* in our lives; that is, they are related to us, on a given occasion, in such a way that we can perceive them to have various properties.

Often the objects that play direct epistemic roles in our lives are also ones that play direct pragmatic roles in our lives. You see an apple; it looks like it is ripe, but perhaps overripe and mushy; you pick it up, and squeeze it a little to make sure it is firm; you put it in your mouth and bite off a piece and chew it; you taste it, and on the basis of what it tastes like, go ahead and swallow it or spit it out.

In thinking about this we find a concept and a term from Howard Wettstein [Wettstein, 1991] useful: 'cognitive fix.' One's cognitive fix on an object is how one thinks of it, in a broad sense of 'thinking.' We like the phrase because it is rather vague, and not tied, like, say, 'mode of presentation,' to a particular theory. Still, we will gradually develop a theory of cognitive fixes, and tie Wettstein's term to our own theory. We think of cognitive fixes on objects as involving epistemic roles, pragmatic roles, or both. Cognitive fixes may be perceptual, in which case they will be expressed naturally with demonstrative phrases: 'that man,' 'this computer.' They may involve the roles the objects play in conversation, in which case they will be expressed naturally with the appropriate indexicals: 'I,' 'you.' Often a mere name seems to do the trick, both in thinking and speaking; we call these *nominal* cognitive fixes, and in Chapter 8 will explain how they are related to epistemic and pragmatic roles. Sometimes we think of things in terms of uniquely identifying conditions; we have a *descriptive* cognitive fix, and descriptions may be the appropriate expressions to use. We think of singular terms as devices for providing hearers with cognitive fixes on objects that are appropriate for the communicate aims of the speaker.

Here the apple plays a number of roles in your life: the thing you see; the thing in front of you that you can pick up by moving in a certain way; the thing in your hands; the thing in your mouth; the thing providing certain taste sensations, and so forth. All of these roles are *linked*; that is, one thing plays all of them. The job of the agent's buffer is to keep track of all these linkages. But there may also be nested roles to keep track of. The apple may be the very one that your office-mate took out of her lunch bag before stepping away for a moment; by eating the apple, you will have an effect on her, perhaps making her angry. And perhaps she has the boss's ear, so the apple is the one that by eating you can anger your office-mate, cause bad things to be said about you to your boss, and get yourself fired.

A sign is an object that plays a direct epistemic role in one's life, the perceivable properties of which are reliably correlated with the properties of other objects, to which it is related. You see the paw print along the trail; on the basis of the pattern and size of the print, you learn that it was caused by a fox. The fox plays a complex, indirect epistemic role in your life; it is the animal that caused the print you are perceiving, and hence the animal you learn about by examining the print.

Nature provides us with many signs; that is, certain events carry information about other objects (or about themselves at other times) in virtue of the way nature made them and the way the world works. Other objects carry information because of structures created by humans, which harness natural information for various purposes. A certain characteristic twitch at the end of your fishing rod tells you that there is, or may be, a fish on the hook tied to the end of the line that feeds into the rod. A ringing doorbell tells you that someone is on the porch.

In interpreting a sign, one basically asks what the rest of the world must be like, for the object perceived to be as it is, or for the event or state perceived to have occurred. As in the case of the effects of one's acts, one doesn't worry about everything; one has in mind certain structures, certain objects that are or might be related to the object seen, and certain ways the world works. I see a paw print of a certain shape and size; I know that given the way the world works there is some animal that made it, and that given the shape and size it was a fox. Interpreting signs is a manner of inferring what the rest of the world has to be like (or probably is like, or may be like), given various structures and constraints, for the sign to have occurred.

So, typically, the interpretation of a sign involves perceiving an object or event as having certain properties, and inferring from those properties what the rest of the world must be like. Paradigmatically, this means inferring that various other objects related to the sign in certain ways have or lack various properties.

3.5   Gricean reference

In this book, we attempt to fit the use of language into this framework of actions, roles, signs, and information, using Grice's idea of a communicative intention. But our terminology differs a bit from Grice's. He distinguishes between natural and non-natural meaning. What he calls non-natural meaning involves an agent doing something in order to change the beliefs, or otherwise affect the cognitions, of a hearer, in virtue of the hearer's recognizing the speaker's intention to effect this change. Language use is a case of non-natural meaning, but not the only case.

According to Grice, if we are talking about natural meaning, 'X means that S' entails that S. This view of Grice's is connected with the use of 'information' by Dretske and others, including one of the present authors in previous writings, to imply truth [Dretske, 1981; Barwise and Perry, 1983]. We adopt a looser view in this book. We use 'information' in the way Israel and Perry use 'informational content' [Israel and Perry, 1990, 1991]. When a bird can see an unobstructed view of an object, it takes this as a sign that it can fly directly to the object. In the modern world, this leads many birds to their death, as they fly into windows and plate-glass doors on the sides of buildings. We regard this as natural meaning; the bird is responding to a natural sign, but one that is not infallible. The importance of this may be mostly terminological; it allows us to use terms like 'natural sign,' 'natural meaning,' and 'information' rather than circumlocutions. But natural meaning, in our weaker sense, is the natural concept to explain how the interpretation of phenomena as signs plays an important evolutionary role; as long as the tendencies involved in interpreting signs lead to good results in a sufficient proportion of cases, the trait of doing so will propagate.

Interpreting the intentions and other cognitions of other people is a natural, evolved ability of humans. From this point of view, there is nothing non-natural about this ability, and the development of language as an extension of it is also a part of nature. We draw approximately the same line as Grice, but we see it as a line between signs that are intentionally produced to be the signs of intentions and other signs.

Now consider an example of Herb Clark's [Clark, 1992, 1996]. A person stands in line at the checkout counter of a grocery store. When his turn comes, he takes a sack of potatoes from his cart and puts them on the counter. The checker will take this as a sign that the shopper wants to purchase the item, and will proceed to ring it up with the expectation of getting paid. This act has at least some of the features of Gricean communication. The shopper wants the clerk to ring up the sack of potatoes. He probably has no great interest in why the clerk does so, but he at least implicitly expects that part of the motivation will be realizing that the shopper wants to buy them. If he doesn't want to buy them, but merely learn the price of the potatoes, he'll have to say something.

It is natural to find a reference–predication structure in this episode, even though no language is involved. The shopper conveys his intention about a certain item, the sack of potatoes. He conveys that he wishes to buy it. If he had held the sack up and asked, "How much?" he would have conveyed his desire to have the clerk tell him the cost of the item. The act of putting the sack of potatoes on the counter is a primitive act of reference. The fact that he put the sack on the counter shows that the desire he wishes to convey concerns the potatoes; the fact that he placed it on the counter and said nothing conveys his desire to buy them. Different aspects of the shopper's act convey different aspects of the desire he wishes to convey.

Clark interprets that act of putting the potatoes on the counter as a demonstration. Perhaps cigarettes are not available for the shopper to put in his cart, but displayed behind the checker, who is not supposed to sell them to those under sixteen. The shopper could convey the same information about a pack of cigarettes that he did about the sack of potatoes by pointing to it. Or he could say, "That pack of Camels, please."

We see a common structure in these examples. The shopper has a desire about a certain item, to purchase it. He wants to convey to the clerk which item it is he wants to purchase. He does so by bringing it about that the item plays certain roles in the clerk's life. That is, he draws the clerk's attention to the item, in such a way that the clerk will realize it is the item the shopper wishes to buy, and will have a cognitive fix on the item that enables him to take the desired action towards the item: to ring it up. The act of reference is the act of getting the referent to play a certain role in the hearer's life, in such a way that the hearer realizes that it is the object that the shopper desires to buy, and has a cognitive fix on the item that permits him to do what the shopper wants him to do with it.

Now suppose that you are eating dinner with a group of people, and you want the salt, which you can't reach. You say to the person next to you, who can reach the shaker,

(3.1)   I'd like some salt, please.

Here you are conveying to your hearer that a certain person would like the salt. The predicate 'like some salt' conveys what the person, to whom you refer, would like. The word 'I' conveys which person that is, but it does more than that. By producing your utterance so that it is heard, you provide the hearer a succession of cognitive fixes on the referent, that is the person of whom wanting the salt is being predicated. It is (i) the person who the speaker is referring to. Your choice of 'I' indicates that that person is (ii) the speaker of the utterance. In this particular situation, the hearer can see who the speaker is: (iii) the person next to him. This puts him in a position to carry out the implicit request, and pass you the salt. Here again your intent is to identify the subject, the person who wants the salt, for the hearer in such a way that the hearer can fulfill your goal in speaking, and pass you the salt.

Suppose now that it is not you who wants the salt, but the woman sitting across from you and your hearer; she is looking at the salt shaker, but is too shy to say anything. You say,

(3.2)   She'd like the salt,

with a glance across the table. Perhaps you nudge the hearer, so that he will turn towards you, and follow your eye gaze and subtle nod towards the woman. Again, you have a referential plan. You want to convey the belief that a certain person wants the salt. The speaker will understand your sentence, and realize that the person referred to by the utterance he hears wants the salt. Other things being equal, he will take it that that person is a female. He will follow your eye gaze and realize that the person you are referring to is the person seated across from you, someone he is in a position to pass the salt to.

These cases illustrate one of our basic theses. The pragmatic aspects of singular reference are largely a matter of *role-management*. We refer to objects in the ways that we do in order to provide our hearers with an *apt* cognitive fix on the people or things or places we want to convey beliefs or other attitudes about, that is, one enables them to take whatever further actions we would like them to carry out with respect to this object.

Suppose now the woman across from you is the movie star Julia Roberts. You say,

(3.3)   Julia Roberts would like the salt.

Your neighbor hears the utterance, and has an initial fix on the person of whom wanting the salt is predicated: (i) 'the person the speaker of the utterance I hear refers to.' He will realize that she is named 'Julia Roberts,' a person he already has a notion of, and can think of as: (ii) 'Julia Roberts.' His is a notion that includes a conception of what she looks like. He will look around the table until he recognizes her. He will then have a cognitive fix on the person who needs the salt as: (iii) 'the person sitting diagonally across from me,' and will pass her the salt. Again, your plan to get Julia Roberts the salt involved providing a path the hearer could take, from having a cognitive fix on the salt-deprived person merely as the subject of the utterance he is hearing, to being the person across from him, an apt cognitive fix that enables him to get the salt to her.

Perhaps the person sitting next to you is a true intellectual, who never sees movies except documentaries; he has barely heard of Julia Roberts, and has no idea what she looks like. Then your plan will fail. Your plan puts a certain cognitive burden on the hearer; in order to follow the path you have in mind, he has to have a notion of Julia Roberts sufficiently detailed that he can recognize her. He may come to believe that Julia Roberts wants the salt, but can't go on from there.

One may want to object that our analyses of these cases are phenomenologically implausible. Neither speaker nor hearers are typically conscious of going through the steps in planning and interpreting that we describe. This is hard to deny. When we produce utterances the process often seems automatic, and so too when we hear and understand them. This is a general phenomenon in the philosophy of action. We want to understand complicated actions and activities as cases of rational, purposeful action, that is, as things that are done in pursuit of goals, and are sensitive to one's beliefs. The reasons we attribute are not always, or even most often, ones that the agent explicitly formulates in consciousness. Nevertheless, they are often accessible after the fact, through query or introspection, when we take apart our actions and ask ourselves, or others, why we do things the way we do. In fact, our attribution of beliefs, goals, desires, and the other elements of reasons is not constrained by a requirement that the agent have consciously been aware of these elements as action unfolds.

To move back to our dinner party, suppose Bob Dole is at the dinner, too. Bob Dole, the Republican candidate for President in 1996, has a habit of referring to himself in the third person. He says to the person next to him,

(3.4)   Bob Dole would like some salt.

This may not work; he isn't as well known as he once was. If instead he had said "I'd like the salt," it would have worked. His choice of words puts an unnecessary cognitive burden on the hearer. It also sounds a bit pretentious. This is because his plan assumes that people will have a rich enough notion of Bob Dole to recognize him, and that's the sort of assumption most ordinary folk won't make, when there is a simpler way of getting the hearer to have the appropriate cognitive fix, by using the first person.

Perhaps it's 1996, and Bob Dole sits next to you at a small dinner party a friend invited you to, without much explanation of who would be there. Dole has been talking politics to you. As he leaves he says, "I hope you vote for me." To vote for someone, you have to know their name. He is putting a cognitive burden on you. If he were more cautious, he would say, "I hope you vote for Bob Dole," or, "I am Bob Dole. I hope you vote for me."

He would clearly add something to the conversation by saying, "I am Bob Dole" that he wouldn't add by merely saying "Bob Dole is Bob Dole," or "I am I." He assumes that the hearer has a notion of Bob Dole, rich enough to include the information that Dole is a candidate. He assumes that the hearer has a notion of the person he has been talking to that includes that he is an intelligent and affable fellow. The effect Dole wishes to achieve is getting these notions merged, so that the hearer has a single notion that includes being a candidate named 'Bob Dole,' being the person he is talking to, and being affable and intelligent. Dole's remark gives the hearer two cognitive fixes on one person, as the person speaking to him, and as the person he thinks of as 'Bob Dole.'

But perhaps it doesn't occur to Dole that he hasn't been recognized, and he simply says, "I hope you vote for me." Later you tell a friend about this puzzling remark. "I was talking to a man at dinner. When he left he said he wanted me to vote for him. I wonder what he is running for." "That man is running for President," your friend tells you. "He is Bob Dole." Your friend plans that you will recognize that the person he is referring to with 'that man' is the very one whose behavior at dinner motivated your remark. He is building on a fix you already have on the man, in order to get the result that you merge your notion of the man you talked to with your Bob Dole notion.

These cases all illustrate our basic thesis that reference involves role-management. The thesis has implications for the semantics of the kinds of expressions we use in singular reference: demonstratives and demonstrative phrases, indexicals, personal pronouns, names, and definite descriptions. The meanings of these expressions are what enable utterances of them to have the role-management uses that they do, and the semantics of these expressions must explain how that is.

4 Elements of reference

4.1 Introduction

Most of the theories we surveyed in Chapter 2 give words and their meanings the key role in determining reference. Especially for those in the logical wing of referentialism, the theory of reference is a relatively autonomous discipline, concerned with referring expressions and the conditions of reference they impose. Contextual factors are modelled as set theoretic objects. Utterances may inspire the theory, but do not make an official appearance in it. Intentions come in around the edges, at most, to resolve ambiguity and nambiguity,[1] supplement incomplete descriptions, and the like. The causal theory of reference is seen more as a story of how names come to have the semantics that they do, rather than as a part of that semantics. Philosophers from the language wing, especially Donnellan, see things a bit differently. He gives intentions of the speaker a leading role in determining the reference of referential descriptions, and focusses on utterances, or at least acts of a person saying something about an object.

In our theory, utterances are the focus of inquiry. The linguistic aspects of the utterance do not operate autonomously; rather, intentions play the major part in determining reference, with words and their meanings playing supporting roles. In this chapter we explain what we see as the basic elements of reference. First, in order to help think about intentions, we provide a rather modest account of minds and cognition. Then we explain the main features of the intentions we see as central to acts of reference.

4.2 Cognition and information: an analogy

An analogy may help give our picture of cognition and information an intuitive basis. Consider an ordinary manilla file folder, the sort that a doctor might use to keep track of her patients. The patient plays a special role in the history of the file. The doctor introduced the file to keep track of that particular patient – the

---

[1] About names and nambiguity, see §7.2 below.

doctor takes it from a stack of virgin folders and assigns it that use. The various tests performed on the patient, notes from consultations, and such things are dropped into the folder, and the patient's name is put on the tab.

The file has two quite different relations to the patient. First, it is the file used to keep track of that patient; it is the one where information about the patient is supposed to be put, and the one consulted in order to deal with the patient. These are facts about the file, and the role it plays in the doctor's office, and the special role the patient plays with respect to it. Second, if things at the clinic and the doctor's office are handled well, the information in the file will be true of the patient – at least most of it. This is a fact about the information in the folder. A descriptive theory might maintain that the file is *of* whatever patient the information in it best fits. A role-based theory says it is *of* the patient it is used to keep track of. If things work well, the two answers will agree. But if we were to try to state carefully the truth-conditions for an item in the file, things can diverge in readily imaginable circumstances, circumstances that mimic the kinds of cases Donnellan and Kripke constructed to impugn the descriptive theory of names. The information in the file may be incomplete, inaccurate, or by coincidence fit someone else better than the patient it is used to keep track of. The doctor may have gotten the name wrong, or it could be a common name, which fits several patients. In such cases, it is not the descriptive theory but the role theory that seems correct.

When she uses the file to consult with the patient, the doctor will engage in what we call role-management. She has a file in her hand. The file in her hand is of a certain patient. It is the same patient that is before her, whom she sees and talks to. The patient plays multiple roles in her life. He is playing an epistemic role, as the patient the file in her hand contains information about. He plays a perceptual role, a second epistemic role, as the person she sees and can observe. He plays a pragmatic role, as the patient that will benefit, or suffer, from her ministrations. The job of the file – the physical, concrete object – is to facilitate her interactions, so her diagnosis and treatment can be guided by more than the information she can gather from perception. The importance of the accuracy of the information in the file is not to *secure* reference to the object, but to enable appropriate treatment of the patient it is a file of.

4.3   A modest theory of ideas

We think the ideas we have of particular objects – we call them 'notions' – are in many ways like files. They are relatively stable, more or less concrete structures in our minds. We establish them, when we meet people, or see buildings, or read about them, or hear about them. We use them to store information, some accurate, some inaccurate, about those things. This information is in the form of ideas of properties, relations, and notions of other things that we associate with the notions. Each association is a cognition – a belief, a desire, a hope, an expectation, a memory perhaps. The notion is a *component* of the cognition. We use that information when we interact with the objects, or engage in conversations about them. A notion is *of* the object it was introduced to keep track of, however poorly or well the associated ideas may fit.

This isn't intended as a cutting-edge piece of cognitive science, but as slightly regimented common sense. In saying they are concrete, we don't claim that notions and ideas are ultimate pieces of the world's furniture. No doubt they are ontologically more like the files we keep on computer disks, and owe their existence to more or less stable structures of more fundamental stuff.

Among notions, we distinguish between *detached notions* and *buffers*. Think of your third-grade teacher. If you can manage this, you have accessed a detached notion, one that is not currently attached to any perception of the teacher, nor even, unless you have cheated, attached to a picture of her or some text about her. It is probably a rather sparse notion, a component of a few memories. You may remember only a little about her appearance, and not even be able to recall her name. Some of the items that seem to be memories may be only false beliefs, based on images displaced from some other interaction with some other teacher. But they are false beliefs about your third-grade teacher, if you accessed the right notion. It could be that the notion you accessed is of some other person, perhaps your second-grade teacher, or a third-grade teacher's aide that made a deep impression. Then you have a false belief, involving the person the notion is of, that she was your third-grade teacher.

Now consider the book you have in your hands. This plays a number of contemporary roles in your life, epistemic and pragmatic. You see it, you are reading it, you are holding it. You can find out things about it – how many pages it has, for example – by performing various operations on it. Your notion of the book is a buffer, and will be so long as you are actively dealing with it, perceptually picking up information about it, holding it, perhaps throwing it across the room in a moment of frustration. Later, after you go on to some more urgent or rewarding task, the notion will no longer be a buffer but a detached notion.

We borrow a couple of terms here from referentialist texts. One, from Donnellan, is the object that someone 'has in mind.' There are various ways one can have an object in mind, depending on what kind of notion one has – detached or buffer – and how it was formed, and what sorts of ideas are associated with it. One may be perceiving the object, remembering it, have just heard it spoken of, be reading about it, and so forth. This is how we conceive of cognitive fixes, the concept we borrowed from Wettstein. One's cognitive fix may involve either a detached notion or a buffer. If it's a buffer, it may be visual, auditory, tactual, or one in which these roles are linked and nested in various ways. It may involve epistemic and pragmatic relations we wouldn't usually regard as perceptual, such as being the person one is reading about, or to whom one is sending a fax. If it is a detached notion, it may involve various key ideas about the object, such as its name, or its present, past, or hoped for role in one's life, or more or less objective, more or less accurate descriptions.

4.4   Paradigm referential plans

The heart of our account of reference is an analysis of the intentions involved in a paradigm case. Such a paradigm case will be a part of a case of Gricean meaning. The speaker S will have a belief, which we'll call *the motivating belief*, with a certain content; he intends that the hearer H will come to have a belief with the same content, in virtue of recognizing S's intention to have H do so. This intention will be in the service of further intentions S has for H; inferences, or other actions, S wants H to perform, or refrain from performing.

When reference is involved, the motivating belief will be about at least one thing X; the belief's content will be a singular proposition about X, to the effect that X meets a certain condition. As part of instilling the belief in H, S intends to get H to think about X, to have a cognitive fix on X, and recognize S's intention to have H believe that X meets the condition. S will intend for H to think about X as the object that plays a role in H's own life, the *target role*, one that is suited to S's further intentions about H's actions and inferences. S intends to accomplish this by exploiting a role X plays in S's life, the *exploited role*, by using an expression whose meaning suits it for helping to identify this role. The expression will be part of a sentence, which identifies the condition X must meet for the utterance to be true. H will infer from the fact that X plays the exploited role in S's life that X plays a role in H's own life, and will think of X in a way suited to thinking of objects that play that role.

In such a paradigm case, there will be a singular term E that is part of the sentence '... E ...' that S utters; S intends to refer to X by uttering E. This intention will be part of a referential plan that involves both the means of and the effects of reference. This is a plan about E, X, the hearer H, an exploited role, and a target role.

Where the content of S's motivating belief is that X meets a certain condition C, we have:

The grammatical intention: S believes that the sentence '... E ...' predicates C of the object identified by E, and intends to assert of that object that it meets C.

The directing intention: S believes that X plays the exploited role in S's life, and that the meaning of E makes uttering E a way of identifying the object that plays that role, and S intends, by uttering E, to get H to recognize that S intends to identify the object that plays that role.

The target intention: S believes that X plays the target role in H's life, and that by thinking of X in that way, and believing that X meets condition C, H will be likely to perform the further inferences and actions S has in mind, and S intends for H to recognize that S intends for H to think of X in that way.

The path intention: S believes that H can infer from the fact that X plays the exploited role in S's life, that it plays the target role in H's life, and intends that H recognizes that S intends for H to make that inference.

It is also useful to note that S may think that by using E to identify X, certain further information will be conveyed to H about X; the intention to convey this information we call the *auxiliary intention*.

We call this the GDTPA structure of paradigm referential plans. We'll explain the GDTPA structure a bit more, and then apply it to a range of examples.

4.4.1   The grammatical intention

When we predicate a property of an object, or a relation between objects, or some more complex condition in the usual way by uttering a declarative sentence, the various argument roles involved in the condition are grammatically specified. In English this is mainly done by word order; in other languages case markings carry the bulk of this information. The predicate 'kills' expresses a relation between a killer, a thing killed, and a time of the killing. To understand S's utterances of such sentences as 'Ruby killed Oswald,' 'Oswald was killed by Ruby,' or phrases like 'Ruby's killing of Oswald,' 'Oswald's killing by Ruby,' and 'the fact that Ruby killed Oswald,' H needs not only to recognize that it is killing, Ruby, and Oswald who are involved in the belief that S wishes to impart, but the roles they play in the killing. The word order combined with the sort of construction used – active or passive – specifies that Ruby is the killer and Oswald the victim. We will take the intention on the speaker's part to convey this information, the *grammatical intention*, largely for granted in this book, without meaning to suggest it is unimportant, semantically trivial, or pragmatically insignificant.

4.4.2   The directing intention

In order to impart his motivating belief to H in an apt way, S has to refer to X. He might, as in Clark's case of the shopper and the clerk, do so by putting X directly in H's line of vision, without saying anything. Or perhaps X is a person who stumbles out of a bar and falls at the feet of S and H. "Drunk," S says; there is no need to get H thinking about X, since he no doubt already is. But we'll focus on cases in which S refers, and uses language to do so.

Our thesis is that the meanings of expressions suit them for use in referring to things that play certain epistemic or pragmatic roles in one's life – that is, things on which one has one kind or other of cognitive fix. In choosing his referring expressions, S's goal is not merely to refer to the object his motivating belief is about, but to refer in a way that is apt for bringing about the right sort of understanding on the part of H. And for aiming at that target S exploits his own cognitive fix or fixes on X. S may have choices here, for he may have (or think he has) different cognitive fixes on the same thing. The *directing intention* is the intention to refer to the object S's motivating belief is about, by using an expression, or some other intention-indicating device, or a combination, that is associated, naturally or conventionally, with some cognitive fix one has on that object. For example, S may use the word 'I' to refer to himself; the word 'I' is suited for that role by its meaning. S may use the word 'that man' to refer to a man he sees; the phrase 'that man' is suited by its meaning for referring to a man with that role in the speaker's life. S may use 'you' to refer to the person he is talking to; the word 'you' is suited by its meaning to refer to that person. These are directing intentions. In each case, S may have further intentions. He may, by using 'you' and referring to the addressee, intend to refer to Elwood Fritchey, and by referring to Elwood Fritchey intend to refer to the next Dean of the College. Those are *not* directing intentions.

Directing intentions are *determinative*. That is, the speaker has referred to whoever or whatever plays the role involved in his directing intention. The further intentions are not determinative. Suppose S thinks he is talking to Elwood Fritchey, but is instead talking to Elwood's twin Christopher. When he says 'you' he has referred to Christopher, not Elwood.

To the question, "Does intention determine reference?," our theory says "Yes and No." Basically, the speaker has authority over which role he exploits. But he does not have authority over who or what actually plays that role; if his beliefs about that are wrong, he may refer to a thing to which he does not intend to refer. When we depart from paradigm cases, and consider ones in which the words chosen are inappropriate for the role the speaker intends to exploit, or when the speaker is misunderstood by careful hearers, things quickly get complicated; we'll look at some of these in the next chapter. Basically, the speaker gets to choose which role he exploits, but then facts take over, and if the speaker's beliefs about those facts are wrong, he may not refer to the thing he intends to.

4.4.3   The target intention

If S is at all adept at using language, he will not only intend to get H to have a belief about some object, but will also have at least a vague intention of the type of cognitive fix on that object that H should have, in order to be in a position to have whatever further thoughts and actions S has in mind for him; that is, an *apt* cognitive fix. This is the *target intention*, one aspect of the referential intention. In the earlier case of passing the salt, the target intention is that the hearer think of the person referred to, the one who wants the salt, in some way that will afford passing the salt to that person. In the case of giving someone information about Cicero, say, to use in an exam, one will likely want the cognitive fix to be via the name that the examiner will use to refer to Cicero.

4.4.4   The path intention

If S is an adept speaker, he will have in mind some *path*, some reasoning, that will lead H from realizing what role the referent has in the speaker's life, that is, from grasping the directing intention, to the target intention, that is to the cognitive fix S wants H to have. When I say, "I'd like the salt," I expect you to realize that the person who wants the salt is the speaker of the utterance you hear, and so the person you see across from you; this is the target cognitive fix, the one that will enable to you pass the salt to the right person.

4.5   Examples

S and H are standing on the east side of Canal Street, just south of Adams, in Chicago. Union Station rises on either side of Canal Street, the main part of the station being underground, running under Canal Street, and connecting the parts above ground. S believes that H's train leaves from Union Station. He intends to impart that information to H, with the goal that H will walk into the nearest part of Union Station. He holds this belief via his notion of Union Station, usually detached, but now connected to perception. In this situation, there are (at least) three ways S could refer to Union Station, exploiting three different cognitive fixes he has on it. He could just say,

(4.1)   Your train leaves from Union Station.

But in order to meet S's goal, H would have to recognize which building was Union Station, and S doesn't think he does. He could point to the part of Union Station which rises on the other side of Canal Street, and say,

(4.2)   Your train leaves from that station.

But that would doubtless lead to H's unnecessarily crossing busy Canal Street. Finally, S could point to the near part of Union Station, which rises on the east side of Canal Street, a short distance from where S and H are talking. This is clearly the way of referring that is most likely to lead to the effect on H that S wants; that is, for H to believe of Union Station, thought of as the building he sees on the same side of the street, that it is the place he needs to go to catch his train.

S's directing intention is to refer to the building he sees as he looks east, by using the demonstrative phrase 'that station.' This fixes the referent. This creates the possibility of a failing to refer to the object he intends to refer to, even though intentions fix reference. Suppose S is in error. Things have changed at Union Station. The above-ground part of structure that used to be the eastern wing of Union Station has been converted to a posh prison for Illinois politicians. Union Station is now just the structure west of Canal Street, plus the part under the street. S points to the structure on the east side, and says "Your train leaves from that station." In this case, even though S's utterance was motivated by a belief about Union Station, and the primary referential intention was to refer to Union Station, he has not referred to Union Station, but to the Illinois Politicians' Prison.

In the original example, S, an adept speaker, chose the way of referring to Union Station that would most likely lead H to have an apt cognitive fix on the station. Here we have role-transfer; the kind of cognitive fix S intended for H to have was basically of the same sort that was involved in S's directing intention, that is, a perceptual fix. That path that S set up for H to follow was short and direct, basically from 'the station S is looking at' to 'the station I am looking at.' S's referential plan, then, is a complex intention to refer to an object, Union Station, in a way that will induce H to recognize S's directing intention, and then following the *path* to a perceptual cognitive fix on the same building – the *target intention*.

But paths are not always simple and direct. S tells H,

(4.3)   Mr. Muggs is wanted on the phone – would you tell him?

Perhaps S answered the phone at a party, and someone asked for Muggs, whom S already knows. He has the sort of cognitive fix on Muggs that one has in such a situation; he isn't seeing or hearing Muggs, just thinking about him in the way one thinks about someone one knows, via a detached notion. But he wants H to have a perceptual fix on Muggs, for this is required to approach him and give him the message. S's plan puts a cognitive burden on H, to know or be able to find out what Muggs looks like.

Or perhaps S is a professor in a large class and Muggs is a student whose name S does not know. Muggs asks him if he can have an extension on his paper, and S agrees. He tells his teaching assistant H, "Make a note that he gets an extension." S is assuming the assistant will know the student's name, for this is required to make a useful note. S's plan, in some detail, is:

- H hears my utterance, and parses it;
- H has the fix: the person the speaker of the utterance refers to with 'he';

- H realizes that I, the professor, am the speaker;
- H has the fix: the person the professor is referring to with 'he';
- H witnessed my conversation with the student, and realizes that is who I have in mind;
- H has the fix: the student the professor was just talking to;
- H is a responsible assistant and knows the names of his students;
- H has a fix on the student via the student's name (whatever it is);
- H will be in a position to make a useful note.

The pronoun 'he' provides auxiliary information about the referent, that he is a male. It may be misinformation. In this case, the professor may not have realized that the student he was talking to was a female; it's not always easy to tell. Or the professor may be a fossil who thinks that girls should dress like girls and boys like boys; he was very aware that the student was a girl, but signaled his disapproval to the teaching assistant by using the wrong pronoun. Or maybe his native language is Basque, which doesn't have a gendered pronoun system, and he always says 'he' rather than think about which English pronoun to use. In this case, it really doesn't matter. The teaching assistant will know to whom he is referring, and disregard the misinformation.

Sometimes it does matter. Perhaps two students have been making requests of the professor. He tells the teaching assistant, "Give *her* an extension, give *him* an incomplete." He is counting on the pronouns to distinguish between the two students, and if he gets it wrong, the wrong students may end up with the incomplete and the extension. This additional information, or misinformation as the case may be, does not affect who or what is being referred to, nor is it asserted of the referent. We say it is *projected*; we'll have more to say about this below, particularly when we get to descriptions.

5   Demonstratives

5.1   Introduction

The demonstratives 'this' and 'that' occupy a rather intriguing place in the history of reference. At one point Russell thought they provided the only true names, what he called 'logically proper names,' ones which were not hidden descriptions, but directly picked out their referents, and contributed those referents to the propositions believed or expressed [Russell, 1912]. Demonstratives, used as logically proper names, had a rather limited use in Russell's view, however, since they serve only to refer to particulars and universals exemplified in one's sense data. Modern referentialism began with a focus on descriptions and names, then moved to indexicals, and more or less halted when it got back to demonstratives. Although Kaplan titled his monograph 'Demonstratives', indexicals dominate the discussion, and only indexicals are treated in the formal part. The monograph nevertheless contains a lot of thinking about demonstratives. Kaplan argues that they are devices of direct reference, and rejects a theory he develops to show how Fregean ideas might be applied to them: the Fregean theory of demonstratives. He adapts a part of that theory, the Fregean theory of demonstrations, but puts a direct reference spin on it. Our acts of pointing incorporate something like a Fregean *Sinn*, but it is the reference, not the *Sinn*, that gets incorporated into the proposition expressed. But he does not seem entirely satisfied with this theory, and adopts, or at least says he is inclined to adopt, a rather different one in the sequel 'Afterthoughts.' This theory holds that it is not the public demonstration that is determinative, but what he calls the 'directing intention' – a term we have borrowed, we hope in a way that does not distort his intentions unduly [Kaplan, 1989b].

In this chapter we consider demonstratives from the point of view of the elements of reference we have identified. We also argue that our ordinary judgements about what is said, and what is referred to, incorporate a forensic element, so that these judgements can be pushed one way or another by judgements about the responsibilities speakers have for cases in which their hearers are misled. We recommend explicating these concepts, in Carnap's sense, somewhat so that we can more cleanly draw a line between the contributions of the speaker's intentions and the contribution of external factors.

5.2 The professor and the portrait

A famous example adapted from Kaplan's earlier paper 'Dthat' [Kaplan, 1979] can help us see the difference he saw between theories in which the demonstration is determinative, and those in which the directing intention is. A philosophy professor is giving a lecture in a familiar lecture hall at UCLA. For years a portrait of Rudolf Carnap has hung behind the podium on the stage of the hall. At one point the professor points behind himself, without looking, and says,

(5.1)   That's a painting of the greatest philosopher of the twentieth century.

But some mischievous graduate students have replaced the portrait of Carnap with one of Dick Cheney.[1] Did the professor say something false about a portrait of Cheney? That seems to be the unequivocal verdict of the theory that holds that demonstrations are determinative. Did he say something true about the portrait of Carnap, the one he intended to point to, in a rather misleading way? If intention simply determined reference, that would be the verdict.

The concepts of directing intentions and target intentions allow a more nuanced view. The cognitive fix on the portrait the professor intended to establish for his hearers was perceptual; that's why he pointed; he wanted the audience to see the portrait behind him, and impart the belief that it portrayed the greatest philosopher of the twentieth century. This intention was successful; the audience did come to have a perceptual fix on the portrait. But he intended that, by having a cognitive fix on the portrait to which he drew their attention, they would have a cognitive fix on the portrait he remembered, which his motivating belief was about, and that he would impart a belief about that portrait; those intentions did not succeed. As in one of our Union Station cases, although the speaker's intentions determined what he referred to, he did not refer to what he intended to.

This is how it works in more detail on our theory. The professor has a detached notion of the portrait, associated with the idea of being a portrait of Carnap, and hence of the greatest philosopher of the twentieth century. This notion is a component of his primary referential intention, to refer to that very portrait. He has a false belief, that the portrait is hanging behind him and is thus playing an epistemic–pragmatic role in his life. It is the portrait he would see if he turned

---

[1] Kaplan's original example had a portrait of Nixon's vice-president, Spiro Agnew, hanging behind the podium. George H. W. Bush's vice-president, Dan Quayle, has often been subsequently used by philosophers discussing the example. Cheney seems a reasonable update. We know of no credible cases in which Gerald Ford, Walter Mondale, George H. W. Bush, Al Gore, or Joe Biden have been used.

around, and that he can point to by pointing behind himself. Thus, he believes it is the portrait he can refer to using the demonstrative 'that,' which is suited by its rather sparse and flexible meaning for referring to things the speaker can draw a hearer's attention to by pointing. If he were actually holding the portrait, 'this' would be more appropriate, although 'that' could still do the job. His directing intention is to exploit this role the portrait is playing in his life, and refer to it with 'that.' The portrait that plays that role is the one he refers to, for the directing intention is determinative. So, although his plan is to refer to the Carnap portrait, he in fact refers to the Cheney portrait.

The path intention is pretty straightforward. He intends that the audience will hear his utterance, see that he is the speaker, notice his gesture, and come to have a perceptual fix on the portrait. He probably has the further intention of getting them to believe that Carnap is the greatest philosopher of the twentieth century (or at least to realize that that is his opinion); some of them will recognize that the portrait is of Carnap, and they will soon tell the others. But things don't go according to plan. Since he doesn't refer to the object he planned to refer to, he doesn't say what he planned to say. In fact he says something quite false, and he is responsible for doing so. This seems to account for the intuitions about the case. However, given this account, the view that intentions are determinative has given the same result as the view that demonstrations are.

5.3   Forensics

Now let's consider some variations. The first is designed to show that Kaplan was correct in coming to think that directing intentions rather than demonstrations are determinative. The original example doesn't show that, since the conclusion we reached was that the professor referred to and said something false about the Cheney portrait, which is the same conclusion that we would come to if we took his demonstration rather than his intention to be determinative.

Suppose there are two portraits on the side wall of the lecture hall – the one closer to the podium is of Carnap, the one further away is of Cheney. Our professor knows this. He is rather careless, and also rather awkward, so without proper care there is a somewhat loose link between his will and the movements he makes. He intends to point to, draw attention to, and refer to the closer portrait, the one of Carnap. He manages to point in the direction of the wall, but a line drawn from his shoulder through his forefinger and beyond would hit the Cheney portrait rather than the one of Carnap. If demonstrations were determinative, it seems he would have referred to the Cheney portrait. He can certainly be faulted for pointing at the Cheney portrait, which is not what he intended to do. But it doesn't seem to us that he has *referred* to the Cheney portait. We maintain, with some qualifications, that he referred to the Carnap portrait, said it was of the greatest philosopher, and misleadingly pointed at the Cheney portrait.

One could protest at this point that surely the best thing to say is that the case is indeterminate. It's clear that the professor pointed at the Cheney portrait, but didn't intend to point at it or to refer to it. It's clear that he intended to point to and refer to the Carnap portrait, but he didn't point at it. On the other hand, he pointed in its general direction. If the Cheney portrait hadn't been there, perhaps it would have been a clear case of referring to the Carnap portrait with an inept gesture. But the Cheney portrait was there. It's really not a clear case of anything. This is hard to argue with.

We believe that there is a forensic element that affects the way we use the concepts of 'what is said' and 'what is referred to' in cases like this – forensic in the sense of having to do with adjudication of responsibility and blame for the results of an act. Suppose that the audience had included a number of alumni innocent of twentieth-century philosophy. They observed the professor's gesture, heard what he said, and concluded that a distinguished UCLA philosophy professor believed that Dick Cheney was the greatest philosopher of the twentieth century. Perhaps one of them, upon returning home, adds a note to the plaque beneath the portrait of Cheney in his living room, 'The greatest philosopher of the twentieth century.' Some of his friends tell him this is an absurd view. Couldn't he reply, with considerable justification, "Professor so and so *said* he was"? The alumnus came to believe the proposition that the portrait of Cheney was of the greatest philosopher of the twentieth century, by a perfectly legitimate process; he assumed the professor was talking about the Cheney portrait, the one he pointed to, and assertively, sincerely, and authoritatively said of it that it was of the greatest philosopher. If saying is all about communication, it seems that one *says* what one *conveys* to semantically competent and attentive listeners who pay attention to the meanings of one's words and gestures.

Suppose the situation were more consequential. Our careless professor is an eye-witness in a law case. There are two defendants at the witness table; the person he saw is in the middle, next to him is the co-defendant, whom the professor did not see, and about whom he has no evidence to give. At the crucial moment in his testimony, he intends to point at the occupant of the middle seat, but given his carelessness and awkwardness points at the co-defendant instead, and says, "I saw that man do it." His testimony is critical in convincing that attentive jury that the co-defendant is guilty; his testimony also seemed to leave the prosecution without a case with regard to the man he actually saw. Surely a member of the jury is entitled to think, and could sincerely and plausibly claim, that the professor referred to the co-defendant, and said that he saw him commit the crime.

We sympathize with the alumnus and the juror. The charges that the professor referred as they said he did, and said what they say he said, are not clearly false. They are not so clearly true either, however. The professor can say that, as a result of his own ineptness, he was misinterpreted. He was taken to say what he didn't say. The aggrieved parties can reply that he didn't say what he intended to.

Here we see the influence of the forensic element. We get credit, and receive blame, for what we say. In general, saying false things is bad, saying true things is good; saying things you have no evidence for in a court of law is especially bad. Since the responsibility and guilt are clear in these cases, we come down on the side of what seems the most straightforward account: the professor said false things, and that had bad results.

For theoretical purposes, however, we think there is much to be said for resolving issues so that the directing intention is determinative as to what is referred to, and so as to what is said. Or, more cautiously, there is much to be said for introducing *explications* of referring and saying, in the sense of the greatest philosopher of the twentieth century (arguably), that leave off the forensic elements [Carnap, 1950].

As we have explained reference, what one refers to is determined by a mix of internal and external factors. The speaker's directing intention determines that the referent will be the object that plays the intended epistemic–pragmatic role. But which object plays that role isn't up to the speaker, but to the rest of the world, which may include pranksters. The concept of the directing intention is the line between the internal contribution and the external contribution. Our concept of reference, faithful to the ordinary one, we think, except for shaving off the forensic elements, follows that line. The speaker has power to choose the role the referent plays in his life, and the referent is the object that plays *that* role. But facts outside the speaker, about which he may have false beliefs, determine who or what plays that role (or whether nothing does). The internal part is the intention, the external part is the facts about which object plays the intended role. Downstream considerations, like the sort of uptake on the part of the audience that the speaker actually achieves in the circumstances, or should have foreseen that he might induce, play no role in determining reference, in our explicated version of it. Their intrusion into our ordinary concept probably makes it useful in certain ways, but being faithful to them would give us a bit of a theoretical mess. The theory needn't ignore them, for they are among the perlocutionary effects the speaker has, and will often be responsible for.

Given this somewhat refined concept of reference, we can explain what we shall call, following Austin, the *locutionary act*. The locutionary act involves referring to an object (or objects) and predicating something of it (or them). For locutionary acts, the reference is determined according to our explication.

The demonstrations theory and the intentions theory gave the same result for the original example: the professor said the portrait of Cheney was of the greatest philosopher. In the variations, however, the two theories give different results. In our version of the intentions theory the professor did refer to the object he intended to refer to, because it did play the role he intended to exploit; he didn't refer to the object he ineptly gestured towards. In each case the professor said something true, but did so in an inept way, and is responsible for the results of that ineptitude. The untoward consequences of inept pointing will be handled at the level of perlocutionary acts, and the issue of responsibility will be seen not as a case of responsibility for what was said, but responsibility for the unintended but in these cases foreseeable consequences of carelessness.

5.4   Walking through Donostia

We'll now look at a less problematic example. Suppose S and H are walking though the streets of Donostia, in order for H to give a talk at the Institute for Logic, Cognition, Language, and Information that is, the ILCLI. S says, looking at Larrazabal Hall, a building down the hill and across a busy street,

(5.2)   That building houses the ILCLI.

As we are imagining the situation, H has already noticed Larrazabal Hall. It's the largest building in view, with a somewhat interesting architecture. Thus the building already plays an epistemic role in H's life; it is a building he is looking at and perceiving and noting various properties of. H hears the utterance (5.2). He believes that S is the speaker of the utterance.

H has the job of intention discovery. Given the situation, he takes S to be saying something he wants H to believe, as opposed to making a joke, or starting to sing an aria. He takes the job of the sentence in (5.2) to be to identify what it is he is to believe: that the building to which S refers is the ILCLI. Although S does not point, it's pretty clear from the direction he is looking, the minimal identification he provides, and the fact that what he refers to is the sort of thing that could house an institute, that he is referring to a large salient building that he assumes H has already spotted or will quickly pick out from the scene before them. H concludes, perhaps tentatively, that S is referring to the large building H has already noted, and that it is the ILCLI.

H's perception and reasoning involves what we call the 'hearer's buffer,' as well as other buffers and notions. H has a perceptual buffer for the utterance (5.2) and a perceptual buffer for S, and he has the belief that S is the speaker of the utterance. He perceives the utterance as being of a certain type, an utterance of the English sentence 'That building houses the ILCLI.' He has a buffer of a large building he sees, and believes that it is the building that S refers to with 'that building.' He links two roles: the role of being the building he sees, and that of being the building referred to by the speaker of the utterance he hears.

In this case, S's primary referential intention is to refer to Larrazabal Hall, the building that houses the ILCLI. He has a notion of Larrazabal Hall, often detached, but now serving as a buffer, since he takes the building he sees to be Larrazabal Hall. It is this perceptual role that Larrazabal Hall plays that he chooses to exploit. This is his directing intention. The permissive conventions of English allow one to refer to a building one sees with 'that building.' His path intention involves H having this series of cognitive fixes on Larrazabal Hall: object referred to by the speaker of the utterance I hear as 'that building'; object referred to by S as 'that building'; building S is looking at; building I am looking at.

S's auxiliary intention is to identify the referent as a building. Thus in constructing the demonstrative phrase 'that building' he predicates being a building of the referent, but does not assert that this is so. Still, he intends H to think of Larrazabal Hall as a building, to go from 'object referred to as "that building"' to 'that building.' If S had had a rather negative view of the architectural merits of Larrazabal Hall, he might have said, "That pile of bricks houses the ILCLI." Larrazabal Hall is not a pile of bricks, but a building with a brick exterior, so S would have predicated something false of Larrazabal Hall in constructing his demonstrative phrase, but not have asserted it. In this case his plan would have involved what we call an identificatory detour:

- the referent = the thing S refers to as 'that pile of bricks'
  - a literal pile of bricks couldn't house the ILCLI
  - S isn't looking at a pile of bricks
  - the referent isn't really a pile of bricks
  - S is looking at a brick-faced building
  - S doesn't much like brick-faced buildings
  - S is most likely using 'pile of bricks' to convey 'ugly brick-faced building'
- the referent = the building S is looking at.

This reasoning of H's is an example of what, in Chapter 1, we called far-side pragmatics in the service of near-side pragmatics. H needs to figure out what S is referring to, before he can identify what S is saying. But he can figure out enough about what S is saying, before knowing what S is referring to, to help him figure out what S is referring to. There are fairly reliable indications that S is trying to be helpful and relevant, and identifying the building to which they are headed seems helpful and relevant, and so a good candidate for what he is trying to do, given the predicate, 'houses the ILCLI.' The word 'that' is suited for referring to an object that one is looking at, and that one's hearer is also in a position to look at. So it seems likely that S is referring to a building, the sort of object that can house a research institute, and of which several are in view.

Buildings aren't really piles of bricks, but an ugly building might appear rather like a mere pile of bricks. So S's auxiliary intention is probably to be helpful in identifying the referent not by predicating something true of it, but something that suggests what it looks like. The most likely explanation of that choice is that he intends to convey, that is to implicate, that he thinks it is rather ugly.

Such reasoning might be reconstructed within a framework that eschews utterances in favor of sentences in formally represented contexts. The context might include a feature of literalness, plus or minus, or something like that. But to us it seems most straightforwardly reconstructed as reasoning to the best explanation for the features of a perceived event. The event is clearly an utterance, an intentional act, and the hearer must arrive at the best explanation, in terms of the intentions of the speaker. Grammatical knowledge plays an important role; H identifies the words, the subject–predicate structure of the sentence, and the structure of the referring expression as involving the expression 'that' with a modifying phrase, 'pile of bricks.' He realizes that 'housing the ILCLI' is predicated of the referent by the whole statement. He takes the whole statement to be a literal assertion, intended to impart the belief that the referent houses the ILCLI by imparting the belief that S believes this.

It does not follow from the assertive nature of the whole utterance that the predication within the referring expression is intended literally. To provide a second example, S might have chosen to refer ironically, while asserting literally, and said 'that little building houses the ILCLI.' In fact he referred metaphorically, while asserting literally.

5.5   Truth-conditions

Earlier we mentioned the problem of Grice's circle. Far-side pragmatics begins with what is said, and looks for the best explanation for it, constrained by Gricean maxims, his Cooperative Principle, or perhaps just reasoning to the best explanation. But then how can far-side pragmatics be used to determine what is referred to, since what is said depends on what is referred to?

Our way out of the Gricean circle is to note that the hearer needn't fully identify what is said in order to commence his pragmatic reasoning; he can reason if he has a way of thinking about what is said, and this doesn't require knowing which proposition is expressed, and so doesn't require knowing which object is referred to. After all, he can start off his far-side considerations by just asking, "Why did the speaker say whatever he said?"

But if this is the only way the hearer has to think about what is said, he won't get very far. The hearer typically needs *semantic* characterizations of what is said, that is, in the case of assertions involving declarative sentences, descriptions of conditions under which the assertion would be true. But now the circle seems to appear again, for what are the truth-conditions of an assertion, if not the proposition expressed by the assertion?

We respond to this with a theory of *relative truth-conditions* and in particular utterance-bound and utterance-independent truth-conditions.[2] The possibility of relative truth-conditions arises naturally from our focus on utterances.

Let's return to the case in which S says, "That pile of bricks houses the ILCLI." Call this utterance **u**. H hears **u** and parses it successfully. He understands what is predicated of the referent by 'houses the ILCLI.' But, until he engages in some far-side pragmatics, he doesn't know what is being referred to.

At this point, H has what we call an 'utterance-bound' fix on the truth-conditions of **u**. He knows **u** is true, if whatever object the speaker of **u** refers to with his utterance of 'that pile of bricks' houses the ILCLI. Let's spell this out. Because of what he understands, and his knowledge of how English works, H knows what the world must be like for **u** to be true:

> *Given* the syntax of **u**, and the fact that the subutterance of 'houses the ILCLI' predicates housing the ILCLI, **u** is true if and only if [*iff*] there is an object that is both the object the speaker of **u** refers to with the subutterance of 'that pile of bricks' and houses the ILCLI.

What follows the 'iff' is a condition for **u** to be true. It is a condition on **u** itself, not on Larrazabal Hall. It expresses a proposition about **u**, not about Larrazabal Hall. It is definitely *not* what S said, not the proposition expressed by **u**. Still, it does get at the truth-conditions of **u**. It tells us how the rest of the world has to be, relative to **u**, for **u** to be true, given certain other facts about **u**.

At this point, H has an *utterance-bound* conception of the truth-conditions of **u**. He understands the truth-conditions of **u** in terms of **u** *itself*, which is why Perry calls them the *reflexive* truth-conditions.

Suppose now we add in the fact that H realizes that S is the speaker. Then he knows what we call the *speaker-bound* truth-conditions of **u**:

> *Given* the syntax of **u**, and the fact that the subutterance of 'houses the ILCLI' predicates housing the ILCLI, *and* that S is the speaker of **u**, **u** is true *iff* there is an object that is both the object S refers to with the subutterance of 'that pile of bricks' and houses the ILCLI.

Here what follows the 'iff' gives the truth-conditions of **u** as conditions on S. It tells how the rest of the world has to be, relative to S, for **u** to be true, given facts about **u** and S. We have a proposition about S, not about **u**. Still, it clearly is *not* what S said; S wasn't talking about himself, but about Larrazabal Hall. But, at this point, H can use everything he knows about S to help him with his

---

[2] Here we basically follow Perry, 2001b. The use of these distinctions to deal with Grice's circle have been discussed in Korta and Perry, 2008. We will return to it in §12.3 below.

far-side pragmatics. He can factor in S's tastes and habits, his dislike of brick buildings, and the like, to engage in the bit of reasoning we mentioned above, which is reasoning about S's intentions:

- the referent of the subject of **u** = thing S refers to as 'that pile of bricks'
  - a literal pile of bricks couldn't house the ILCLI
  - S isn't looking at a pile of bricks
  - the referent isn't really a pile of bricks
  - S is looking at a brick-faced building
  - S doesn't much like brick-faced buildings
  - S is most likely using 'pile of bricks' to convey 'ugly brick-faced building'
- the referent of the subject of **u** = building S is looking at.

H realizes that the building S is looking at is the same building he is looking at, the one he can think of as 'that building.' Now H knows:

> *Given* the syntax of **u**, and the fact that the subutterance of 'houses the ILCLI' predicates housing the ILCLI, and that S is the speaker of **u**, *and* that S refers to *that building* with the subutterance of 'that pile of bricks,' **u** is true *iff that building* houses the ILCLI.

Now the condition to the right of 'iff' is a condition on Larrazabal Hall, the building H is looking at and thinking of as 'that building.' It expresses neither a proposition about **u** nor one about S. The proposition it expresses is true in some worlds in which neither **u** nor S exists, and some in which S exists but never said a word to H, or anything about Larrazabal Hall.

Since we have terminology for the utterance-bound and the speaker-bound truth-conditions, we'll introduce some for this level of truth-conditions; they are the *referential* truth-conditions of **u**. We take ourselves to be referentialists, in holding that what is said by speakers employing demonstratives, indexicals, and proper names are propositions encoding the referential truth-conditions of their utterances. However, as *critical* referentialists we maintain that these are not the only truth-conditions of utterances that speakers and hearers take into account, in planning and interpreting utterances. If they were, the differences in the ways that different singular terms refer would have no bearing upon what people say or understand.

5.6   Demonstratives and the problems of cognitive significance

In §2.2 we noted a somewhat puzzling thing about the history of reference. In adopting the descriptive theory of proper names, Frege and Russell were motivated, at least in part, by the problems of cognitive significance: the co-reference and no-reference problems. The referentialist theories that have now largely supplanted their theories as standard views in the philosophy of language seem to provide no solution to these problems. In these theories, the two statements "Tully is Tully" and "Cicero is Tully" express the same proposition, that a certain Roman bears the relation of identity to himself, and, assuming there is no monster in Loch Ness, "Nessie is huge" doesn't express any proposition at all. Is this progress?

The term 'cognitive significance' is used in a variety of related ways. For us, of course, it is utterances that *have* cognitive significance. We use the term to get at the beliefs that motivate the speaker to make an utterance, and the beliefs that the competent hearer of it acquires; these properties of two utterances can be quite different, even if their referential contents are the same.

5.6.1   Co-reference

The co-reference problem can be illustrated with just one demonstrative. Return to the example of §4.5, involving Union Station in Chicago. S and H can see two parts of Union Station from their vantage point, the eastern part and the western part. S can refer to Union Station by pointing at either part. Consider two utterances, **u-1** and **u-2**, of

(5.3)   That is the same building as that.

In the first, S points twice at the eastern part of Union Station. In the second S points first at the eastern part, and then at the western part. The statements clearly differ in cognitive significance; the first is trivial, the second conveys a rather surprising fact.

It seems hopeless to develop a pragmatic theory, a theory about how language is used, on the basis of a semantics that cannot explain such a fundamental fact as the difference in cognitive significance between **u-1** and **u-2**. But we think the difference can be explained, within a recognizably referentialist theory of utterances, given the concept of relative truth-conditions developed in the last section, which is a key part of our approach to pragmatics. This will be a continuing theme, but we'll start at Union Station.

Consider **u-2**, S's second, non-trivial utterance – indeed, one whose truth is rather surprising. S has two cognitive fixes on Union Station, one when he looks east, the other when he looks west. He assumes that H has two corresponding cognitive fixes. S's goal is to get H to realize they are cognitive fixes on the same building. What is his plan?

S plans to exploit the speaker-bound truth-conditions of **u-2**:

> *Given* the syntax of **u-2**, and the fact that the subutterance of 'is the same building as' predicates being identical buildings *and* that S is the speaker of **u-2**, **u-2** is

true *iff* there is an object that is a building the S refers to with his first use of 'that' and his second use of 'that.'

S's plan is that H will observe the way he looks at and points to the eastern wing with his first utterance of 'that' and the way he looks at and points to the western wing with his second utterance of 'that.' So H will realize:

> *Given* everything above, and in addition that S is referring to the building he sees and points at to the east with S's first utterance of 'that' and to the building he sees and points at to the west with his second use of 'that' **u-2** is true *iff* the building he sees and points at to the east is the same building he sees and points at to the west.

S assumes it will be obvious to H that the buildings S sees to the east and west are the same ones that H sees to the east and west, so he will transfer the roles, and realize, if he believes S, 'The building I see to the east is the same building I see to the west.' And, no doubt, he will be surprised to learn that.

With respect to **u-1** it's a little hard to flesh out S's full motivation plausibly, unless he is a philosopher making a point. But suppose he is. Then he wants H to reason as above, substituting '**u-1**' for '**u-2**,' and 'east' for 'west,' thus arriving at, 'The building I see to the east is the same building I see to the east,' which S assumes he will find quite trivial.

The general point is that one can be a referentialist about what is said by a speaker, the proposition expressed by the utterance she makes, without assuming that that proposition, the one corresponding to the referential truth-conditions, is the only one made cognitively accessible by the utterance. This is not only important with regard to the problem of cognitive significance, but is the key to using referential semantics in the service of pragmatics. We'll return to this theme often in what follows.

5.6.2   No-reference

Angus and Fiona are sitting on the banks of Loch Ness. There is a flurry of activity near the middle of the loch. Fiona says

(5.4)   That monster can really stir things up.

Assuming there really is no Loch Ness monster, Fiona has not referred to any-thing. Yet she seems to have a motivating belief, and an intention for Angus to have a belief with the same content.

The speaker-bound content of Fiona's utterance, given the way she intends to use 'that monster,' is that there is a monster that she is perceiving, or at least perceiving an effect of, and it can really stir things up. Since there is no such monster, what she says is false.

The motivating belief can be assigned a *notion-bound* content. It has notion as a component that is not a notion of anything. It's one Fiona formed in response to hearing about the monster, and she has associated new ideas with it as she heard more about the monster and made her own observation. The notion is associated with the ideas of being a monster and living in Loch Ness and a number of other things. So the reflexive or notion-bound content of her belief is that there is a monster, that this notion is of, that lives in the loch and can really stir things up. There is no such monster; this belief does not meet its notion-bound truth-conditions, so it too is false.

Perhaps Angus has never heard of the monster, or has heard of it but was skeptical until now. Hearing the credible Fiona refer to it, he decides that there must be such a monster, and that surely it can stir things up, as they have just witnessed. So now he too has a belief with the notion associated with being a monster and living in Loch Ness, but his notion, like Fiona's, isn't of anything.

The levels of utterance-bound, speaker-bound, and notion-bound truth-conditions allow us to assign contents and truth values to Fiona's utterance and Angus and Fiona's beliefs. We assume the gullible Fiona also has a notion of the yeti, the Himalayas' Abominable Snowman, which is distinct from her notion of Nessie, the Loch Ness monster. The beliefs cannot be distinguished by their referential content, for they have none – or at least so we assume. But we can distinguish the notion-bound content of Fiona's belief that Nessie can stir things up from the notion-bound content of her belief that the yeti can stir things up.

Still, there seems something unaccounted for; at the level of utterance-bound and notion-bound contents, Fiona's belief and Angus' belief don't have much in common. If there were a monster, their beliefs would have referential contents that were about the same monster, but since there is no monster, they don't stand in that relation. But they still seem to have something important in common. For one thing, in roughly the same counterfactual circumstance – there being a real monster who is the origin of all the monster talk, who can really stir things up – their beliefs would both be true, in virtue of the same facts about the same monster.

The missing part of the account is what we call 'conditional co-referring' or 'coco-referring.' The basic idea is that there can be a connection among notions and utterances, such that if any of them have a referent, they will all have the same one. This is the relation that obtains among Fiona's notion, the utterances on the basis of which she formed it, her own utterances of 'that monster,' and Angus' notion and utterances. All of these are part of the same network, linked locally by intentions to refer to the same thing if one refers to anything, and more distantly by series of such local links. If that network had an appropriate origin, they would all have a referent, and it would be the same for all of them. Coco-referring is important in anaphora and with proper names; we will provide more details in Chapter 7.

6   Context sensitivity and indexicals

6.1   Role-contexts

The word 'context' is often, perhaps most often, used to mean the linguistic context, that is, 'the parts of a written or spoken statement that precede or follow a specific word or passage, usually influencing its meaning or effect.' This is what is meant when we say someone has 'taken a remark out of context.' It is what we mean when we say that speech-recognition systems look at the contexts of the words they are identifying. It is not too far from the original idea behind a 'context-free grammar,' i.e., one in which phrases can be taken out of context; the syntactically important properties don't depend on what goes on in other phrases.

In the philosophy of language, however, a more general meaning is common: the set of circumstances or facts that surround a particular event, situation, etc.[1] From the point of view of a theory of utterances, things quickly get a bit complex thought of in this way. As we have said, we are thinking of utterances as intentional acts of speakers at times, involving beliefs, intentions, and other mental states causing bodily movements of a sort appropriate to make sounds, write letters, type, and the like. Where do such events occur? What counts as inside them, and what counts as being in their surroundings?

We think of context mainly as what we will officially call the 'role-filling context.' The utterance is comprised of the mental states and movements that are involved in the production of the token. The context starts on the far side of the speaker's plan, at the point where the world takes over from the intentions to determine what the locutionary content will be. That is, given the words the speaker uses, and the directing intentions with which he uses them, which objects play the appropriate roles to be the referents?

The role-filling context needs to be distinguished from what might be called the 'evidential context' – all the facts that the hearer has at her disposal to figure out what the speaker's intentions are, and what he has actually said.

---

[1] Both definitions are from Dictionary.com.

The role-contextual facts about the utterance are part of what a hearer has to figure out, to completely understand what is going on. But of course she also has to figure out a lot more. Joana and Larraitz, in Chapter 1, had to figure out which language John was speaking. The hearer needs to figure out the intentions that resolve ambiguities and nambiguities, detect any irony that is there to be detected, and so forth. All of this requires evidence, and the evidence surely comes from the context, in the ordinary sense, of the perception. However, these are not what we will call role-contextual facts, and it will not be what we have in mind when we use the word 'context.'

By 'context-sensitive,' said of expressions, then, we will mean that factors beyond the meanings provided by the language and the intentions of the speaker that are involved in determining reference. So understood, context-sensitivity is not the same as indexicality, in the way we shall use the term.

6.2   Indexicals

Philosophers sometimes use the term 'indexicality' for any kind of context sensitivity. For example, when Hilary Putnam wanted to express his insight that the reference of a natural kind term like 'water' depends not only on the 'stereotype' associated with it by those who understand the term, but on the facts about the chemistry of liquids in the part of the universe where the term is used, he refers to 'hidden indexicality.' We distinguish among a number of types of context sensitivity, and use the phrase 'indexical' more narrowly, for what Kaplan calls the 'true indexicals.' These include 'I,' 'here,' 'now,' 'today,' and 'tomorrow.' Indexicality, as we use the term, is not that common, and is hard to hide; context-sensitivity, on the other hand, has many forms, and is ubiquitous, although sometimes hard to notice. In this chapter we begin with a discussion of context sensitivity, and then discuss semantics and pragmatics of indexicals.

There are basically two contextual issues that need to be resolved, and it is the way that the meanings of indexicals contribute to resolving these issues that marks their difference from demonstratives. First there is the issue of what epistemic/pragmatic role the speaker intends to exploit. Indexicals constrain the options narrowly. When I say "that man," I may have in mind the man that I see, the man we have been talking about, the man the television newscaster has just mentioned, and so forth. But when I say "I," I am basically limited to exploiting the role of being the speaker of the utterance, or perhaps the thinker of a thought. When I say "today," I am limited to the role of being the twenty-four-hour period during which the utterance takes place. The meaning of the indexical specifies the contextual element that is relevant, the utterance-relative role. An utterance of 'I' refers to the speaker of the utterance; an utterance of 'today' refers to the day on which the utterance occurs; an utterance of 'now' refers to the time at which the utterance occurs; a use of 'here' refers to the place at which the utterance occurs.

Second, once the exploited role is fixed, there may be the issue of which of several objects that play the exploited role the speaker intends to refer to. The context may make it evident that when I say "that man" I intend to refer to a man that I see across the street. But there may be a couple of candidates. I may point or otherwise gesture to make it clear; even so, it may not be clear. You may have to ask. With regard to this issue, indexicals differ amongst themselves.

With 'I,' the meaning fixes the role, and there is only one candidate to play the role, and any further intentions about reference can have no effect at all. If I say "I," I refer to myself, whatever further intentions I might have. Elwood may think that he is Barack Obama or Napoleon or Socrates, and may intend to refer to one of them when he says the word 'I.' Nevertheless, he refers only to Elwood. Thus 'I' is perhaps the word in English most suited to obscure the role of intentions in language. The speaker must intend to use English, and intend to use the sound or letter 'I' to express the first person, rather than merely as part of the acronym 'CIA' or as part of the refrain 'E-I-E-I-O.' But given that he intends to use the word with its first-person meaning, there isn't much left for intention to do. The meaning determines the role the speaker exploits; and there is only room for one object to play that role – the speaker himself or herself.[2] Thus understanding the reference of a use of 'I' places minimal demands on the hearer's intention-discovery abilities.[3]

---

[2] At this point, the two authors, who insist on using the word 'I' in examples as if there were only one of them, may seem to be struggling to provide a counterexample to their own claim. We ignore this complication.

[3] While 'I' is least susceptible to indeterminacy, philosophers can disagree about which stretches of personhood constitute a single person. According to David Lewis [Lewis, 1976] and Ted Sider [Sider, 2001], a person is a momentary or perhaps instantaneous stage of what are usually thought of as persons. Galen Strawson thinks that, strictly speaking, the referent of 'I' is a self, a short instance of consciousness, lasting considerably less than a second [Strawson, 2009]. If one of these philosophers, in the mood to speak strictly, said "I didn't exist a moment ago," and a hearer, unaware of the theoretical context of the remark, denied this, we would seem to have a misunderstanding. The problem wouldn't be with the meaning of 'I,' or with the role that its referent plays with respect to its utterance. Moreover, both the speaker and the hearer would suppose that, among persons, it is the one who spoke the word 'I' that the utterance of it refers to (although it might be hard for an instantaneous person or a person who lasts only a micro-second to complete the task). The misunderstanding rests on the difference of opinions as to what persons are, and the disagreement will remain when the misunderstanding is cleared up. That is, the listener, unless persuaded by the speaker's view, will still think the speaker's remark is false, because he will think that the speaker, whatever his philosophical opinions and intentions, referred to himself, a being that did exist a moment before.

Another relevant philosophical position is that of Derek Parfit [Parfit, 1971], who maintains, more or less, that uses of 'I' can refer to different stretches of psychologically connected personhood. We'll leave discussion of this issue for another occasion.

The other indexicals are more demanding. There is clearly some intention discovery involved in interpreting utterances of 'here' and 'now.' They aren't always used indexically; one can point to Elba on a map and say "Here is where Napoleon was exiled." In the course of a narrative, one can say, "Now it was time for Lincoln to assert his authority as commander-in-chief." But even in indexical uses, the period of time that counts as 'now,' or the region that counts as 'here,' seems to depend on the intentions of the speaker. When Obama says, "I want a vote on healthcare reform now," he means this week or this month. When he says, "Now it is time to act on the problem of global warming," he may be a little more patient. When the coach tells the team, arriving at the stadium, "Here is where the game will be played," he means they have arrived at the field of battle. When he assembles the defense on the 10-yard line and says, "Here is where we will depend on you to be unyielding," he means the last 10 or so yards before the end zone.

A different sort of indeterminacy can creep in with 'today.' Kepa emails John: "I need the draft today." John emails Kepa: "I'll definitely send it to you *today*." Unless he gets it there the same day as he sends his emails, he emails falsely. And days are twenty-four-hour stretches of time, whatever one's intention or metaphysics. But is it the same day in Donostia or the same day in California that John is committed to? Or is he trying to convey one thought to Kepa, to placate him, while harboring another standard for himself that will give him more time? One way to look at the problem is that there are really twenty-four twenty-four-hour stretches of time officially counted, given modern time-keeping practices, that envelop any given instant.[4] In a conversation, one usually sticks to the one determined by the speaker's position, or the hearer's, or explicitly brings in the time-zone parameter, as John would have done if he had said more candidly, "I'll get it to you today, my time."[5]

So we see the sort of semantic context dependency that true indexicals exhibit, in their indexical uses, as significantly different from their use in the case of demonstratives, where the meanings of 'this' and 'that' only mildly constrain the role the referent has to play. It has to do instead with what counts, in the conversation, as the relevant units of times or places, or perhaps even what kinds of things speakers are supposed to be. Given the decision as to what counts, which object is the reference of 'I' or 'today' or 'now' or 'here' is determined by meaning and the occupants of the role mandated by meaning.

---

[4] Ignoring the non-standard time zones, as in Myanmar, which are a half hour off of the standard ones.

[5] In what is sometimes called the real world, as opposed to the world of philosophers, getting something to a person 'today' might suggest getting it to them by, say, five o'clock. This seems very odd to us.

6.3   Using 'I'

Let's start with 'I,' the philosophically important paradigm indexical, although, as we noted, a somewhat misleading paradigm. The semantics of 'I' is exhausted by our adaptation of Kaplan's character rule: an utterance of 'I' refers to the speaker of the utterance. That is, 'I' is a device a speaker can use, no matter who he is, or how self-deluded he is, to refer to himself or herself; that is, to refer to the person with whom he or she is identical.

Identity is an epistemic relation, and self an epistemic role, in the sense of Chapter 3. There are certain ways of knowing about oneself that we call 'normally self-informative ways' of knowing. There are ways of knowing if you have a headache, or if your arm itches, or if you are hungry, or if you see a bear in front of you, or if you'd rather have a Heineken or a Budweiser, that aren't available to others to know these same facts about you. We each have what we call a *self-notion*, where information about ourselves discovered in these ways is kept. It's a buffer that never needs to be detached, since we are always in a position to find out things about ourselves in these ways. But it can serve the role usually reserved for detached notions; since we never use these methods to find out about others, so we can accumulate information gotten in these ways in a single notion; no one else will ever play the role of self relative to us.[6]

The same notion is used for information we find out about ourselves in other ways, as long as we are aware that we are finding out about ourselves. When Barack Obama consults his daily schedule, distributed to all in the White House inner circle, he founds out what he will be doing at 10 a.m. in the same way that everyone else does, by seeing an entry like: "POTUS meets with potato-chip industry leaders in Oval Office" in the row marked '10 a.m.' He knows that he is POTUS, so this information goes in his self-notion. When Biden reads the same entry, it goes in his Obama-notion.[7]

Identity is also a pragmatic relation. If Obama wants Biden at the Oval Office at 10 a.m., he tells him, or emails Biden's aide. If Obama wants Obama there at that time, he gets up and starts walking to the office a bit before 10. There are ways of getting yourself to move, of scratching your own head, of chastising yourself, of changing your own mind, of getting food to your stomach, that aren't ways for anyone else to accomplish those things, although they can use them to have the same effects on themselves. Indeed, the first person is just such a device; it is a way we each have of referring to ourselves that we can't use to refer to anyone else, and that no one else can use to refer to us.

---

[6] See Perry, 2001a *passim*.

[7] POTUS being an acronym for President Of The United States, apparently widely used by the Secret Service and in the White House.

There is a way of knowing about an utterance that is self-informative, namely, being aware of the utterance as one's own act, involving one's will and one's mouth. In normal situations, in fact in all but very extreme situations that involve severe mental illness, or a philosopher's made-up examples, or both, we know that an utterance we are aware of in this way is our own.

We can't always be sure that an utterance known of in other ways isn't our own. You shout, "I love Yosemite" from the top of the falls, and hear the echo. Is that your own utterance you hear, or is there someone else in the distance expressing their love of the park? Technology can confuse things; you type in a response to a query using iChat, and you see the words you used appear on the screen – but maybe someone else gave the same response; you need to check the icon next to the text to make sure it is your own utterance you are seeing, or seeing an effect of, on your screen.

This all makes 'I' a very useful tool for the speaker, for imparting beliefs to others about himself, in certain situations; that is, an utterance of 'I' often provides the first step on a kind of path down which one often wants the hearer to travel. We've already considered its utility in getting the salt; now we'll look at some more consequential examples.

The first person is standardly used to convey to others the content of beliefs about oneself with one's self-notion as a component. The directing intention is to use the first person to convey a belief about oneself; the target intention will be to have the hearer have a belief with the same content, but a different cognitive fix – except in the case where a person leaves a reminder to himself. The intended path will begin with the fix the hearer has on the speaker as the speaker of the perceived utterance, and then, if it is a face-to-face conversation, as one the hearer is perceiving and interacting with, and from there to whatever the target role is. Let's look at some examples.

Bush and Cheney in the Oval Office
Bush enters the Oval Office by his private door, joining a meeting of his close counselors that is already in progress. Cheney is arguing strongly for a certain decision, so strongly that Bush feels his role as the Decider is in danger of being forgotten. Bush says to Cheney:

(6.1)   I am in charge.

Bush is trying to impart to Cheney a belief that he, George Bush, is in charge – or, more optimistically, remind him of and reinforce a belief he already has. Bush's motivating belief is that Bush is in charge, but he holds this belief in the special way people usually hold beliefs about themselves: Bush's cognitive fix on Bush is via his self-notion; his self-notion is a constituent of his primary referential intention. The role he exploits, when he uses 'I,' is the utterance-relative role of being the speaker. As noted above, he can be quite certain that the person playing the role of being the speaker of the utterance he is making is the same one whom he believes, via his self-notion, to be in charge. So his directing intention is to refer to the person who his self-notion is of, and the meaning of 'I' suits it to exploit this role, given the effect he wants to produce on Cheney.

Cheney will also recognize that the referent of the utterance of 'I' in (6.1) is its speaker. In order to keep the various elements involved in Cheney's understanding separate, imagine that his back is turned to Bush, there are other people in the room with whom he has been vigorously arguing, Cheney didn't hear Bush enter, and he doesn't immediately recognize his voice. He will realize that the referent is the speaker, and thus that the statement he hears is true if and only if the speaker is in charge. At this stage, there is a *nesting* of roles. Cheney hears (6.1) and attends to it. His fix on (6.1) is based on the role it plays in his life at that moment, as the utterance he hears and attends to. His initial fix on the referent of 'I' is as the speaker of the utterance he hears and attends to; the role of being the utterance heard and attended to is nested in the more complex role.

Cheney turns and sees a figure behind the famous Resolute desk, looking at him. This person is clearly the speaker. At first, perhaps, Cheney's fix on Bush is simply as the fellow he sees and attends to. Cheney *links* three different roles involved in his thinking; the person his current perception is of is the speaker of the utterance he just heard and attended to, and the person of whom being in charge has been predicated. At this point, we may suppose, he recognizes Bush.

Cheney has a notion of Bush that he acquired when he met Bush many years earlier. With subsequent experiences of Bush, reading about Bush, and the like, he has associated a great deal of information with this notion. He can use this notion to think about Bush when Bush isn't present, when it is detached. All of this information, all of the ideas he has associated with his Bush notion, now become attached to the roles of being the speaker of the utterance and the man that he sees. His notion becomes a buffer.

This is all according to Bush's plan. Bush wants to remind Cheney of something he already knows, that Bush is the President, and he is not, and he wants thereby to calm Cheney down, and to make it clear to his other counselors that in spite of Cheney's age and experience he remains the Decider. This he might have accomplished by saying, "Bush is in charge." But he wants them to have this thought in a certain way, the way one has a thought about a person who is present and at whom they are looking. Perhaps he hopes for a tinge of awe.

Thus the role assigned by English to 'I' plays an important role in Bush's plan. His use of 'I' puts a cognitive burden on his hearers. To identify to whom the speaker refers, they must identify the speaker. In doing this, they will come to realize that Bush has joined them. 'I' is a device of role-management, because getting them to think of him via the fix *speaker of the utterance I am hearing* will lead them to think of him under the fix *person I am looking at*. At that point they will recognize him as Bush, and realize that the President has joined them – and Cheney will moderate his tendency to take charge.

In this case, Bush's motivating belief is his belief that he is in charge, or perhaps his belief that he should be in charge and ought to act as though he is in charge. His directing intention is to exploit the standard meaning of the word 'I,' and so to refer to himself as the speaker of the utterance he is producing. He wants Cheney to notice that he has returned to the oval office, and to have the sort of cognitive fix on him that a person has when they see someone, recognize that person, and realize that that person is addressing them. His path intention is that Cheney will hear the utterance, recognize the voice, or look up and recognize the speaker. His communicative intention, of course, isn't to get Cheney to come to believe that Bush is commander-in-chief, but mostly to remind him of that fact, and call attention to his presence in the Oval Office, and his annoyance at Cheney's behavior.

Introducing oneself
Consider a simpler version of our opening example. When Larraitz meets John she says,

(6.2)   I am Larraitz.

If we assume a referential semantics for indexicals and names, Larraitz could have expressed the same thing by saying,

(6.3)   I am I

or

(6.4)   Larraitz is Larraitz.

But neither of these utterances would have achieved what she achieved with (6.2). John's first fix on on the subject will be as *speaker of the utterance I am hearing*; then he will link this role with *person I am seeing before me*. Then he will realize that if the statement is true, the person he sees before him is Larraitz, and this is Larraitz's goal.

Larraitz here exploits the fact that she has two cognitive fixes on herself. She has her self-notion. But she also, like her friends, neighbors, and associates, has her name. She wants to impart to John two cognitive fixes, one as the person talking to him, one as Larraitz.

There are cases where it's best not to refer to yourself with 'I' or to supplement it. Consider, the following two.

Send me a fax
Kepa needs the ILCLI secretary to send him a fax at home. (Perhaps his internet connection isn't working.) He calls and says one of the following:

(6.5)   This is Kepa. Please fax me the colloquium schedule.

(6.6)   Please fax me the colloquium schedule.

When he hears (6.6), the secretary will know that he is to fax the schedule to the utterer of (6.6), the person at the other end of the line. To do this, he will have to know the right fax number. This means he will have to look up the number for Kepa's home fax, or at least hit the right button on the autodial list on the institute fax. In either case, he will need the name of the caller. Kepa's plan in uttering (6.6) requires that the secretary recognize his voice and remember his name. The first part of (6.5) reduces the cognitive burden. If the secretary, or Kepa, were new to the institute (6.6) would be a bit pretentious, and (6.5) a better choice.

Note the difference generally between telephone and person-to-person communication. The caller usually announces himself by name on the phone. In America one says, e.g., "This is Kepa"; in other countries one might say "I am Kepa" or "Kepa here." We sometimes do this in face-to-face communication, as in Larraitz's case, sometimes not, as in the salt case of §3.6. The difference is whether (i) we have a goal in mind that requires the hearer to know who we are and what our name is or knowing our relative location suffices; (ii) whether we can count on the hearer recognizing us and knowing our name. Tasks like passing the salt to someone at the same dinner table don't require knowledge of names, only relative location. Tasks like sending a fax, looking up information in one's file, and the like, require one's name.

David and the federal agent
Our next example is from *Reference and Reflexivity*. David Israel is a computer scientist at SRI. We imagine that computer scientists at SRI have come under a dark cloud of suspicion in some future American regime, for being pointy-headed intellectuals that get government money to pursue goals unrelated to America's manifest destiny and religious roots. David is meeting with a federal agent in his role as manager of a group; he doesn't think the agent actually caught his name, since he refers to David as 'Mr. Big Shot.' The agent goes down a list of names and asks Israel if the person named is or ever has been a computer scientist. He asks, "Is David Israel a computer scientist?" David could answer:

(6.7)   I am a computer scientist.

(6.8)   David Israel is a computer scientist.

David chooses (6.8). To use (6.7) would be more natural, and conform better with Grice's maxims of cooperation. If he utters (6.7), and the agent naturally takes him to be providing an answer, the agent will link the roles of being the utterer of (6.7), and being the referent of 'I,' and being the person named 'David Israel' that he asked about. He will conclude that the person he is talking to is David Israel, is a computer scientist, and will probably treat him more contemptuously than he already has. Why would David want to bring that upon himself? He doesn't really want to be cooperative, beyond what is necessary to avoid whatever consequences there are of lying to a federal agent. So he utters (6.8), telling the truth in the least cooperative way he can think of.

6.3.1   *Misidentifying oneself*

In spite of the tight connection between the meaning of 'I' and the speaker, mistakes are still possible, with a little imagination. Suppose Fred is a young graduate student who admires John Searle greatly. He admires him so much, he often pretends to be Searle. And, as time goes by, he begins to occasionally fall into fugue states, where he believes he *is* John Searle. In such a state Fred walks into the philosophy lounge, and hears another student say, "*Intentionality* is a great book. Who wrote it?" Fred says proudly, "I wrote *Intentionality*."

Fred intends to inform the student that John Searle wrote *Intentionality*. His plan is that the student will recognize him as John Searle, and as the speaker of the utterance, and so come to have the belief in an apt way, a way that will answer the original question. Like George Bush, he wanted to elicit a little awe too, conveying that the author was in the very room, and so chose the first person. Fred's directing intention was to refer to himself, and he succeeded in this, and so said something false. He thought he would thereby refer to Searle, and say something true, but this intention was not fulfilled.

Fred might have said, "John Searle wrote *Intentionality*," with the plan that the student would recognize him as John Searle, realize the speaker was John Searle, and be awed. From Fred's point of view, it seems that he would accomplish about the same either way, convey information and produce awe. But in the latter case he would have merely referred to Searle and said something true.

In both cases, Fred intends to refer to Searle. In the first case, things go awry because his directing intention is based on a false belief, that he is Searle, and so can refer to Searle by referring to himself using 'I.' In the second case, he is using a proper name to exploit a rather more complex role Searle plays in his life, which we'll explore in the next chapter, very roughly being the person he is thinking about when he thinks 'Searle.' Searle does play this role, and he refers to Searle.

We are fudging a bit here. Fred's psychology is a mess. When he is not in a fugue state, his remarks about Searle are motivated by beliefs that have his Searle-notion as a constituent – a notion he formed when he first heard of Searle, and has added to on the basis of reading things by Searle and about Searle, and perhaps some encounters with him. If Fred were completely delusional, we might suppose that this Searle-notion had been completely absorbed into his self-notion. But then would he still have a notion *of* Searle at all? Could he refer to Searle?

We have finessed things, by imagining that Fred isn't that badly off. Most of the time he doesn't believe he is Searle. The fugue state, as we are imagining it, brings with it a temporary connection between two notions, his self-notion and his Searle notion, and with it the belief that he is Searle. So his use of 'Searle' gets to refer to Searle, in virtue of his Searle-notion, even when he is in the fugue state. If Fred were completely delusional, his self-notion would be a particularly troublesome case of what Perry calls a 'mess,' using that word as a technical term. We'll have a bit to say about messes below, but if anyone wants an elaborate theory, he'll have to look at *Reference and Reflexivity*.

6.4   Indexicals, dates, and time

Most people don't have Fred's problem, and this accounts for something rather special about 'I' and the self. There is only one object that plays the role of *self* relative to a given person, namely, that person himself or herself. This means that the self-buffer, the notion assigned to store information received in normally self-informative ways, can also serve as the permanent self-notion, as long as one doesn't have a problem like Fred's. Most people know who they are.

With 'now' and 'today,' things are quite different. Everyone at some point loses track of what time it is, or what day it is, and sometimes even what month or year it is. Utterances like, "It is five o'clock," or "Today is July 17" provide useful information. We will give a somewhat more detailed account of these.

We assume that relative to any given place (or, in modern times, any time zone), there are days, twenty-four-hour periods from midnight to midnight. There are special epistemic and pragmatic methods connected with the present time and the present day. To find out what the weather is like at a given time, in the place one is at, one has only to open one's eyes and look around. To see what someone is wearing at a given time, one has only to look at them. And so on. One can find out a lot about the present day by consulting one's relatively short-term memory and one's plans for the rest of the day. When one says 'now' or 'today' in face-to-face conversation, the path intention is almost sure to be simple role-transfer; S seeks to get H to engage his 'now' or 'today' buffer, to think about the present moment or the present day in the same way that S does.

And of course there are quite distinctive pragmatic methods connected with the present moment and the present day. To do something now, you just do it. To get something done today that takes an hour, you can get started anytime before 11 p.m.

There are also special epistemic and pragmatic methods connected with indexicals like 'tomorrow' and 'yesterday.' One can usually remember what happened yesterday, even if one does not know yesterday's date. One can make plans for what one is going to do tomorrow, even if one doesn't know its date.

Dates provide another way of referring to days, in terms of their systematic connections with other days, months, and years. Given the institution of calendars and other sources of information that use dates, such as newspapers, minutes of meetings, diaries, and the like, a date provides an epistemic method of finding out about the events of a given day. A systematic person can find out what they did on, say, April 7, 2007, by looking in their diary. They can find out what happened in their city, or in the world, by looking in the archives of a newspaper. So the two methods of reference to days, in terms of 'today' (or 'yesterday' or 'tomorrow') and with dates, can provide quite different cognitive fixes on the same day.

A typical case in which the question of what day it is arises when you start out your day and wonder what appointments and commitments you have for the day. These you have typically recorded on a calendar – an old-fashioned calendar that is taped to your refrigerator, let's suppose. Suppose in fact it is March 18, 2010. You know what month it is – the month whose page is at the front of the calendar, pages for previous months having been ripped off. Maybe you know it is Thursday. But which Thursday? If it is Thursday the 18th, you have an appointment with the dean. If it is Thursday the 25th, you are going fishing. So which is it? A momentous question; in the one case you put on a tie and go to the office; in the other you dress casually and drive to the lake. You know, of course, that today is today, and March 18th is March 18th. But is today March 18th? A substantial question. You hope it's the 25th, but sadly you can't remember having met with the dean, and conclude it must be the 18th. What do you learn? And what information do you convey to your sleepy spouse, who arrives in the kitchen with the same question on her mind, when you say, "Today is March 18"?

As we construct the situation, there are two notions in your mind, and in your spouse's, a buffer for the present day, connected with the pragmatic and epistemic methods for that role, and one for March 18, 2010.

This phenomenon of having two notions of the same individual and coming to discover that they are notions of the same individual is characteristic of recognition. And in the most familiar cases of recognition, one of the notions will be a buffer. You were talking to a man at the party; you have a cognitive fix on the man as the person you're talking to, listening to, seeing, and so forth.

It turns out that you already have a notion of this person; perhaps it is Elwood Smith, the famous author, many of whose books you have enjoyed. It is a fact about the world that your two notions, the buffer and the old notion of Elwood Smith, are of the same person. But this fact is not reflected in your mind. When it comes to be reflected in your mind, that's what we call recognition. The flow of information changes. The information in your Elwood Smith file flows into your buffer, and has an effect on the way that you treat the person you're talking to.

Similarly, when you or your spouse recognize what day it is, that it is March 18, the information written on the calendar, which amounts to an external addition to a detached notion of that day, flows into your 'today' buffer, and has an effect on the way you act; you, for example, begin psyching yourself up for your meeting with the dean.

6.5   Technology and indexicals

Most of the languages that people speak – English, Basque, French, Chinese, etc. – are old compared to the individuals that use them, and even compared to many of the nations and cultures to which those people belong. The basic vocabulary of reference – indexicals, demonstratives, personal pronouns, and the like – evolved not only long before email, iChat, answering machines, and such modern tools were available, but even before there were written languages. These tools were basically fashioned for face-to-face communication, but have survived into an age where they serve a number of other uses.

We distinguish between tokens and utterances. Utterances are human acts, with all the mental and intentional properties that such acts have. Tokens are basically traces of utterances that can be perceived by hearers. The distinction is scarcely worth making with face-to-face communication. You see me utter my words; you hear them. You perceive the utterance and you perceive the token. These perceptions occur at the same time, and constitute a single experience as far as you're concerned. But as soon as we have written language, the distinction becomes important. You perceive the token, the marks on the letter you received, and infer there was an utterance at some earlier time. The most basic facts about the utterance – the speaker, the time, the place – may not be apparent. The difference was more dramatic before sound-recording was possible. Now in the case of hearing spoken speech, as in the case of reading written texts, years can pass between the utterance and the perception of the token.

When we talk of truth and falsity, and truth-conditions, it is utterances and the beliefs that motivate them that we have primarily in mind, and tokens only derivatively. Utterances are acts, and it may seen odd to think of acts as being true or false, and having truth-conditions, however, that is how we think of things. In logic and philosophy, truth and falsity are attributed to a variety of entities: sentence types, sentence tokens, propositions, statements, and beliefs, to provide a partial list. We think that tokens, conceived of as mere patterns of ink or sound, do not have enough properties to be considered true or false. They must be connected to things and properties in the world to admit of truth and falsity, and we can't see where these connections come from other than the circumstances of their intentional production, that is, the utterance, which is in turn connected to the mind which produces it, which is in turn connected to the objects and properties, interactions with which have given it the form and structure it has.

In face-to-face communication, roles are linked that are theoretically separable. The time of the utterance, the time of the perception of the utterance, and the time of the perception of the token produced by the utterance are all basically the same. There is no sense to the question which of these times an utterance of the word 'now' refers to. With writing, the roles can be separated. The time of the utterance may be Monday; the reader may never perceive the utterance; the time of his perception of the token may be Wednesday. It seems there is some latitude here for the speaker or writer. Usually an occurrence of 'now' will refer to the time of utterance; "I am having a good time now," on a postcard, means that the writer is enjoying himself at the time he writes, not at the time the postcard is received and read. To convey the latter thought, one might say "I will be having a good time, by the time you read this," or something like that.

Consider, however, this example from Stefano Predelli.

Jones . . . suddenly decides to flee the country. Before leaving home at 8 in the morning he writes a note to his wife who will be back from work at five in the evening.

[P]. As you can see I am not home now. If you hurry, you'll catch the evening flight to Los Cabos. Meet me in six hours at the Hotel Cabo Real.

Here Jones intends for his wife to take the reference of the word 'now' to be the time at which she reads the note, which he believes will be around five o'clock. Is this an abuse of language? Or a natural accommodation allowed by the meaning of the word 'now' to the phenomenon of written communication, and the possibility that the roles of being the time at which a word was written and being the time at which the word is perceived may not be linked?

In David Kaplan's 'Demonstratives' the sentence 'I am here now' is taken to be a theorem in the logic of demonstratives. In that work, a context is modeled as a quadruple of agent, location, time, and world. Proper context is one in which the agent is at the location at the time in the world. By the time 'Demonstratives' was published, a number of years after it was written, answering machines were common, and it wasn't unusual to hear a message that violated Kaplan's theorem: "I am not here now; please leave a message." One can handle this phenomenon in various ways. Perhaps the speaker intends to say something obviously false, but to suggest, by means of a Gricean implicature, the actual state of affairs. Perhaps a speaker merely misuses language, but as misuse becomes standard use, the meaning of 'now' changes. Perhaps it is just an idiom, it has a meaning as a whole, that one cannot derive compositionally from its parts. From the point of view of a theory of utterances, however, it seems natural to say that the word 'now', well designed for a world in which the roles of being the time of utterance and the time of perception of utterance were universally linked, has a meaning that can be used for either role in situations where their linkage has been broken.

7 Names

7.1 Introduction

Speaking of David Kaplan, he once complained that proper names were a nightmare for semantics, and if it were not for their use in calling the kids for dinner, he would as soon junk the whole category. We are quite fond of proper names, since we think they fit well with our approach, and approve of feeding children. In calling the kids for dinner, one illustrates language as technology. Once the habits of responding to 'Jordan' and 'Valerie' were instilled in Kaplan's children, he had a new way of doing something, a new pragmatic method for getting them to come home for dinner. And Valerie and Jordan had a new epistemic method for determining their father's wishes. It's just as important not to lose sight of the very features of names that make them useful, in considering their semantics and pragmatics.

The classic treatment of names and definite descriptions in philosophy and semantics was inspired by their more straightforward mathematical cousins, individual constants and functional expressions. Because of this, the very features that connect names and descriptions with the practice of planning utterances so as to manage roles in particular conversations have been obscured. When one looks at the way we use these expressions to manage roles, some of the problematic cases become central and straightforward. We'll begin with names. In this chapter we'll also continue to develop our modest psychological vocabulary for describing how role-management works.

7.2 Names and nambiguity

Individual constants differ from ordinary proper names in that only one individual is assigned to them. This is not the way ordinary proper names work. Family names like 'Kim' and 'Jones' are the names of millions of people, and can be used to refer to each of them. Full names often belong to more than one member of the same family – George Bush, for example – as well as many unrelated people. Google the name of anyone you know, and you will probably find that many people have that name. In our terminology, names are *nambiguous*.

Individual constants are assigned to a single object, so that every occurrence of the constant designates the individual. Names don't work like this. They are permissive conventions; if you name your new child 'Larraitz,' you seek to establish a practice that makes it possible to refer to the child with that name; you don't make it impossible to use the name to refer to other people named 'Larraitz.' Ambiguity is supposed to be a bad thing; a verb or noun with half a dozen unrelated meanings can be confusing. It seems that using the same name for indefinitely many people should be even more confusing. But in practice, it usually is not. It's usually possible to limit the number of people whom a speaker might be using a name to refer to by consideration of the probably quite small percentage of people with that name she knows of, can expect the hearers to know of, and about whom she might have something to say relevant to the conversation.

Even if the plausible referents are limited in such ways, there may be a number of candidates for the referent of an uttered name. In the late 1980s there were three people named 'John' in the Stanford philosophy department – four including Jon Barwise, whose first name sounded exactly like that of John Perry, John Dupré, and John Etchemendy. Nevertheless, if, in a certain situation, the department chair said,

(7.1)   If John would quieten down, John could hear what John is saying,

what he said might have been clear to everyone. Each use of 'John' provided an utterance-relative role: being the person the speaker intends to refer to with *that* use of 'John.'

When we give a person the name 'John' we do not associate it with a role, but with a person. Perhaps then names should be a nightmare for us, with our emphasis on role-management, as well as for Kaplan, who would like them to be more like individual constants [Kaplan, 1990]. But roles play a role with names. The convention, whether established by some official act of baptism or by a usage that simply develops, is permissive; it allows one who knows the convention to refer to that individual with that name. When the chair uses the name 'John,' the permissive conventions and the conversational situation narrow the possible referents down to three (or four). The question is which of them plays the role of being referred to by the speaker with each use of the name. So, in our view, even though the permissive conventions that govern our use of names assign individuals to names, not roles, nevertheless roles are crucial in understanding the way names work.

Still, it would be quite misguided to think of names as working like indexicals or demonstratives. We can refer to a certain person as 'I' or 'you' or 'that man' or 'that woman' because of some role they play relative to us; being ourself, or the person we are addressing, or a man or woman salient in some way, perceptually or through conversation or in some other way. But having a name is a property a person or place or thing has independently of the role they play in the life of the speaker who uses the term at the time that they use it. We can refer to Obama as 'Obama' because that is his name, wherever he is in the world.

7.3   Networks and reference

Actually, our last remark is too simple, although most likely true. If 'we' is limited to the authors and readers of this book, it is certainly true that we can all refer to Obama by using the name 'Obama' wherever he is, and wherever we are, and this is an important difference between 'I,' which only Obama can use to refer to Obama, and 'you,' which only someone who is addressing Obama can use to refer to Obama. We can say that Obama is *referentially accessible* via the word 'I' only to himself, and referentially accessible via the word 'you' only to those who are addressing him. Clearly, Obama is referentially accessible via 'Obama' to a lot more people than he is via 'I' or 'you.' Still, there are limits. It is likely that there are people in the world who have never heard of Obama, never read about Obama, never been in a conversation in which Obama was referred to. These people cannot use 'Obama' to refer to Obama, even if they use the name to refer to other Obamas that they know or know of.

For Obama to be referentially accessible to a given speaker via the name 'Obama,' that speaker needs to be able to utter 'Obama' as a part of what we officially call a 'name-notion network,' but usually just call a 'network.' Networks are our take on what Kripke calls 'chains of communication' and Donnellan calls 'referential chains,' and closely related to what Chastain calls 'anaphoric chains' [Chastain, 1975]. For our purposes at present, a rather simple and idealized picture of networks will suffice.

To explain networks, we need a concept which we'll call 'conditional co-reference' or 'coco-reference,' which we have already mentioned at the end of Chapter 5 (§5.6.2).

7.3.1   Coco-referring

A later utterance *co-refers with* an earlier one, if both utterances refer, and refer to the same thing. So an utterance of Saint Augustine, referring to Plato, and one of François Recanati's, referring to Plato, co-refer. This would be true even if (contrary to fact, we're certain) Recanati had never heard of Saint Augustine, or had but was unaware that Augustine had ever referred to Plato.

A later reference *intentionally co-refers* with an earlier one, if it refers to the same thing as the earlier one, and this is the second speaker's intention. Perhaps Recanati is lecturing on Saint Augustine. He quotes a passage from

Saint Augustine about Plato, and then comments on it, referring to Plato as he does so. Now we have not only co-reference, but intentional co-reference.

Suppose Recanati is lecturing on Saint Augustine, and quotes a passage in which Augustine makes a rather obscure reference to Plotinus, which Recanati takes to be a reference to Plato. He then comments on it, referring to Plato as he does so, thinking wrongly he is referring to the same person that Augustine did. Then we have attempted co-reference that failed. It was intentional attempted co-reference, but not intentional co-reference.

Now change the situation a bit. Recanati is lecturing about Plato's philosophy of language, and quotes a passage where Plato talks about Homer. Recanati has no idea whether or not there really was such a person as Homer. When he uses the name 'Homer' he intends to refer to the same person Plato did, *if there was such a person*. This is what we call 'conditional co-referring,' or, for short, 'coco-referring.' A later reference *conditionally co-refers* or *coco-refers* with an earlier one, if the second speaker's intention is to refer to the same thing as the earlier utterance, if there is anything it referred to, and to refer to nothing, if it refers to nothing.

The later speaker may believe his utterance coco-refers for three reasons. The first operates in the case of anaphora. You say,

(7.2)   Robert lost his job,

and I reply,

(7.3)   He must be very worried.

I use the pronoun 'he' as an anaphor for your use of 'Robert'; I intend to 'pick up' the reference of your use of 'Robert'; my utterance only refers in virtue of your utterance referring. My utterance coco-refers because the mechanism of reference I exploit for my utterance is the same as for your utterance, plus the small additional anaphoric step. When I say 'he' I intend to refer to whomever you referred to, if you referred to anyone.

I could also reply,

(7.4)   Robert must be very angry,

using the very nambiguous name 'Robert' in such a way that it is intended to coco-refer; I intend to refer to whichever Robert you referred to, via the same convention you exploited. This is second kind of coco-referring: a person uses a name with the intention of exploiting whatever naming convention was exploited by an earlier use. Note that I may coco-refer with your utterance in conversation with someone who didn't hear your utterance. I may say to a third party, "Robert must be very angry," intending to refer to the Robert you told me about.

Now suppose Anissa is talking to her younger brother Everett about Santa Claus. Everett believes in Santa Claus; Anissa isn't sure whether or not he exists. Everett asks, "Does Santa Claus live right on the North Pole, or just nearby?" Anissa replies, "No one really knows exactly where he lives." Her use of 'he' would be anaphoric coco-reference. If she had replied, "No one knows exactly where Santa Claus lives" her use of 'Santa Claus' would have been same-name coco-reference.

In both cases her intention is that her utterance and Everett's will have a certain relationship, a relationship such that if Everett's utterance refers to something, hers will refer to the same thing. In the first, anaphoric, case, the dependence of her utterance on his guarantees this relationship. In the second case Anissa uses the same name as Everett did. She has a directing intention to use 'Santa Claus' in the same way that Everett did, so that the facts sufficient to make a certain object the referent of his utterance would suffice to make the same object the referent of hers. If, contrary to her suspicions, there is someone suitably related to Everett's utterance of 'Santa Claus' to be its referent, that same person will be the referent of her utterance of the same name.

Now suppose Anissa says "No one knows exactly where Kris Kringle lives," with the intention of conveying to Everett that Santa Claus has another name too. This is neither anaphoric nor same-name coco-reference. The facts are more complicated. Anissa believes that the two names are parts of the same myth, so that, if contrary to her beliefs the myth has a factual basis and 'Santa Claus' refers, then 'Kris Kringle' also refers, and refers to the same person. This is the third kind of coco-reference, which we'll call 'convergent coco-reference.'

The three kinds of coco-reference differ in the possibility of, or at least the relevance of, confusion and misunderstanding. Suppose S says, "Oxford is a fascinating city" and H replies, "It's a dry, boring little town, although the people are nice." H is thinking of Oxford, Nebraska, where he used to deliver shingles, although S referred to Oxford, England, where he used to go to school. Even though H was confused, his use of 'it' clearly referred to Oxford, England. His directing intention was to use 'it' anaphorically, and so used it refers to Oxford, England. This is a case like those considered in Chapter 3, of intentionally referring to something you didn't intend to refer to.

If H had replied, "Oxford is a dry, boring little town," things are a good deal less clear. His motivating belief is about Oxford, Nebraska. But what is his directing intention? Does he intend to same-name coco-refer, in which case the directing intention is to use 'Oxford' in the same way that S did? In that case, he refers to Oxford, England, and doesn't say what he believes.

But perhaps his directing intention is to use 'Oxford' in the way he did growing up, for the small town in Nebraska; he happens to believe that by doing this, he will be using it in the same way that S did, but he is mistaken. In this case, he says what he believes, referring to Oxford, Nebraska. We have attempted co-reference, but not coco-reference. Of course, the ranking of the intentions in a real case is unlikely to be clear cut, and apprised of the facts, H would no doubt admit as much, unless a sum of money turned on whether he said something true or false.

We'll return to these kinds of misunderstandings and miscommunications later. For now we set them aside, to focus on the networks that result from problem-free coco-referential links between utterances.

7.3.2   Networks

We'll say that an utterance is a *coco-descendant* of an earlier utterance, if there is a chain of coco-referring utterances from it to the earlier one. Elwood tells you that Jack drank the last beer. You leave me a note saying "Jack drank the last beer." I tell Marsha, "Jack should be whipped." She tells Fred, "Jack's becoming unpopular because of all the beer he drinks." Your note coco-refers with Elwood's utterance. My utterance coco-refers to your note, and Marsha's utterance coco-refers to mine. Marsha's utterance doesn't coco-refer with Elwood's utterance, but it is a referential descendant of it, because of the chain of coco-references. Being a coco-ancestor is the inverse of being a coco-descendant. None of this depends on Jack existing; I could have made Jack up in order to blame him for drinking the missing beers that I actually had taken.

The intentions involved in coco-referring needn't be full-blown conscious ones; it is a practice that comes naturally to those who know how to refer, most of whom have no explicit concept of reference, much less coco-reference.

We can stipulate that referential utterances coco-refer to themselves. Coco-reference is then reflexive but neither transitive nor symmetrical. Being a coco-descendant of (or ancestor of) is reflexive and transitive but not symmetrical, and is many-one and one-many.[1]

Start with an utterance. Every utterance you can reach by going forwards (from ancestor to descendant) or backwards (from descendant to ancestor) on a coco-reference chain, belongs on the same coco-network as the starting point. So we have three relations between utterances:

- **Coco-referring**. An utterance u' of a singular term coco-refers with an earlier utterance u, when the later utterance is made with the intention to conditionally co-refer with the earlier utterance.
- **Being a coco-descendant (ancestor)**. If there is a chain of coco-referring utterances stretching from u' back to u, u' is a coco-descendant of u, and u is a coco-ancestor of u'.

---

[1] Whether it is asymmetrical is a more interesting matter that would require further discussion of the connection between utterances and tokens.

- **Network-sharing**. The utterances u and u' *share a network*, or *occur on the same network*, if there is a path from u' to u, where each leg of the path is from an utterance to a coco-descendant of it, or from an utterance to a coco-ancestor of it.

We can think of the typical network having a trunk with roots and branches. Roots begin with references that are not intended to co-refer. I see a new person at the department meeting, and ask you, "Was she appointed while I was on leave?" Perhaps you don't know either, and pose the same question to the person sitting next to you. After a while someone can answer the question with a name: "That's Alice Fritchey, our new logician." The root begun by my question joins the trunk, and my original reference to Alice Fritchey comes to share a network with thousands of references to Alice most likely going back to the day she was born, at least. That evening I tell my wife about Alice Fritchey and some of the interesting things I noticed about her; she tells her friends the next day at lunch; this is a branch that may continue growing for years if the things I noticed were interesting enough, without feeding back into the main trunk.

A network for a person like Alice Fritchey will typically begin with a number of roots, begun by references to the new-born Alice by her mother, father, the midwife, and so on. Their descendants soon form a network of coco-referring utterances. Alice, the object at the beginning of these merging roots, is the *origin* of the network. As time goes on, Alice meets new people, moves to new neighborhoods, enrolls in new schools, and new branches with her as origin begin.

There can be networks with Alice as the origin that neither branch off from or merge into the main Alice-network. Perhaps some students see Alice at the Student Union; they don't meet her, they don't learn her name, but they chat about her among themselves later, and then forget all about it. So there is a little independent Alice-network, which doesn't involve her name, and never joins the main network.

Of course, networks need not begin with a reference to a real object; they can begin, as in the case of Jack a couple of paragraphs above, with an act of invention. In this case we have what Donnellan calls a *block*; none of the utterances in the network refer, although they do coco-refer. In such cases, we talk about referring to the same person, and having the same person in mind. But there is no reference, and no identity of referents; it is a loose way of talking about coco-referring.

This is the picture of networks we will have in mind for the rest of this chapter. It is an idealization. The complications come from misidentifications. These occur when an utterance is both intended to be part of a coco-chain but independently refers to something other than the origin of the chain. In these cases, we have what we call a *mess*. Because of messes, there are several kinds of blocks in addition to the sort of intentional invention involved in the Jack case. We consider these complications in the next chapter. Roughly, in this chapter we look at how things can go right, and later, how they can go wrong.

Now we can provide an account of permissive conventions for the use of proper names. A convention for name N is *supported* by a network, if there is a practice along the network to use N to coco-refer. A use of a name that exploits a convention refers to the origin of the network that supports the convention, if it has one; otherwise the convention and the use are empty.

A practice is inaugurated when a name is used as part of a network. It may be explicitly introduced for this purpose, by reference to an existing, salient object. Perhaps Alice's mother says, "Let's call her 'Alice.'" Or perhaps she just starts using the name, coco-referring with other references to Alice. The practice is continued when others use the name as a part of the Alice-network. The permissive convention to call Alice 'Alice' is supported as long as the practice is continued.

The network contemplated above supported a convention for the use of 'Jack.' The convention permits one to coco-refer with other acts of reference on the same network. If there is an origin, then by coco-referring, one will refer. In this case, we have a permissive convention to refer to the origin with the name. Recall that by 'permissive' we mean to emphasize that the convention doesn't prevent one from using the same name to refer to other individuals, or to coco-refer on other networks. The convention that permits me to use 'Jack' for the beer-drinking guy I invented doesn't preclude me from using 'Jack' to refer to other people I know by that name, or to coco-refer with people talking about Jack Frost, Jack Sprat, or the Jack found in the beanstalk.[2]

A convention can support more than one name for an individual in this sense. New naming conventions can come into being with only indirect connections to the named object. The English word 'Aristotle' doesn't look anything like the name that Aristotle's parents gave him, and probably doesn't sound all that much like it either. The same goes for the different-sounding and -looking names for him in other languages, such as the French 'Aristote.' These two names developed within the alphabetic and phonetic systems of English and French to give people a way of referring to Aristotle. People can still invent new names for Aristotle. Imagine that in an ancient philosophy class, a beginner student asks a question about 'Ari-whats-it.' Soon everyone in class is calling Aristotle by his new name, 'Ariwhatsit.'

When a speaker uses a name in accordance with a naming convention supported by a given network, the speaker (and his utterance) *exploits* the convention which is supported by or resides in the network.

---

[2] Megan Stotts points out that modern institutions require naming conventions, or something like them, that are not so permissive. No more than one person is supposed to have a given social security number, for example.

7.4   Names and roles

Let's grant that when a person uses a name to refer to an individual, he does so in virtue of exploiting a convention, which is part of a network, along which his referential act lies. If a person can coco-refer by a referential act that uses a name, the origin of that network is referentially accessible via that network. This imposes a very weak condition on the use of a name to refer; in the ordinary sense one doesn't need to know who the individual referred to is; one need not be able to furnish a non-trivial, utterance-independent description of the referent. One need not even know what sort of thing it is; not even whether it is an abstract or a concrete object. A rather lackadaisical set-theory student might ask his more diligent classmate: "Aleph-null was a Hebrew logician, right?" A reasonable answer is, "No, it's not a person at all, it's a number." We can use names to ask the most basic of questions about what they stand for, and to make statements about them that reflect ignorance of the most basic facts about what they are or who they are.

The relation one has to another individual, in virtue of being able to coco-refer with utterances that refer to that individual, may seem rather thin. And in and of itself, it is. Nevertheless, being accessible via a name supported by a network is an epistemic role. Our example of 'Aleph-null' illustrates why this is so. The ability to use a name supported by a network gives one – at least in many cases and the most typical cases – the ability to ask questions about the object in a way that can elicit more information from others.

Kaplan's remark suggests one way the institution of names might have begun; a practice evolves of making different-sounding grunts outside one's cave, depending on which of one's kids one wants to return to help clean the fish or skin the wild pigs or gather ants for dessert. The practice is extended to other uses; telling which kids to sit where, and so forth. And soon any adult can get one or other kid's attention by making the appropriate sound. Suppose you were invited for dinner at the cave-Kaplans, and heard cave-David use the name 'Valerie' to get one of his cave-kids to do something. Then by making the same sound, you could get cave-Valerie to turn around, and learn which of his kids Valerie was, and what she looked like, and the like.

The point can be made with an old joke. A and B have a good time at a party. As the party draws to an end, A says to B: "I've really enjoyed getting to know you. Can I give you a call?" B replies: "Certainly. My number is in the book." "But what's your name?" A asks. "It's in the book too!" B replies. Without B's name, A cannot find out B's number; without B's number, A cannot call B. Knowing a person's name, or that there is a person with a certain name, potentially unlocks all sorts of information. One can call the name, and see who responds, as the bellboy does in the famous Philip Morris commercial.[3]

[3] www.youtube.com/watch?v=2BVvjfzgZrc.

One can ask other people about the person; one can look them up in various directories; one can google their name. Most of these methods require having a bit of information about the person named, but not enough to identify them without the name. Googling 'David Kaplan' returns more that 1.9 million hits; only 3 of the top 10 concern the UCLA philosopher. Just adding 'logician' reduces the hits to under 6,000, and 9 of the top 10 concern the philosopher.

The picture that names need a backing of utterance-independent and name-independent descriptions has some motivation, but it is quite misguided. The name of a person or thing is an extremely important property from an informational point of view. It doesn't have to be a name it has had from invention, birth, or construction. If it is the name used in the conversation you are joining, by using it to coco-refer you can learn what others in the conversation think about the object. If it is a famous person or object, and you know just enough to resolve the nambiguity – to know, for example, that the David Kaplan you want to find out about is a logician rather than a physician or a movie director – you can use the name to find out more in an encyclopedia or by googling.

Names also unlock information a person already has about an object. Consider the example of S and H and the building that houses the ILCLI. H already has in his mind a notion of the ILCLI. Perhaps H acquired his notion of the ILCLI from reading about it and conversations with S. But even when he is not in an epistemic relation to it – not reading about it, and not talking about it with others – he retains the notion and the beliefs of which it is a constituent.

When S says "That building houses the ILCLI," then, both of the singular terms he uses, the demonstrative phrase and the name, serve to manage H's roles. S's remark links two fixes H has of the building across the street: as the building he sees, and as the building that he has a notion of. This puts H in a position to learn things about Larrazabal Hall by looking across the street, and to learn things about the building across the street by realizing it is Larrazabal Hall.

7.5   Names as role-coordination devices: examples

Julia and the salt
Let's return to the example of §3.5 about the famous actress Julia Roberts. She sits at our table. S sees she is looking around the table, presumably for the salt. H is well positioned to reach the salt and pass it to her; she sits directly across from H. S tells H, "Julia Roberts would like the salt." What do roles have to do with this?

When S says

(3.3)   Julia Roberts would like the salt,

H learns that the person S intends to refer to bears the name 'Julia Roberts.' Here the background situation is quite different from the case where an indexical might be used. Everyone at our dinner party knows that the beautiful actress seated at our table is named 'Julia Roberts.' Of course she is not the only person with that name; there are probably hundreds, perhaps thousands, of people named 'Julia Roberts' living in the United States alone. Still, in the situation, common sense and the added information that the intended referent is named 'Julia Roberts' will enable H to identify the person S is talking about in a manner that is linked to various roles she is playing in their lives, that is, the person they see sitting near them, and, in the case of those sitting near her, the person they can pass the salt to.

A name, like an indexical, provides supplemental information that enables hearers to link the role of being the speaker's intended referent with various roles people are playing in their lives. Although names are not, like indexicals, associated by meaning with utterance-relative roles, they nevertheless provide tools with which the speaker can coordinate roles.

So here S's plan is as follows. His motivating belief is that Julia Roberts wants the salt. His primary referential intention is to refer to Julia Roberts, via his notion of Julia Roberts, which, since S has recognized her, is also a buffer for information gained perceptually. He assumes that H also has a notion of Julia Roberts, which is also serving as a buffer: everyone is aware that Julia Roberts is at the table, and steals a glance at her from time to time. S's strategy is a simple role-transfer, to get H to have the same sort of cognitive fix on the referent as he does. His target intention is to get H to have a perceptual fix on Julia Roberts, suitable for getting the salt to her. The path is trivial, assuming that his Julia Roberts-notion is already serving as a buffer for H.

When S utters (7.5) S will create the roles of being the person referred to by the speaker of that utterance and being the person of whom the speaker predicates wanting the salt. By using the name 'Julia Roberts' S specifies a role the referent plays in his life, the person he is thinking of via the name 'Julia Roberts,' and so one person by that name of whom S has a notion. Things might go wrong if H doesn't grasp which Julia Roberts S has in mind, but that's unlikely in this situation. She will get the salt.

Even though names are not loosely linked to perceptual and other epistemic roles the way demonstratives are, or tightly linked to utterance-relative roles the way indexicals are, the name serves as a role coordination device; it provides the incremental information necessary for H to link the roles of being the person across from him and being the person of whom wanting the salt is asserted by S.

Of course, often we communicate not with the goal of enabling a specific action, like passing the salt to someone who wants it, but simply to modify beliefs. S and H are talking about their favorite movie stars; Julia Roberts is nowhere in sight; S says "Julia Roberts won an Academy Award." S's goal is simply to change or reinforce H's beliefs. S wants to be sure H can correctly and confidently reply to such questions as, "Has Julia Roberts ever won an Academy Award?"

Elwood and François
S meets Elwood the philosopher at a cocktail party. S is talking about world events, cognitive science, and other subjects in a way that presupposes that both are knowledgeable. In order to convey that he really doesn't know much about any of this, Elwood says, "I am just a philosopher." S learns that the person he is talking to is just a philosopher, and moves to simpler (but perhaps more profound) topics.

If Elwood had said, "Elwood is a philosopher," that wouldn't have achieved his purpose, since S doesn't know his name yet. The indexical 'I' was the appropriate role-management device.

Suppose on the other hand S and Elwood are discussing the works of François Recanati. Recanati, whom S hasn't met, happens to be at the party, over by the bar ordering a drink. Elwood says, "Recanati's earliest work was on performatives." His intention is to have an affect on S's Recanati-notion; to get the role of being the origin of that notion linked to being the person he is talking about, and hence associated with the idea of having done his early work on performatives. If Elwood had pointed to Recanati, and said, "That man's earliest work was on performatives," he wouldn't have succeeded. S would have linked the role, 'being the man Elwood is talking about' with the role, 'being the man I see at the bar' but not, unless he already knows what Recanati looks like and recognizes him, with the role of being the person he has just referred to with 'Recanati.'

In the simple case of introducing oneself, the different role-linking strategies are both involved. Elwood says, "I am Elwood." What S learns is that the man he is talking to is named 'Elwood.' More precisely, he learns that the person he is talking to thinks of himself via a notion that is associated with being named 'Elwood'. He thinks about himself via his self-notion, and most likely knows his own name. So S learns that Elwood's name is Elwood. It wouldn't have worked for Elwood to have said "I am I" or "Elwood is Elwood."

7.6   Names and cognitive significance

In §2.3 we noted,

> On the referentialist view of proper names, the statements "Cicero was an orator" and "Tully was an orator" express the same proposition, the singular proposition about the Roman who had both names, the proposition true in just those worlds in which that person was an orator, whatever his name in them. But then what does

someone who knows that Cicero was an orator, but doesn't know whether Tully was, learn when he is told that Cicero is Tully, that he wouldn't learn by being reminded that Cicero is Cicero, or Tully is Tully?

As with demonstratives and personal pronouns, from the point of view of a theory of utterances it is natural and we believe essential to acknowledge that when we make statements using names, their truth-conditions can be assigned in different ways, depending on what is taken as given. This provides the basis for dealing with the problem of cognitive significance.

The problem has to do with identity, not only with identity-statements. Imagine a rather uninquisitive student, Alice, who has learned in her classics class that Tully was a Roman orator and in her philosophy class that Cicero was a Roman philosopher, but hasn't realized that Cicero and Tully were the same person, and who doesn't know that Tully was a Roman philosopher. If a friend tells her, perhaps just before the mid-term, "Tully was a Roman philosopher" she will learn something of potential value to her, that she wouldn't have learned had the friend said, "Cicero was a Roman philosopher." What does she learn? Call the friend 'Fred' and Fred's utterance **u**. Call the Tully-network that Fred exploits, the one that stretches from his use back to the famous Roman, N_{Tully}. We distinguish among:

Utterance-bound truth-conditions
Given that **u** is English, has the syntax it does, and 'was a Roman orator' means what it does in English, **u** is true *iff*

(1) $\exists x, \exists N, \exists y$ such that x is the speaker of **u**, N is the network x exploits with 'Tully,' y is the origin of N and y was a Roman philosopher.

Speaker-bound truth-conditions
Given that **u** is English, has the syntax it does, 'was a Roman orator' means what it does in English, AND Fred is the speaker of **u**, **u** is true *iff*

(2) $\exists N, \exists y$ such that N is the network Fred exploits with 'Tully,' y is the origin of N and y was a Roman philosopher.

Network-bound truth-conditions
Given that **u** is English, has the syntax it does, 'was a Roman orator' means what it does in English, Fred is the speaker of **u** AND N_{Tully} is the network Fred exploits with 'Tully,' **u** is true *iff*

(3) $\exists y$ such that y is the origin of N_{Tully}, and y was a Roman philosopher.

Referential truth-conditions
Given that **u** is English, has the syntax it does, 'was a Roman orator' means

what it does in English, Fred is the speaker of **u**, $\mathbf{N}_{Tully}$ is the network Fred exploits with 'Tully' AND Tully is the origin of $\mathbf{N}_{Tully}$, **u** is true *iff*

(4) Tully was a Roman philosopher.

This seems like a rather elaborate scheme, but it is all really necessary to get at the various things that might happen when Alice hears Fred's remark, assuming only that she is a semantically competent user of English, and hears and parses the utterance.

Suppose she doesn't realize it is Fred that made the utterance. It's clearly an assertion in English, that's all she is sure of. Alice is deeply suspicious, and thinks the speaker might have just made up the name 'Tully,' by utter coincidence using the same name as her classics professor uses, but not doing so as part of the relevant network or any network. Then all she gets out of Fred's utterance is (1). She knows it is true if it meets certain conditions, but she doubts very much if it does.

Still, (1) might intrigue her enough to figure out who made the utterance. She discovers that the speaker is Fred. But Fred has often deceived her in the past. She is still very suspicious. All she gets out of the utterance is (2); it is true if Fred meets certain conditions, which she doubts.

Suppose she is not all that suspicious of Fred. She is sure he is talking about someone and using the name 'Tully' as part of an established network. She knows his utterance is true if that network meets certain conditions, which (3) reflects. Having gotten this far, whether she can go further depends on how much she knows about $\mathbf{N}_{Tully}$. If she knows nothing except that it is the network that Fred exploits, she still won't have gotten much help with her exam. But she is in a position to refer to the same Tully Fred refers to, that is, to coco-refer with his utterance. She can ask, "Is Tully the orator the professor in my class talks about?" for example. She might even ask, "Is Tully Tully?" using 'Tully' first to coco-refer with Fred's utterance, and then to coco-refer with the professor's.

If she believes, correctly as we are imagining things, that Fred is exploiting the same network as her classics professor, then she will learn (4). We might say that she learns that Tully was a Roman philosopher. But we are supposing that she already knows that Cicero was a Roman philosopher. On a referentialist analysis, "Tully was a Roman philosopher" and "Cicero was a Roman philosopher" express the same singular proposition, so just citing this proposition doesn't get at what Alice learns. The crucial information, which explains how Fred's remark might put her in a better position for the exam, comes when she realizes that $\mathbf{N}_{Tully}$, the network Fred exploits, is the same one her professor exploits. When she sees the question, "True or false: Tully was a Roman philosopher" on the exam, she realizes that her answer will be graded on the basis of the properties of the origin of the network her professor exploits. Since that's the same network Fred exploited, if his statement was true, she can mark the question 'True.' The knowledge that she had before Fred spoke, that Cicero was a Roman orator, as she would have put it, wouldn't help her.

Our knowledge about objects is held relative to, or via, modes of presentation, to use Frege's term in an intuitive way. Alice's knowledge that Cicero was a Roman philosopher was held via the name 'Cicero' before Fred spoke; she also knew it via the name 'Tully' afterwards. But in the sense of modes of presentation in which this is true, they are not the *Sinne* of Frege's theory of names, or the hidden descriptions of Russell's. They are what we call cognitive fixes. A nominal cognitive fix involves a name, a notion with which the name is associated, and a network of which that notion, and the utterances it motivates, is part. The object plays an epistemic and a pragmatic role in the life of a person, in virtue of having such a notion. They can pick up information about the object by reading and hearing statements using the name on that network, and they can say things and answer test questions about the object by using the name on that network.

As we are imagining things, Alice still doesn't know that Cicero is Tully. If Fred had simply said, "Cicero is Tully," it is the network level that would be crucial:

Given that **u** is English, has the syntax it does, 'is' is used to express identity, Fred is the speaker of **u** AND N_{Cicero} is the network Fred exploits with 'Cicero,' AND N_{Tully} is the network Fred exploits with 'Tully,' **u** is true *iff*

(5) $\exists x, \exists y$ such that x is the origin of N_{Cicero} and y is the origin of N_{Tully} and $x = y$.

(5) is what Alice will believe on the basis of understanding and believing Fred. If, in addition, she assumes that N_{Cicero} and N_{Tully} are the same networks her philosophy professor and her Classics professor exploit, then the notions she acquired of Cicero in the two classes will be linked, or even merged.

7.7   The no-reference problem

Perhaps in the classics class Alice also learns things about the Roman gods, that Jupiter and Juno are married, perhaps. But, most likely, Juno and Jupiter never existed. If we could trace the use of the names back, we would find blocks, in Donnellan's sense; at some point the names began to be used, and coco-refering chains took shape, without there being real individuals serving as the origin. There are two problems here. First, is it true that Jupiter and Juno were married, given that they never existed? It seems that the right answer is no, it isn't true; there were no such beings, and the marriage never happened.

Still, in certain circumstances we would call it 'true' – if for example we were talking about myths. In such talk, someone who says that Jupiter and Juno were not married, but Jupiter was Juno's administrative assistant, would be, in some sense, wrong. The statement that Jupiter and Juno were married has some sort of favored status, which we'll just call 'accuracy.'

The second question is what is this 'it' that we just said wasn't true, but had a favored status? It doesn't seem that it can be a singular proposition, with Jupiter, Juno, and the relation of being married as constituents, because Jupiter and Juno don't exist. Unless the referentialist can find some other objects to serve as Jupiter and Juno – a strategy we don't favor – it looks as if he has no plausible candidate for the proposition that Alice comes to believe when the professor says that Jupiter and Juno were husband and wife, and no candidate for the proposition whose accuracy, whatever that may amount to, accounts for the fact that the correct answer to the exam question, "Were Jupiter and Juno married?" is "Yes."

On our approach, there are network-bound truth-conditions for the statement the professor makes when he says "Jupiter and Juno were married." There have to be origins of the two networks he exploits, and they have to have been married. The network-bound truth-conditions for this statement are different from if he had said "Mercury and Juno were married," because the Jupiter-network and the Mercury-networks are different, even if they are both blocked.

We assume that in cases like this, that is, myth and fiction, the accuracy of a statement is in some way a function of the utterances, documents, and minds that are to be found along along the relevant, blocked networks. The statement "Sherlock Holmes and Doctor Watson shared rooms on Baker Street" is accurate, though not true. It is accurate because there are canonical texts, the stories that Conan Doyle wrote, that say so. What counts as canonical? Everything that Doyle wrote, even the unpublished stories, the remarks to his friends, and the like? Or just the published texts? What about inconsistencies? What about things he didn't explicitly say, but everyone takes as true, as for example that Holmes had a great-grandmother? Whatever the right theory about such things might say, if there is one, it seems that the principle that accuracy must be grounded in facts about the networks, whereas truth is grounded in facts about the origins of the networks, remains plausible.

So we think that a referentialist can account for the fact that different statements about different fictional and mythological beings have different truth-conditions, even though there are no referential truth-conditions. And we think that referentialism does not preclude a reasonable theory of the accuracy and inaccuracy of statements about things that do not exist, without inventing some special sort of beings to do the job of being the referents. We don't, however, offer any detailed theory of this kind, at least not for now.

8 Definite descriptions

8.1 Introduction

Definite descriptions are phrases of the form 'the F.' Since Russell, at least, possessives like 'Caesar's wife' have also usually been thought of as definite descriptions. Russell saw definite descriptions as members of a class he called 'denoting phrases' that includes 'an F,' 'some Fs,' 'every F', and so on. In the general case of denoting phrases, the denotation is the set of objects of which the descriptive phrase is true. In the case of definite descriptions, if there is a unique member of the denoted set, it too is often called the denotation. We'll adopt a somewhat different terminology. For us, the denotation is always a set; we use the term 'designation' for the object picked out by a definite description that denotes a singleton set. So, 'The present king of France' denotes the null set, but doesn't designate anyone, since that set is empty. 'The senator from California' denotes the set consisting of Barbara Boxer and Dianne Feinstein, but doesn't designate anyone, because that set doesn't have a unique member. 'The largest state in the United States' denotes the singleton set consisting of Alaska, and so designates Alaska.

Given this, Russell's famous theory of definite descriptions can be summarized as follows:

(1) Definite descriptions are not real syntactic units in a logical language, and are misleadingly so in natural language.
(2) A statement of the form 'The F is G' is true if there is a unique F and it is G.
(3) Such statements are false if there is no F, or if there is more than one F, or if there is exactly one F and it is not G.
(4) The proposition expressed by such a statement does not contain the designation of the definite description, if any, as a constituent; anachronistically put, it is true in worlds in which there is a unique F that is G, but the unique F doesn't have to be the same individual in each such world.

One of Russell's motivations for the syntactic thesis was his distrust of the subject–predicate form. The treatment of quantifier phrases like 'every man' in the predicate calculus also abandons subject–predicate form. In the English sentence 'Every man is mortal,' the phrase 'Every man' is a syntactic unit. But in '$\forall x(\text{Man}(x) \rightarrow \text{Mortal}(x))$' it is not. The noun 'man' is part of an open sentence, and the universal quantifier is an operator appended to that sentence. 'The philosopher is mortal' is primitively rendered as

$$\exists x\{\text{phil}(x) \, \& \, \forall y[\text{phil}(y) \rightarrow x = y] \, \& \, \text{mortal}(x)\}$$

where the effect of 'the philosopher' is distributed across the first two conjuncts. However, Russell augments his primitive notation with defined notation. Once the primitive notation has been augmented we can render our sentence that suggests, misleadingly in Russell's eyes, that it shares the form of $F(a)$, as

Mortal($\imath x[\text{phil}(x)]$).

Thesis (1) has largely been abandoned for definite descriptions, even in the design of many formal languages, and especially as a thesis about natural language. Generalized quantifier theory permits languages in which the syntactic unity of quantified phrases in natural language is preserved in formal languages [Peters and Westerståhl, 2006]. In the contemporary semantics of natural language, quantifier phrases are usually treated as syntactic units, consisting of a determiner (*all, every, some, a, the, most, at least five*, etc.) and a noun phrase. Roughly, the determiner is interpreted as providing a relation between sets, and the determiner together with the noun phrase as a condition on sets. So 'Every man' gives us the condition of having the set containing all men as a subset; "Every man is mortal" is true if the set of mortal things meets that condition, that is, the set of men is a subset of the set of mortal things. "No man is immortal" is true if the set of immortal things and the set of men do not intersect.

We'll use 'Russell's theory of descriptions' for the semantic part of his theory of definite descriptions, theses (2)–(4), even though Russell attached great importance to (1) [Kaplan, 1970].

Donnellan's theory of referential and attributive uses of definite descriptions challenges theses (2) and (4). On his account, referential uses express a proposition about a particular object, contrary to thesis (4), and that object need not fit the description, contrary to thesis (2). An utterance of 'The man with a martini is wanted on the phone' might be attributive; the speaker conveys that the unique man with a martini, whoever it is, is wanted on the phone. More likely, however, is that the caller asked for someone by name and the speaker is using the description because it is a helpful way of identifying that man for the person he is sending to fetch him. He has a particular man in mind, and wishes to convey that that man is wanted on the phone. This is a referential use. In this case, the speaker might successfully use the description to refer to the man in question, even if he is not the only man with a martini, or even if he is drinking a gimlet instead of a martini.

Our strategy is as follows. First, we adapt Russell's theory to our utterance-based approach. Within the theory, as adapted, there is a natural way of dealing with Donnellan's reservations about thesis (4), given our pluri-propositionalism. We handle his reservations about thesis (2) in a different way.

8.2   Incomplete descriptions

As soon as one looks at actual discourse with Russell's theory in mind, one is faced with the problem of incomplete definite descriptions, that is, descriptions that seem to successfully pick out an object, but do not designate the unique object they pick out. Language seems to be full of incomplete descriptions: "Please bring me the book," "I left the can-opener in the kitchen," "The senator from Connecticut is being inconsistent." There is not just one book, one kitchen, or one senator from Connecticut in the world, so each of these descriptions, taken literally, doesn't designate anything in Russell's theory.

From our point of view, incomplete descriptions are a natural phenomenon, an illustration of the incremental nature of language. The speaker uses a descriptive phrase to convey his communicative intention, often assuming that the hearer knows quite a bit about his intentions already. In a natural situation, if I say, "Please bring me the book," I assume the hearer knows quite a bit about the object I want, independently of the descriptive information provided by the word 'book.' He knows that it is the object I am asking for, and that I believe he is in a position to bring me. Even if there are a lot of books within reach, he is in a position to infer which of them I want, perhaps because we have been discussing it. Once he knows that it is a book I want, rather than a bottle of Scotch or a pen or an apple, he will grasp my intention.

S's plan is that if H knows the kind or type of thing to which S is referring, H will know which thing, of that kind or type, S is referring to. The book is, perhaps, the book that H has been asking S about; the kitchen is the kitchen of the house S is in, or the house H is in, or the kitchen of some other house that has been under discussion, or will easily come to mind once H realizes it is a kitchen where the missing item may have been left. The senator in question is doubtless whichever senator from Connecticut has just had the floor, or been quoted, or appeared on television. These additional properties of the object referred to, that S plans on H already knowing or quickly grasping, seem to provide the necessary augmentation.

The apparent problem applies to attributive as well as referential descriptions. Consider a slight alteration of Donnellan's famous example. One and only one man is actually drinking a martini at a party that is supposed to be alcohol-free. The host tells his butler, "The man with a martini is breaking the rules." In the referential case, he intends to refer to the man. In the attributive case, he has learned that someone is drinking a martini, but he doesn't know who. He wants the butler to inform whoever it is that is drinking a martini that he is breaking the rules. In both cases, he clearly has a more restrictive condition in mind than his words provide: being the man *at this party* who is drinking a martini.

This problem, or phenomenon, is not limited to descriptions, but occurs with all quantifiers in natural language. Consider this conversation between Fred and Ethel, who are throwing a party for the adult residents of the apartment building they manage:

(8.1) Fred: Have you invited Lucy and Ricky?
       Ethel: Every adult has been invited to the party.

Ethel is clearly talking about the residents of the apartment house; she has invited all of the adults that live there, not all of the adults in the world. If the host at the non-alocholic party thinks there might be more than one offender, he might tell his butler, "Everyone drinking a martini is breaking the rules." He means everyone at the party, not every one in the world drinking a martini at that moment.

With respect to descriptions the usual strategy, which goes back at least to Russell's reply to criticisms from Strawson [Russell, 1957], is that additional descriptive material is available from context, and, once augmented by this contextual material, the descriptions denote what they should denote. The same strategy seems applicable to the cases involving other quantifiers.

This strategy fits well with our incremental approach; utterances have many properties from which this contextual augmentation can be drawn. In our theory, when a speaker uses a description or other quantifier phrase, he will typically have a domain in mind, and intend to specify a subset of that domain. The use of the definite article imposes the condition that the subset will be a singleton. The domain that the speaker has in mind is what we call an 'unarticulated constituent' of the truth-conditions of the utterance – we say more about unarticulated constituents in the next chapter. Ethel has in mind the set of residents, and intends to denote the set of adult residents. The host has in mind the set of people at his would-be alcohol-free party.

Given this, we modify Russell's theses (1), (2) and (3) as follows:

(1) Definite descriptions are real syntactic units in natural language.
(2a) A speaker S uses a definite description 'The F' to narrow down a set of objects B that S takes to be contextually available to the hearer H. The use of the description denotes the subset of Bs that are also Fs if that set is a singleton, otherwise it denotes the null set. If the use of a description denotes a singleton whose only member is x, the use of the description *designates x*.

(2b) A statement "The F is G" is true if "The F" designates an object x, and x is G.

(3) Such statements are false if "The F" does not designate an object, or it does but the object is not G.

We also need to modify thesis (4) in the light of our pluri-propositionalism; this requires some discussion, which will allow us to explain the first part of our treatment of Donnellan's distinction.

8.3   Designational truth-conditions and referring*

So far we have recognized four levels of truth-conditions: utterance-bound, speaker-bound, network-bound, and referential. Now we introduce a fifth level, which we call *designational* and also at times *referential**. This level of truth-conditions gets at what the world has to be like for an utterance to be true given its referential truth-conditions, *plus* the facts about denotations and designations of descriptions. Call S's utterance of 'Smith's murderer is insane' **u**:

Referential truth-conditions:
Given that **u** is in English, its syntax, the meanings of the words, and the fact that Smith is the origin of the exploited Smith-network, **u** is true iff there is a unique person who murdered Smith, and that person is insane.

Designational truth-conditions:
Given that **u** is in English, its syntax, the meanings of the words, the fact that Smith is the origin of the exploited Smith-network, AND the fact that Jones murdered Smith, **u** is true iff Jones is insane.

One can use a description with the intention of having one's hearer form a belief *about* the object the description designates. Suppose S says to H, "The person speaking to you would like a bit of your attention." The aim is to have H look at S, and pay attention to him. The plan is to have H realize that the unique person talking to him would like his attention, and then to look around, if necessary, to find that person, and perceptually attend to him, and have the cognitive fix on him that one would naturally express with 'you'. This is an example of what we call 'reference*'. The intention is to bring about a 'referential' cognitive fix, the sort of cognitive fix that would naturally be expressed with a name or demonstrative or indexical, in virtue of having a descriptive fix, and realizing who the description designates.

Consider examples where S says "Smith's murderer is insane." In the paradigm attributive case, S and H are looking at Smith's body. S makes his assertion based on the way the body has been mutilated. He doesn't have anyone in mind. His remark is based on general principles. He means to impart to

H the belief that whoever it was who murdered Smith, that person is insane. His target cognitive fix is descriptive.

In the paradigm referential case, S and H are at the trial of Jones, who, for now, we assume did actually murder Smith. At the trial, however, Jones is exhibiting very strange behavior, and that is the basis of S's assertion. In this case, S intends to impart to H the belief that Jones is insane. His target cognitive fix is perceptual; he wants H to be in the state he could naturally express with "that man is insane." He could have done this by saying "that man is insane" or "Jones is insane." But he chooses to do so with a description; he intends to get H to the target cognitive fix, by way of a descriptive one. This is what we call referring*. The content of the target belief is not the referential content of the utterance – a singular proposition about Smith – but the designational content – a singular proposition about Jones.

Donnellan says that in the attributive case, the description is essential to S's intentions, where this is not so in the referential case. In our view, this is a case of a common sort in the philosophy of action. There is more than one way to accomplish a goal; the goal is what is essential, the method used to accomplish it is not.

In both of these paradigm cases, S's use of 'Smith's murderer' denotes the set consisting of Jones, and so designates Jones. This is so, whether or not S is using the description referentially* or attributively. The difference between referential* and attributive lies, pretty much as Donnellan pointed out, in the structure of S's intentions.

In the first case, the attributive use, S's motivating belief is a general one, that whoever murdered Smith is insane. This is the belief he intends to impart to H. S has no belief about Jones, or at least no belief that is relevant to his communicative intentions. It is a fact about S's utterance that it has the desig-national truth-conditions that it does; given that "Smith's murderer" designates Jones, the utterance is true if and only if Jones is insane. But S is unaware of this fact, and it plays no role in his plan.

Note, however, that S could use the description attributively, even if S were aware that Jones murdered Smith. He still might not intend to communicate this to H. Perhaps Holmes has already figured out that Jones murdered Smith, but thinks it will be good for Watson to figure this out on his own, given a hint or two. He wants Watson to figure out that Jones murdered Smith, but he does not want Watson to come to believe this as a matter of recognizing his intentions. Holmes' belief that Jones murdered Smith may even be an important part of his motivation, but it is not his motivating belief, in the sense we have assigned that phrase.

In the referential* use, S wants H to come to believe the singular proposition that Jones murdered Smith. Here S really has a *pair* of motivating beliefs; he wants H to come to have a belief in a singular proposition *by* coming to have a belief in a general proposition. His plan is to make a statement whose referential content is that Smith's murderer is insane, and whose designational content is the proposition that Jones is insane. His path intention is that in virtue of having the merely descriptive cognitive fix provided by the description 'Smith's murderer' and realizing that Jones, the man he sees in court, is Smith's murderer, H will come to have a referential cognitive fix, and a belief whose referential content is the singular proposition that Jones is insane.

Thus, in our use of the phrase, the term 'referential*' in 'referential* use of a definite description' does not imply that the speaker *refers* to the object in question, but that he designates the object in question with the intention of imparting a belief with a referential cognitive fix. It is not a matter of the speaker referring, but a matter of the speaker designating with a target intention of imparting a referential belief. (We use 'reference*' simply to keep track of the difference between our Donnellan-inspired view and his own view, according to which in such cases the speaker actually does refer.)

'Smith's murderer' is a complete description, so S's plan doesn't involve H's recognizing a contextually supplied set that the description further limits. This is fairly typical of possessives. S's path intention is that H will grasp that by designating Jones, S intends to refer* to Jones, the defendant he is looking at and has just observed behaving bizarrely, and so recognize S's intention to impart the belief that Jones, thought of as the man H is looking at, is insane.

In our theory, cases in which the description is used both referentially and attributively do not present a problem.[1] In the attributive case of "Smith's murderer is insane" as described above, S and H did not know that Jones murdered Smith. But suppose they did. S wants H to believe, on the basis of the mutilated body, that Smith's murderer is insane, and on the basis of that belief to realize that Jones is insane. Here his use of 'Smith's murderer' *is* essential to his plan, and not just a means to his referential* goal, so his use is attributive. But he also intends to impart the referential* truth-conditions, so his use is also referential. So, in our view, the essentiality of the description for imparting the intended belief(s) is a necessary condition for the attributive use and not for the referential use, but the absence of such an intention is also not a necessary condition for the referential use.

8.4   Inaccurate descriptions

Now let's return to Donnellan's 'the man with a martini' case, in its original form, where the man is a man *without* a martini. Let's suppose that Muggs is drinking a gimlet, from the kind of glass ordinarily used for martinis, with an olive, and at a casual glance anyone would take him to be drinking a martini.

---

[1] See O'Rourke, 1994.

S says to his butler H, "The man with a martini is wanted on the phone." He intends to impart to H the belief that Muggs is wanted on the phone, with a perceptual cognitive fix on Muggs, appropriate to S's further goal, that H go tell Muggs he is wanted on the phone. So the case has much in common with a straightforward referential* case, which it would be except for the inaccuracy of the description. Assume that Muggs is wanted on the phone. Has S then said something true? Has he, as Donnellan sometimes says cautiously, said something true *of* Muggs? Or has he merely managed to convey something true, while saying something false?

Our basic position is the last, but we see another possible treatment for some cases.

Suppose, as our first variation, that S believes that Muggs is drinking a martini, and believes that H believes this too, or will as soon as he looks around the room. S intends to truly say that the man with a martini is wanted on the phone, and, by doing that, to refer* to Muggs and convey to H that he is wanted on the phone, in a way that involves, or can easily lead to, a perceptual fix. Then it seems that S will likely succeed in imparting a belief of just the sort he wants to H, and H will likely tell Muggs that he is wanted on the phone, just as S wishes. In this case, it seems to us that S's utterance will not be true. S has said something false, but by doing so imparted a true belief to H, which had the effect on H's behavior that S desired.

This sort of thing isn't that uncommon. S and H may both falsely believe that Calvin Coolidge was America's greatest President. S tells H, "America's greatest President reduced income taxes and pursued a policy of noninterference in foreign affairs," and H comes to have the belief that Calvin Coolidge did these things. Communication occurs, S's Gricean intentions are satisfied, and H comes to believe something true, but not because S said something true. S intended to refer* to Calvin Coolidge. There is no one who is both Calvin Coolidge and the greatest President of the United States, so S didn't designate anyone, and so did not refer* to anyone. He conveyed a truth to H, by saying something false.

Now consider the case in which S believes that Muggs is drinking a martini, but H, S's butler, actually poured the drink, and knows it is a gimlet that looks like a martini. Here again it seems as if S manages to convey a true belief to H, by saying something that is false. He intended to refer* to Muggs by designating Muggs, and say something true. In this he failed. It's just that H could figure out what he meant to say.

Now consider the case in which S doesn't believe that Muggs is drinking a martini but assumes that H will think that he is. He plans on H mistakenly thinking that he said that Muggs is wanted on the phone, and coming to believe this in the appropriate way, and delivering the message. He plans on conveying a true belief by conveying a false belief, by saying something untrue. It's not really deceit, or at least not harmful deceit, for the false belief he intends to instill as part of his plan to instill a true belief is totally transitory and inconsequential.

Finally, consider the case where S knows it's a gimlet, and thinks that his butler H knows that too, and knows that S knows it. Perhaps right at that moment S can't remember the word 'gimlet.' He wants to impart the belief that Muggs is wanted on the phone, via a perceptual cognitive fix, and he succeeds. Perhaps the simplest thing to say is that S knows that you can sometimes impart a true belief by saying something false, because the hearer will recognize the falsity, think that you are intentionally flouting the maxim of quality, and come up with the correct view of the belief you intended to impart as the best explanation of this.

Still, there is another way of looking at the last case. First note that a conversation like this is not especially puzzling:

(8.2)   H: I told him that he was wanted on the phone.
        S: Thanks.
        H: He wasn't drinking a martini, it was a gimlet with an olive.
        S: I know.

We saw in §4.5 that incorrect characterization of the intended referent does not block reference. You can mistakenly call a woman 'he'; it doesn't mean you haven't referred to her. The gendered pronoun is to provide auxiliary information that may help the hearer figure out to whom you refer, but it doesn't really affect reference. In §5.4 we looked at a case of referring to Larrazabal Hall as 'that pile of bricks.' The key point was that we can provide auxiliary information non-literally – metaphorically, ironically – to provide a hyperbolic insult while making an assertion that is intended literally. In such cases there is a bit of a detour for the hearer to take, in order to extract any helpful auxiliary information.

It would be but a small alteration in the Larrazabal Hall case to have S use a description: "The ugly pile of bricks across the street houses the ILCLI." One might suppose that the correct explanation is that S intends to say something obviously false, flout the maxim of quality, and implicate that the brick building across the street houses the ILCLI. This does not seem to us to be the only plausible analysis of S's plan. One could bring in pragmatics not at the level of what is said, but on the near-side, as an explanation of what the speaker is trying to do with the obviously false description.

In this view, S intends for H to recognize that he does not intend the words 'the ugly pile of bricks' to designate an object which he is trying to impart a belief about, but to suggest another description for that object, that is, 'the brick building across the street' or perhaps 'the ugly brick building across the street.' That is, the definite description is not to be taken literally, although the statement as a whole is to be taken literally.

In this view, it is not the falsity of what S says that provokes H's pragmatic reasoning, but the emptiness of the description when taken literally. There is something like a maxim of referential uses of descriptions, to the effect that the description that one uses to identify the object of which one intends to assert something, should designate that object. S flouts that maxim. H engages in near-side pragmatic reasoning: S is trying to get me to believe of some object that it houses the ILCLI, by saying that it does; S's description is empty (or at least doesn't designate any appropriate object); he clearly knows this; he is not using 'the ugly pile of bricks' literally, but using it to suggest some other identifying conditions. The hypothesis that S intends H to realize that he is speaking non-literally, and intends for H to figure out that he has the brick building across the street in mind, accounts for everything; the implicated description designates the building, and the building is an appropriate candidate for housing the ILCLI.

Similarly, in our last case, where S neither believes himself that Muggs is drinkng a martini, nor intends to impart that belief to H, and in fact fully expects H to realize that Muggs is not drinking a martini, it seems gratuitous to insist that S says something false. His plan is rather to implicate an alternative description, something like "the man who appears to be drinking a martini," by which he refers* to Muggs, and conveys the singular proposition that he is wanted on the phone.

From our perspective, it is important to keep in mind that language provides the speaker with tools to help the hearer discover his intentions. Definite descriptions, like referring expressions and phrases, provide the speaker with tools for getting the hearer to identify the object about which the speaker intends to assert something. As a matter of fact, in many situations descriptions can be used non-literally to achieve the right effect. In using the phrase 'the man with a martini' to direct the hearer to a man without a martini, but who looks as if he might have a martini, the speaker exhibits a certain facility in the use of the equipment language offers.

So we are inclined to recognize implicative directing intentions, to use a description that neither the speaker nor hearer thinks accurately picks out the speaker's intended referent, as an invitation for the hearer to come up with an alternative description, or identifying condition, in the course of figuring out the speaker's intentions. We do not believe that there has to be a sharp line between the different sorts of cases involving inaccurate descriptions.

A speaker can refer* to an object by uttering a description that (incrementally) designates that object. A speaker can also intend to refer* to an object by uttering a description that (incrementally) and non-literally designates the object. In this case the speaker plans on the hearer recognizing his intention to non-literally designate and working out an appropriate identifying condition.

8.5   Conclusion

Here then is our final theory of descriptions (at least for this book):

(1)   Definite descriptions are real syntactic units in natural language.

(2a)   A speaker S uses a definite description 'The F' to narrow down a set of objects B that S takes to be contextually available to the hearer H. The use of the description denotes the subset of Bs that are also Fs if that set is a singleton, otherwise it denotes the null set. If the use of a description denotes a singleton whose only member is x, the use of the description *designates x*.

(2b)   A statement "The F is G" is true if "The F" designates an object x, and x is G.

(3)   Such statements are not true, and at least in some cases false, if "The F" does not designate an object, and false if it does but the object is not G.

(4a)   The referential content of such a statement does not contain the designation of the definite description, if any, as a constituent; anachronistically put, it is true in worlds in which there is a unique F that is G, but the unique F doesn't have to be the same individual in each such world.

(4b)   With such statements, however, we also recognize the designational content of statements. This is the proposition that encodes the designational truth-conditions, that is, what has to be the case for the statement to be true given not only the facts of reference, but the designations of definite descriptions. When there is a designation, this proposition will be a singular proposition about that designation.

(4c)   An intention to use a description to refer* is an intention to induce the hearer to have descriptive cognitive fix on its designation, and thereby, in the light of knowledge the hearer has or can acquire, come to have a cognitive fix on it of the sort standardly imparted by names, demonstratives, and indexicals. The speaker intends, that is, for the hearer to come to have a belief with the designational content of the speaker's utterance, in virtue of coming to have a belief with its referential content.

(5)   A speaker may use a definite description to intentionally communicate a belief about an object which the description does not designate, and will do so successfully if the hearer, for one reason or another, correctly infers that the speaker intends to communicate a belief about that object. Two rather different mechanisms may be involved, which, assuming the belief is true, can be described as follows: (i) the speaker may be conveying the true belief, in a singular proposition, by saying something false, relying on false beliefs of the hearer, which the speaker may or may

not share, that the speaker has referred* to that object; (ii) the speaker may be relying on common knowledge, or belief, that the description does not fit the speaker's intended referent*, and thereby implicate an alternative identifying description which does fit it. In the latter case, following Donnellan, we say the speaker has said something true *of* the object that fits the implicated identifying condition.

9   Implicit reference and unarticulated constituents

9.1   Introduction

Until now, we have been dealing with acts of reference in which the speaker uses an expression with a fairly complex intention to talk about some particular object. In our approach, the various referential devices are paradigmatically suited to exploit different types of cognitive fix the speaker may have on the object he intends to refer to. Demonstratives paradigmatically exploit perceptual buffers – e.g., 'the object I'm seeing' – indexicals exploit specific utterance-relative fixes – 'the speaker of the utterance' – names exploit nominal fixes – involving a notion, and a network – and descriptions, when used referentially, can exploit any sort of epistemic or pragmatic role.

Now, we also hold that there are cases in which a speaker refers to an object without using any of these expressions or any expression at all. There are cases of *implicit reference*. We take implicit reference, or at least a central form of it, to involve a sort of mismatch between the referring expressions used in an utterance and the proposition that classifies its referential truth-conditions. Objects appear in the latter with no corresponding expression in the former. We call this phenomenon 'unarticulated constituents.'[1]

In this chapter we explain the idea of an unarticulated constituent and defend it from some objections to show how well it fits into the perspective of this book.

9.2   Unarticulated constituents and the supplemental nature of language

If we think of language as a species of action, it is natural to adopt the view that utterances are typically intended to add to or supplement a pre-existing

---

[1] See Perry's 'Thought without Representation' [Perry, 1986]. The concept was originally intended to shed light on self-knowledge. Several examples, especially the use of 'It's raining' to say that it is raining in Palo Alto, drew far more attention than his deep thoughts about self-knowledge. Subsequently Mark Crimmins and Perry [Crimmins and Perry, 1989; Crimmins, 1992] used the concept in their account of belief reports, and that use also has attracted a great deal of attention, favorable and unfavorable.

Type of cognitive fix exploited by the directing intention

Type of expression	Type of cognitive fix
Demonstrative	Perceptual (broadly)
Indexical	Utterance-bound
Name	Network-bound
Description	Descriptive

situation, in some manner that will help complete the circumstances necessary to achieve some goal. Suppose it is your job to set the table for dinner. What you have to bring about is that there is a table, a tablecloth, four plates, and silverware, napkins, a water glass, and a wine glass next to each plate. To achieve this goal, you start with what is there, and add to that whatever is necessary to finish the job. If you live in a cramped apartment, you may have to get a folding table from the front-hall closet and set it up. If you live in a house with a room and a table devoted to dining, the starting point may be a table with a tablecloth already in place. Perhaps someone has already put down some or all of the plates. Whatever you find, you don't start over, but add to it.

It seems to us that purposeful language use is like that. You usually have the goal of changing someone's thoughts; instilling new beliefs, or reinforcing old ones, or implanting new desires, or extinguishing old ones, or of course any of dozens of other things. In all likelihood you are attempting to affect thought in order to affect action; you want to change the way your audience acts by changing what they want or what they believe. But maybe not; perhaps you are just telling an anecdote, to bring pleasure.

In any case, you have a starting point. The hearer already has certain beliefs and desires, certain perceptions, certain concerns and thoughts that are present in her mind. Among these will usually be some that concern the purposes of the conversation. Your goal is to build a bridge between where the mind of the hearer is and where you want it to be, in the hope that the hearer will cross the bridge and wind up where you want her to be.

In some cases, where it won't be obvious, you need to go out of your way to make it clear what words you are using, or with what meaning. Consider an example due to Ivan Sag. Just back from Saudi Arabia, you say, "I'd forgotten how good beer tastes." You are probably using 'good' to modify 'taste' and mean 'pleasurable,' not to modify 'beer' and mean 'of good quality.' You probably don't need to explain yourself. But perhaps you are intending to make a somewhat debatable point about the bottle of Budweiser you are drinking. Then you are likely to be misunderstood unless you add something like "I really do think this stuff is good beer, although I know you regard it as an American abomination."

Unarticulated constituents continue the same picture. If it's pretty clear that your conversation pertains to the plan you and your conversational partner have had to play tennis on a given day, at the usual place, a court in Palo Alto, and you say "It's raining" he will understand that you are talking about Palo Alto. You don't need to tell him what place you are talking about, because he knows, or can easily figure out, what place you are talking about. There is no more need to use language to introduce the subject matter, than there is to explain that what you mean by 'rain' is moisture condensed from the atmosphere, rather than merely a great quantity of something or other.

9.3   Three kinds of unarticulated constituents

There are three patterns that seem to call for unarticulated constituents, which we will discuss in turn.

First there are utterances of sentences that are not grammatically complete, and because of that do not articulate everything that is needed for the proposition the utterance expresses. John has been looking for his cell phone. At one point Frenchie says, "On the mantle." The phrase she uses is not a grammatically complete sentence, and she does not articulate all the items involved in the truth-conditions of her utterance. But she and John both know she is talking about his cell phone, and her utterance is true just in case his cell phone is on the mantle.

There are a couple of variations on this. One sort of case is of the Herb Clark genre. Frenchie might hold up the cell phone and show it to John, saying it was on the mantle, relying on her gesture and the cell phone itself to identify it as what she is talking about. Or she might just leave it where it is, find him, and say "On the mantle." It's just obvious to John what she's talking about, and she plans on this.

Second, there are cases like "It's five o'clock," that are grammatically complete but truth-conditionally incomplete. The sentence uttered is grammatically complete. And yet, if true, it will be because there is some time zone such that at the time of the utterance it's five o'clock in that time zone, and that's the time zone relevant to the truth of the utterance. This is typically the time zone in which the utterer is situated at the time of the utterance, but not always.

Finally, there are utterances like the one considered in the last chapter, when Ethel says to Fred, "I invited everyone to the party," meaning to convey that she has invited everyone in the apartment building to the party. Her sentence is grammatically complete. And it also articulates all the material one needs to provide the utterance with truth-conditions: that she invited everyone (in the world) to the party. But the fully articulated truth-conditions are not the correct ones; they do not match her motivating belief.

9.3.1   Unarticulated and grammatically incomplete

Consider the case of John and Dikran, who have the habit of smoking a small cigar before going home after work. It's usually Dikran's job to provide the 'cigarrillos.' It's 5 p.m., and John enters Dikran's office. Dikran says:

(9.1)   On the top shelf.

John reaches the top shelf and finds the packet of cigarrillos next to a pile of books. We can imagine that John grasps immediately the referential truth-conditions of (9.1): namely, that the cigarrillos are on the top of Dikran's bookshelves, but, of course, he might not. Perhaps John forgot about their smoking habit, and simply intended to invite Dikran to try a coffee from his new espresso machine. He grasped only what we call the speaker-bound truth-conditions of the utterance, something like:

Given that Dikran is the speaker of (9.1), (9.1) consists of the English predicate 'on the top shelf,' and he refers with 'the top shelf' to the top shelf of the bookshelves in this room, (9.1) is true if and only if the object Dikran is referring to is on the top shelf.

Understanding the speaker-bound truth-conditions is enough to prompt John to look for what Dikran is referring to and find the packet of cigarillos, and be reminded of their pleasurable, if unhealthy, habit.

From our point of view, this is the most natural view once you take utterances as acts that are intended to supplement the information already available in the situation. The speaker exploits that information, and he can successfully refer to objects without using specific expressions to do that in complete or incomplete sentences.

This goes against what we might call the 'sententialist' view, which claims that if there is anything said, any proposition expressed by an utterance, then necessarily it must be the utterance of a sentence [Corazza and Korta, 2010]. So, if by uttering X Dikran manages to refer to the packet of cigarrillos then necessarily X involves an elliptical sentence like '[The packet of cigarrillos is] on the top shelf.' The problem is that these examples (and many others discussed by Elugardo and Stainton [Elugardo and Stainton, 2004; Stainton, 2006]) do not meet the usual definition of ellipsis, according to which the elided material is copied from a previous utterance, so the elliptical sentence cannot occur in the initial discourse position. There are various philosophical arguments for a sententialist view, which we reject [Perry, 1994]. In some cases there are linguistic arguments that favor the postulation of an unarticulated phrase, rather than merely an unarticulated referent. But in many cases, there is no reason for the speaker to use language to get the hearer to think about an object, if he is already thinking about the object, and can be expected to easily move to the targeted cognitive fix, on the basis of common sense, perhaps with the help of the predicated condition.

9.3.2   Unarticulated, grammatically complete, but referentially incomplete

Utterances like "It's raining," or "It's five o'clock" are grammatically complete. But their referential truth-conditions seem to require a place where it is raining or not, and a time zone in which it is or isn't five o'clock. These cases typically involve leaving factors that are, broadly speaking, a part of the perspective of the thinker or speaker unarticulated. Thoughts and utterances typically occur in places on earth, each of which is a part of one time zone or another. These serve as the default values. While sophisticated speakers are aware of this relativity, less sophisticated speakers may not be. Basic mastery of language does not require being aware of the relativity, but only the ability to make and assess judgements relative to the default value. A young child might know how to use the sentence 'It's raining' to report what she sees out the window, without having ever considered that it might be raining where she is, but not some place else. And time zones are really a rather sophisticated device, which many people no doubt never learn about.

Consider a young child, call her 'Jamaica,' who has learned to tell time. That is, she can look at a clock or a watch and report, based on the position of the hands, "It is nine o'clock," or "It is quarter to one." She knows that at least some 'o'clocks' occur twice in a day; she has been up both at 7 a.m. and 7 p.m., and knows the difference. She knows that when it is light and twelve it is noon, and when it is dark and twelve it is midnight. She may have only the vaguest idea that there are such things as 1, 2 and 3 a.m., since she has never been allowed to stay up that late. And she has no idea about time zones, and the general relativity of o'clock properties to locations.

Suppose Jamaica and John are at the lake fishing. They both know they should be back at the cabin for lunch at one. They both look at their watches and see the big hand at nine and the little one a bit before one. They both think "It's quarter to one, time to start back." They both say to the other kids, "It's quarter to one, time to start back." Neither of them thinks, "It's quarter to one Pacific time." Jamaica can't think it, because she doesn't have the necessary knowledge and concepts. John could think it, but he doesn't because this more complicated form of thought is triggered only when the difference in time zones is relevant to the use he is making of the information.

The Pacific time zone is an unarticulated constituent of both of their thoughts and utterances. But there is an important difference. John has the requisite concepts to articulate the time-zone factor in thought and language, while Jamaica does not. When such considerations are relevant, John is capable of employing what we might call 'time-zone introduction and elimination rules.' If his thought, "It is quarter to twelve" is true, then the more complicated thought, "It is quarter to twelve in Z" is also true, where 'Z' designates the time zone about which he picked up information. In the case in question, where he looked at the watch on his own wrist, this will be the time zone he is in.

This pattern is characteristic of factors involved in one's perspective. One might hypothesize that language was developed for the service of people unaware of the relativity involved. Later, when science or philosophy discovered the relativity of the sorts of judgement in question to the perspectival factor, explicit mention of it, and so the ability to explicitly handle judgements made from other perspectives, was handled with adverbial modification.

To take a rather extreme case, suppose you are what David Lewis calls a 'modal realist' about other possible worlds. You think they are concrete realities, differing more or less from the actual world in what happens in them, but not in their basic metaphysical status. When you are thinking about it, you realize that *your* thought or utterance, "It's raining in Palo Alto" is true because it is raining in @, where '@' is the name of the actual world – the one both authors and readers of this book are in. You might be careful to be explicit about this when talking about complicated modal examples with other realists. But mostly, in day-to-day life, you just forget about it. And the possibility to forget about it is recognized, indeed encouraged, by natural language. If you just say or think "It's raining in Palo Alto" nothing seems to be missing; it's not like saying "The Giants beat today," which seems to syntactically demand an expression that refers to the beaten team.

Another example is the relativity of all judgements about things happening at the same time to inertial frames. If John says, "The New Year's Eve ball dropping in Times Square on New Year's Eve happened exactly as the clock in our living room in Palo Alto chimed nine times," what he says is true, because these events were simultaneous relative to the inertial frame defined by his position in spacetime. But the sentence feels complete as it stands. Language evolved long before the relativity of simultaneity was established, and that fact remains irrelevant to most conversations.

There are probably more people who believe in time zones than other concrete possible worlds, and more people who are aware of time zones than are aware of the relativity of simultaneity. But the same phenomenon is present with time zones. "It's twelve o'clock" sounds fine; even one, like John, who is aware that his thought or utterance is true because it is twelve o'clock Pacific time, won't worry about time zones in conversations about local affairs with local people.

In these cases, the time and place of an utterance provide a default value for the unmentioned factor, and this serves for most mundane purposes, such as thinking about what one is going to do, or discussing such issues with people that share the same possible world, inertial frame, or time zone. We will say that one who has mastered that part of language that assumes the default value, has thoughts and makes utterances that *concern* that value. Jamaica's thoughts and utterances about what time it is concern the Pacific time zone. In contrast, we'll say that John's thoughts and utterances are *about* the Pacific time zone (unless he's travelling), because he has the ability to exercise time-zone introduction and elimination rules. Most people have thoughts that concern only the actual world (if David Lewis was right about it being only one of an infinity of worlds) and concern only their own inertial frame. Teenagers and adults who have access to telephones, talk to distant relatives, watch television, travel in airplanes, and the like, need to be capable of explicit thought about time zones, and so when they are involved in such activities their thought are about time zones. At other times, when checking their watch against their clock, or talking face-to-face with their family and friends, they face less of a cognitive burden in dealing with time, and their thoughts need only concern time zones, or at any rate the ability to explicitly represent this contingency need not be engaged.

9.3.3   *Unarticulated, even though grammatically and referentially complete*

When Ethel says to Fred, "I invited everyone to the party," her utterance is grammatical and provides everything one needs for a truth-evaluable (referential) proposition, the proposition that Ethel invited everyone to the party. However, it seems implausible to say that she said something false, because in fact she didn't invite the Obamas or Queen Elizabeth and Prince Philip. Given that they had been talking about a party for the people in their apartment building, and Fred had just asked Ethel about Ricky and Lucy, residents in the building, it seems clear that Ethel's motivating belief was that she had invited everyone in the building to the party, and that is what Fred will take her to have said.

This is the sort of treatment favored by those who favor what Recanati calls a 'contextualist' approach to the issue of the pragmatics/semantics interface. 'Minimalists,' like Cappelen and Lepore, favor an alternative treatment which would be to suppose that Ethel did express the proposition that she invited *everyone* to the party, but she is intentionally expressing something false: she is intentionally and blatantly flouting Grice's maxim of quality. Her plan is that Fred will recognize this, and take her to have implicated that she invited everyone in the apartment building.

But Gricean reasoning doesn't seem very well suited to do the job in cases like this. If Fred takes Ethel to be saying something false, the most natural inference would be that she *didn't* invite Ricky and Lucy – she would as soon invite everyone in the world. That would be the natural inference for Fred to make if she said, for example, "Oh sure, and I've invited Queen Elizabeth and Prince Philip, too" – a statement which is, if anything, less obviously false than that she invited everyone in the world. The natural inference would be that she only makes as if to say that she invited Queen Elizabeth and Prince Philip as well as Lucy and Ricky; she is being ironical, and would no more think of inviting Ricky and Lucy than inviting British royalty. Surely, the contextualist argues, bringing what we would ordinarily take Ethel to have said, that she invited everyone in the building to the party, only as an implicature generated by blatant falsity is, in Hume's happy phrase, an 'unexpected circuit' in Fred's pragmatic reasoning.[2] It's much more plausible to simply credit her with saying, with respect to the domain of people Fred is worried about, that she has invited all of them.

In Chapter 12, when we develop our account of the pragmatics/semantics interface, we will show how some of the ideas about that issue that motivate minimalists can be handled in a way consistent with the unarticulated approach to cases like this one.

9.4 Whence unarticulated constituents?

9.4.1 Deep lexicalization

Someone who says "It is raining" will not be understood, in any normal situation, as asserting that it is raining *somewhere on earth*, much less *somewhere in the universe*, although we could construct settings in which that's what is meant and what is understood. To understand the utterance, we supplement what is given by language with an unarticulated constituent. On the other hand, as Ken Taylor points out, if we say "Betty was dancing" we do not usually regard it as part of what is asserted that she was dancing in a particular place, even though she must have been [Taylor, 2007]. Why is the place a constituent of the remark about rain, but not the remark about Betty?

In his original article [Perry, 1986] Perry relied on metaphysics here; he claimed that it was a metaphysical fact that rain always occurred in a place, so if one just says, "It is raining" the propositional components provided by 'rain' and the present tense will leave a gap. The speaker must have a place in mind, and the hearer knows this. Taylor's dancing example shows that this isn't going to do. The metaphysics of dancing requires that dancing occurs at some

---

[2] Hume is discussing Descartes' strategy of proving the existence of God as a way of assuring himself that, e.g., he has feet and hands: 'To have recourse to the veracity of the supreme Being, in order to prove the veracity of our senses, is surely making a very unexpected circuit.' [Hume, 1748, XII].

place, but we don't suppose that our report about Betty expresses a proposition with the place she was dancing as an unarticulated constituent. It is consistent with the metaphysics of rain that when we say, "It is raining" we ordinarily just mean that it is raining somewhere. The fact that 'it is raining' doesn't normally work that way has to do with the roles that rain and reports about rain play in human discourse. These facts are contingent, but grounded in pervasive and enduring facts about our world. In a world, as François Recanati imagines, in which there is severe worldwide drought, it might be so important to us that it is raining somewhere or other, that the standard use of 'it is raining' might simply be to say that it is raining somewhere or other [Recanati, 2007a]. The same would be true in the Rain-Ache universe, where, as Cappelen and Lepore imagine, people get severe headaches when it is raining anywhere, unless they are wearing magic caps [Cappelen and Lepore, 2007] . But our world isn't like these fantasies. It is always raining somewhere, and hardly worth mentioning. If we did want to say that, we would doubtless say, "It is raining *somewhere*" to indicate our intention. We are usually interested in the issue of whether it is raining where we are, or where we plan to be, or where some person or thing we care about is.

In thinking about our linguistic knowledge, the right place to delineate the differences between, say, raining and dancing seems to us to be, as Taylor suggests, the lexicon. Metaphysics says rain is a binary relation with places and times as parameters; it says the same thing about dancing, although there is also a parameter for the dancer. So metaphysics doesn't tell us the difference. But part of knowing how to use these words is sensitivity to the sorts of situations and information we use them to deal with. A good dictionary will tell us that 'rain' can be used to describe a torrent of oil coming down on us from a gusher, or even a torrent of cats and dogs. But it will also tell us that the ordinary use is to describe water falling from clouds. An ordinary dictionary won't tell us that people usually have a place in mind for the rain, but the sort of lexicon one would have to put together in AI, to develop a program that could interpret ordinary conversations, would have to have that knowledge in it. In Wittgensteinian terms, the language game we play with 'rain' is part of the form of life where we share information about what is happening at particular places, where we might be, might be planning to go, or are otherwise concerned about.

Taylor calls this sort of thing 'deep lexicalization' [Taylor, 2007]. We take it that deep lexicalization is not a matter of brain cells in each speaker, but a social phenomenon involving deference, differences between idiolects, differences between casual and more official uses of language, and many other things. People may have more or less understanding of the way the words they use work. Jamaica, for example, has only a partial understanding of her 'o'clock' vocabulary, because she hasn't learned about time zones.

9.4.2   Logical form

Another issue is whether there is, in the 'logical form' of 'it is raining' (to take that example), a variable for the place at which the rain occurs. This issue engendered a debate between François Recanati and Jason Stanley, for which they comandeered the term 'unarticulated constituent.' Stanley thought there was such a variable, by which he meant that the place constituent was articulated after all. Recanati thought that there wasn't such a variable, and that the argument for the place came through a process of enrichment. But he seems to have accepted Stanley's redefinition of 'articulated,' so that it doesn't require what Perry thinks of as articulation, that is, that there be a spoken or written symbol of some sort that stands for it [Recanati, 2004, 2007a; Stanley, 2000].

Some linguistic theories insist on a level of logical form. Our personal favorite, HPSG [Ginzburg and Sag, 2001], does not require it, although it can allow for it if wanted. We are somehow skeptical about logical form as something that is a part of syntax, but don't wish to claim mastery of this complicated issue. It is certainly useful, for certain purposes, to postulate a level of logical form which in the present case will include an invisible and unspoken variable for time zones. But if we do that, we would just be representing a fact about the way other people use the 'o'clock' vocabulary, a lexical fact, as part of a logical formalism we are using as an analytical tool.

Time zones are a rather interesting phenomenon. As we understand it, they were introduced into ordinary time-keeping in the nineteenth century, mostly as a consequence of the development of railroads. It was convenient to give up the old system, where 'noon' meant that the sun was directly overhead, so no two towns shared exactly the same o'clock properties, for one in which broader swaths of territory agreed on what time it was. The first time zone in the world was established by British railroad companies, using Greenwich Mean Time, which had been established almost two centuries earlier, in 1675, to aid sailors to determine longitude at sea. The clocks at local stations in Britain were adjusted to GMT. The clock on the town hall might still use the old system, but if you wanted use the railroad's schedule to catch your train, you had to adjust to their practice, and go by the one at the station. As American railroads extended across the broad continent, the modern system of time zones emerged. If there is a variable in logical form for time zones, it must have crept into syntax in the nineteenth century.

9.5   Are unarticulated constituents a myth?

Cappelen and Lepore maintain that unarticulated constituents are a myth [Cappelen and Lepore, 2007]. They acknowledge that if one utters "It is raining" one will in all likelihood 'saliently assert' a proposition that has a location as a constituent, a location that is not referred to by any word, morpheme, or even any less audible and visible syntactic creature. So it sounds a lot as if they agree with Perry's doctrine of unarticulated constituents. Their reason for denying it is that they think there is a 'location-neutral' proposition that does not have a location as a constituent, nor involve any sort of quantification over locations, that is 'semantically expressed' by the words 'It is raining (at t)'. At a first pass, one might say that they think that semantics determines what is strictly and literally said, and what is strictly and literally said does not involve a place constituent; that comes in later, from pragmatics. That's an oversimplification because, as we will see in the next chapter, they demote the concept of what is said from semantics completely, in favor of their concept of semantic content.

Let's call the 'location-neutral' proposition that Cappelen and Lepore take to be semantically expressed by an utterance at t of 'It is raining' R. We can't figure out what R is supposed to be. It's pretty clear that R is true if it's raining somewhere on earth at t. But is it true or false if it's not raining anywhere on earth, but it is raining on Venus, or one of the moons of Jupiter, or a planet in a distant galaxy? To be location neutral, it seems it ought to be true if there is rain anywhere at all; if, as they say, "rain is going on at t." But so understood, R doesn't fit the description of their Rain-Ache universe. In order to know when to put on their magic hats and avoid headaches these folk place rain-detectors around 'the entire globe.' Where did the restriction to the globe – presumably our earth? – come from? It sounds to us like an unarticulated constituent of R.

Still, as far as their explanation goes, it doesn't much matter exactly what R is. The role R plays in their theory doesn't require much of it; its truth-value, and truth-conditions, whatever they are, are irrelevant to what the speaker meant to convey in the tennis example; they stand outside the whole informational transaction, which began with his looking out the window, and ended with the hearer's giving up on playing tennis, and going back to bed. What is needed for R is a semantic content that depends only on the components of the sentence, and is so wildly irrelevant that the hearer can begin trying to figure out what else, other than the semantic content, the speaker might have been trying to convey.

This irrelevance is our main problem with their theory. Granting the existence of R, why would we describe this proposition as the 'semantic content' of an utterance of 'it's raining at t'? To be sure, the proposition is constructed of constituents (rain, and the time t) that are articulated in the utterance. But so what? As Perry showed in the original paper, there is nothing in the nature of a compositional semantics for utterances that requires the clause in our semantics that assigns contents to sentences to confine the constituents of the contents to items articulated in the sentence. This point is intended not merely as one about the weather, but is used in a variety of settings, from issues involving the self to criticisms of Davidson's arguments against reference [Perry, 1994], connected with the supplemental view of language. To suppose that if such a proposition as R can be found, it must be assigned the honorific 'semantic content' is just to assume that this is not so, without, as far as we can see, any reason having been given.

According to Cappelen and Lepore (2007), when I say "It's raining today" I am semantically expressing R, a proposition I don't believe, "in order to communicate a proposition [I] do believe." But what reason is there to assign R any role at all in my plan? My utterance introduces some propositional constituents, today and the relation of raining at a location. And the hearer figures out what location, if any, I am talking about. My plan for his reasoning, and his reasoning, don't require anything like R.

The hearer needs a proposition to get started with any sort of Gricean pragmatic reasoning. What other candidate is there besides R? This is a question to which the reflexive–referential theory provides a nice answer. If a person is talking about location l, his utterance at t of 'it is raining now' will be true iff it rains at t in l. His contemporary hearer will know that what the speaker has said is true iff: there is a location l such that (a) the person is talking about l and (b) it is raining at l now; i.e., the utterance-bound proposition.

If they are in Palo Alto, and have been discussing whether they can play tennis, the assumption that the speaker is being relevant and helpful will lead the hearer to the conclusion that S is talking about Palo Alto. If they are in Palo Alto and it is obviously sunny and bright, the quality maxim will lead him to wonder where else S might be talking about. In neither case does S or the hearer need to worry about R.

10 Locutionary content and speech acts

10.1 Introduction

Given our concept of reference, we can explain what we shall call, following Austin, the *locutionary act*. The locutionary act involves referring to an object (or objects) and predicating something of it (or them). The locutionary content, our explication of 'what is said,' is the referential content of the locutionary act. For the purposes of the locutionary act, the referent is the object that occupies the epistemic–pragmatic role the speaker intends to exploit, whether or not it is the object to which he intends to refer. Similarly, the locutionary content may not be what the speaker intended to say, as in various of the examples we have discussed. The untoward consequences of inept pointing, the usual basis of what we called the forensic element of saying in such cases, is handled at the level of perlocutionary acts, and the issue of responsibility will be seen not as a case of responsibility for what was said, but responsibility for the unintended but in these cases foreseeable consequences of carelessness.

Our plan for this chapter is as follows. In §10.2 we give an overview of our reasons for distinguishing locutionary content from what is said. In §10.3 we explain locutionary content in the context of speakers' plans. In §10.4 we look at a number of examples to show how locutionary content can diverge from what is said. In §10.5 we compare our concepts to Austin's, and consider Searle's misgivings about locutionary acts. (We should emphasize that, although there are some differences between our concept of locutionary act and Austin's, and although we disagree with Searle's rejection of locutionary acts, we see our concept of locutionary content as a friendly amendment to the basic ideas of the Austin–Searle theory of speech acts.)

10.2 Locutionary content versus what is said

Pragmatics and the philosophy of language have put a number of pressures on the concept of what is said by (the speaker of) an utterance. First, David Kaplan and others grounded the concept of the proposition expressed in intuitions about what is said, to support arguments that the contribution names, indexicals, and demonstratives make to the proposition expressed is the object referred to, rather than some identifying condition that the referent meets.

Kaplan distinguishes between the character and content of a sentence in a context. The character of the sentence, together with the context, determines the content; semantics spells this out. Since the content of a sentence is the proposition expressed, which is explained in terms of what is said, it creates a second pressure: what is said is (more or less) equated with what semantics provides.

A third pressure comes from Grice's [Grice, 1967a] distinction between what is said and what is implicated by an utterance. In the standard case, the hearer takes what is said as the starting point in inferring implicatures. So what is said has another role to fill, serving as the starting point of Gricean reasoning about implicatures.

These combined roles for what is said give rise to what we will call the classic picture of the relation between semantics and pragmatics. Semantics provides what is said as the input to pragmatics. In both speech act theory and Gricean pragmatics, as originally developed, pragmatics is focussed on what is done with language beyond saying.

We don't think the ordinary concept of saying is quite up to meeting all of these pressures, and that this has obscured some issues about the interface between semantics and pragmatics. There are (at least) the two following difficulties.

On the one hand, as we argued in 'Three Demonstrations and a Funeral' [Korta and Perry, 2006a] and will further explain in the next chapter, it is not always the referential content of an utterance that provides the input to Gricean reasoning about implicatures. Often it is some of the other kinds of content (utterance-bound, speaker-bound, network-bound). In §10.5 we extend this point to speech act theory. Information that is required to determine the illocutionary force of an utterance is sometimes lost at the level of referential content, but available at the level of reflexive content.

On the other hand, and our main point in this chapter, it is necessary to distinguish between acts of saying and locutionary acts. Our locutionary content is, like the classic picture of what is said, a form of referential content, and is intended to give grounding to the ubiquitous concept of the proposition expressed. The problem is that the ordinary concept of saying is shaped by the everyday needs of folk psychology, folk linguistics, and attributions of responsibility, and so does not quite carve phenomena at their theoretical joints, in the following ways.

First, saying is naturally taken to be an illocutionary act, of the same species as asserting, with perhaps somewhat weaker connotations. A speaker is committed to the truth of what she says. But propositions are expressed in the antecedents and consequents of conditionals, as disjuncts, and in many other cases without being asserted.

Second, to repeat, the concept of saying is to a certain extent a forensic concept. One is responsible for the way one's remarks are taken by reasonably competent listeners. But locutionary content is not sensitive to actual and hypothetical mental states of the audience.

Finally, the ordinary use of 'what is said' or 'what a speaker said' is quite flexible; what we take as having been said is often sensitive to the information that the speaker is trying to convey. Intuitively, Joana doesn't say the same thing when she utters "I am Joana" as she does when she utters "Joana is Joana" or "I am I." An utterance of 'I am I' would not commit her to having the name Joana, but this might be the main information she is trying to convey when she says 'I am Joana.' Locutionary content does not have this sensitivity to the information the speaker is trying to convey to sort this out. Our theory is quite sensitive to such matters, but we do not handle this by stretching the concept of what is said to cover all needs, but replace it, for theoretical purposes, with a number of other concepts.

These three differences we illustrate and discuss by going through a number of examples in §10.4.

10.3   Locutionary acts and locutionary content

The central concept in our approach is that of a speaker's plan. This is a natural outgrowth of the Austin–Searle concept of language as action, and of Grice's concept of speaker's meaning. Paradigmatically, a speaker utters a sentence with the intention of producing an utterance with certain truth-conditions, and thereby achieving further results, such as conveying information to a hearer, and perhaps thereby getting the hearer to do something. So, for example, Kepa might say the words "I'm hungry" with the intention of uttering the English sentence 'I'm hungry,' so that his utterance is true if and only if he, the speaker, is hungry, and so informing John that he is hungry, implicating that he'd like to break off work to go to lunch, and eliciting John's response as to whether that seems like a good idea.

For our purposes, we assume that we are dealing with competent speakers who can utter (speak, type, write, or sign) meaningful words, phrases, and sentences of English at will, as a part of a plan that marshals the requisite intentions to perform locutionary acts. We will focus on that part of the locutionary act that consists in referring to a certain individual. This involves:

(1) producing singular terms of English, by speaking, writing, typing, signing or other means;
(2) doing so with appropriate intentions that resolve:

(a) which words, of those consistent with the sounds uttered (or letters typed ...), are being used
(b) which meanings of those permitted by the conventions of English for the words and phrases being used are being employed
(c) nambiguities; that is, issues about the reference of names which various persons, things, or places share
(d) the primary reference of demonstratives and other deictic words and issues relevant to the reference of indexicals
(e) anaphoric relations.

In addition, the speaker will have:

(3) (possibly quite minimal) beliefs about the facts that resolve the semantic values of indexicals, and which objects play the various roles exploited by demonstratives, which objects are the origins of exploited networks, and which objects fit the descriptions used;
(4) the intention of producing an utterance that will have certain certain referential truth-conditions, in accord with these beliefs, in virtue of having utterance-bound truth-conditions;
(5) (possibly quite minimal) further intentions to accomplish other results by producing his utterance: conveying implicatures, performing illocutionary and perlocutionary acts, and the like;
(6) (possibly quite minimal) intentions to accomplish other results by doing all of this: getting salt for his steak; influencing votes; starting wars; etc.

In determining the locutionary content, the speaker's intentions and the facts that determine reference are determinative; actual and possible misunderstandings, however easily the speaker could have foreseen and prevented them, are not relevant. Thus the intended utterance-bound truth-conditions will be what the speaker intends them to be, so long as the meanings and structures the speaker intends are allowed by the conventions of English. So the utterance-bound contents of a locutionary act correspond to the internal contribution. The speaker's beliefs in (3) are not determinative for locutionary content, however. The intended locutionary content will be the referential content of his utterance given his beliefs in (3). But the actual locutionary content will be determined by the facts, not by the speaker's beliefs about them.

Suppose, for example, that absent-minded John is in the philosophy lounge, but thinks that he is in the CSLI lounge. "Kepa is supposed to meet me here," he says. He intends to use 'here' indexically rather that deictically, and intends the referent of 'here' to be the room he is in, not, say, the campus he is at or the nation in which he resides. These intentions are determinative. The locutionary content of his utterance is that Kepa was to meet him in the philosophy lounge, the actual referent of his use of 'here'. The intended locutionary content, however, is that

Kepa was to meet him in the CSLI lounge, the place he thought would be the referent of his use of 'here.'

10.4   Locuted but not said: some examples

Grice's main distinction in his analysis of utterance meaning is between what is said and what is implicated. Grice also remarked that there are implicatures in cases in which the speaker says nothing, but only 'makes as if to say.' Irony is a case in point.[1] Let's assume that Elwood, with whom John has been on close terms until now, has betrayed a delicate secret of John's to an academic rival. John and Kepa both know this and they both see Elwood passing by. John utters:

(10.1)   He is a fine friend.

The utterance-bound and speaker-bound contents will not work:

> That the person that the speaker of (10.1) is referring to by his use of 'he' is a fine friend.
> That the person that John is referring to by his use of 'he' is a fine friend.

Assuming John's voice is not dripping with irony, to grasp the irony, Kepa has to grasp that John is referring to someone Kepa knows John no longer thinks of as a fine friend; he must grasps the locutionary content of (10.1).

> That Elwood is a fine friend.

Independently of what John might intend to communicate – typically, the opposite, or something implying the opposite, of the locutionary content of his utterance – and how the understanding process exactly works, it seems clear that for Kepa to take the utterance as ironic he has to identify the referent of 'he' and the property of 'being a fine friend,' i.e., the locutionary content. Without identifying Elwood and the property ascribed to him in the locutionary content of John's utterance, and as the Elwood that has betrayed John's confidence in him, Kepa will not grasp John's utterance as ironic, and will miss the point. John may be making as if to say [Grice, 1967a, 1967b], pretending [Clark and Gerrig, 1984], or echoing [Sperber and Wilson, 1986] a proposition, but he is definitely not *saying* it, he is not committing himself in any way to the truth of the locutionary content. However, this content has a role to play in the understanding of John's ironic utterance.

However the difference between saying and just making as if to say should be characterized, it seems clear that when a speaker is being ironic she refers

---

[1] For an account of irony that makes use of the basic concepts of Critical Pragmatics see Garmendia, 2007, 2010.

to objects and predicates properties so as to provide content for her utterance that the hearer is intended to grasp [Garmendia, 2007]. From the perspective of the speaker, this content plays a role in her utterance plan; from the perspective of the addressee, it plays a role in understanding the utterance. This content does not count as what she said, because, possibly among other things, she is overtly not committed to its truth, and she expects the hearer to understand that she is not so committed, but it is content anyway; a content that is locuted but not said.

In the case of many logical operators and other sentence-embedding constructions, propositions are locuted but not said, as Frege pointed out and Geach reminded a generation of ordinary-language philosophers [Geach, 1965]. When someone says, "If Hillary is ever elected President, Bill will enjoy his return to the White House," she doesn't say either that Hillary will be elected, or that Bill will return to the White House. These seem to us like sufficient reasons for keeping a place for locutionary content in a theory of utterance content.

The forensic element is not limited to the case of reference. Consider the following case. In a discussion with alumni about politics on campus, Kepa says,

(10.2) John is turning red.

He means that JP's face is turning red, perhaps from anger, or eating a hot pepper. The alumni take him to say that JP is becoming a communist. Kepa should have seen that people were likely to interpret his remark that way. Later he may protest, "I didn't say that." John might retort, "You didn't mean to say it, but you did, and I had to do a lot of explaining." Perhaps this retort is not correct. But the fact that the issue is debatable suggests that our ordinary concept of what is said is to some extent responsive to uptake on the part of the audience. What is said seems to have both illocutionary and perlocutionary aspects. In contrast, our concept of locutionary content will not depend on effects on the listener.

Suppose now that Kepa produces the sounds necessary to say

(10.3) Flying planes can be dangerous.

He intends to be producing a token of 'planes,' not of 'plains.' He intends to be using 'plane' with the sense of airplane, not flat surface. He intends to use 'Flying planes' as a gerund with its direct object, rather than as a verbal adjective modifying a noun. These intentions are all determinative for the locutionary act.

They might not be determinative for what is said. Suppose Kepa and John are flying kites on a hill near the airport with some other folks. People have been discussing the dangers that birds, power lines, electrical storms, and other phenomena pose for kite flyers. Kepa hasn't really been paying attention, but is daydreaming about being a pilot. He utters, "Flying planes can be dangerous," somewhat loudly, to remind himself of the reasons for forgoing his dreams. Everyone takes him to have used 'flying planes' as a noun phrase, and to have added a warning to the list generated by the conversation about the dangers of flying kites on the hill. Any semantically competent listener who had been listening to the conversation would have understood what Kepa said that way, and Kepa himself would have realized this if he hadn't been daydreaming.

When Kepa realizes how he has been understood he can surely protest, "I didn't mean to say that." But it is at least arguable that he did say it. Our ordinary concept of saying has a forensic element; Kepa would be responsible if a member of the group, frightened by his observation, quit flying kites. A discussion of whether he did say what he meant to, or said what he didn't mean to, would likely devolve into a discussion about his responsibility for the effects of his remarks on others. But, to repeat, with respect to our theoretically defined concept of locutionary content, there is no room for debate. There are no uptake conditions, and no forensic dimensions, to consider.

10.5   Locutionary versus propositional content

Our concept of a locutionary act is intended to be similar to Austin's. His definition was:

> The utterance of certain noises, the utterance of certain words in a certain con-struction, and the utterance of them with a certain 'meaning' in the favourite philosophical sense of that word, i.e. with a certain sense and with a certain reference. [Austin, 1961, p. 94]

According to Austin, locutionary acts are what saying consists in in its full general sense. They are the acts of saying something in contrast with the acts performed *in* saying something. We formulate it as the difference between the act of 'locuting' something (with a certain content, in our favored sense of the word) and the act of 'saying' it (telling it, asking it) to some-one. How faithful to Austin this is depends on just what he had in mind, which has been a matter of debate [Forguson, 1973; Searle, 1968; Strawson, 1973].

Surprisingly, Searle rejected Austin's distinction between locutionary acts and acts of (illocutionary) saying, arguing that it cannot be completely general, in the sense of marking off two mutually exclusive classes of acts [Searle, 1968, p. 143]. From our point of view, this would mean that the same act could be an instance of two different actions, locuting and saying, and wouldn't constitute a problem. Setting this argument aside, it seems that Searle followed

Austin's lead, and offered a concept of locutionary act under a different label: the propositional act.

So, in order to clarify our concept of locutionary content, a comparison with Searle's propositional content will help. In (10.4) through (10.8) Kepa and John are conversing; John is the speaker in (10.6), Kepa in the others, and all occur on Monday, May 14.

(10.4) Will I finish the paper by tomorrow?

(10.5) I will finish the paper by tomorrow.

(10.6) Kepa, finish the paper by tomorrow!

(10.7) [I hope] to finish the paper by tomorrow.

(10.8) If I finish the paper by tomorrow, [John will be pleased].

According to Searle, the same propositional content is expressed by the unbracketed parts of all of these utterances.

Within Critical Pragmatics, there is more than one candidate for this content. For each utterance except (10.6) we can identify an utterance-bound content:

(10.x1) That the speaker of (10.x) finish the paper referred to by the speaker of (10.x) before the day after (10.x) is uttered.

But this will not do. First of all, since the reflexive truth-conditions are conditions on the utterance itself, the reflexive truth-conditions for each utterance are different. Second, a proposition of this sort will not do for (10.6), where John is the speaker. So it seems our candidate for the common propositional content must be the referential content:

(10.x2) That Kepa finishes the paper by May 15, 2006.

That seems to work for all of the utterances. They are all about a person and his finishing a certain paper by a particular date. They use this content in different ways but all locute or express it. It fits well our intuitions that, on Wednesday, May 16, Kepa could express it uttering:

(10.9) I finished the paper yesterday,

or by John addressing Kepa,

(10.10) You finished the paper yesterday [as you promised].

It seems, then, that our locutionary content is just another label for Searle's propositional content. But there are some points where Searle's propositional content diverges from our locutionary content. First of all, according to Searle's original view [Searle, 1969], there would be no difference in the propositional content of utterances (10.4) through (10.8) on the one hand, and (10.11) on the other:

(10.11)   I promise to finish the paper by tomorrow.

Thus, the content of the (sub-)utterance of 'I promise' would vanish from the content of (10.11) because its meaning, he thought, determines the illocutionary force and that is what we are trying to contrast the proposition with.

In our view the locutionary content of the subordinate clause in (10.11) is the proposition (10.x2), but the whole of (10.11) has a more complex locutionary content:

(10.x3)   That Kepa promises at the time of (10.11) to bring it about that Kepa finishes the paper before the day after the time of (10.11).

However, Searle changed his view on this point in his later essay, 'How Performatives Work' [Searle, 1989], where the propositional content does include the content of the 'performative verb' and its subject, so this is a moot point.

There is a second and more important difference between propositional content and locutionary content, however. An important concept in Searle's theory is that of the *propositional content conditions* of a speech act. Some of these conditions are determined, according to the theory, by the illocutionary point. The commissive illocutionary point, for instance, establishes that the propositional content of a speech act with that point – e.g., a promise – must represent a future act of the speaker. The directive illocutionary point, in contrast, determines that the propositional content of a speech act with that point – e.g., a request – must represent a future act by the addressee.

We think that the locutionary content (or Searle's propositional content) is not the content that could satisfy the 'propositional content' conditions of the speech act. Recall our basic picture: a speaker plans to produce an utterance with certain utterance-bound truth-conditions, and intends to thereby produce an utterance with certain referential truth-conditions, i.e., locutionary content. The level of utterance-bound content is crucial, because many of the effects that a speaker will intend for his utterance to have will depend on the hearer's recognition of the utterance-bound (or speaker-bound or network-bound) content.

We call the constituents of the locutionary content, the places, things, and people that are constituents of the proposition expressed, the subject matter of the utterance. So Joana is the subject matter of her utterance, "I am Joana." Often, the elements of the subject matter play a role in the utterance situation. Indexicals, of course, are the most explicit means of conveying this information. When Joana says "I am Joana," she conveys not only the trivial locutionary content, but the important fact that the person in the subject matter of the locutionary content is also playing the role of the speaker of the utterance itself. When John says to Kepa, "You must finish the paper," Kepa is an element of the subject matter, the paper-finisher, but also a part of the utterance situation, the addressee. This information is conveyed by John. This sort of information is lost at the level of locutionary content. If the speaker doesn't get the utterance-bound content right, even if the locutionary content is grasped, important information will be lost.

We agree with Searle that the illocutionary point of an utterance is not part of the locutionary content or propositional content. It is a fact about the utterance that it is important for the listener to grasp, but it is not part of the proposition expressed. And we agree that certain illocutionary points (and forces) of utterances put conditions on the content. But it is up to the utterance-bound content, not the locutionary content, to satisfy these conditions.

It is in grasping the utterance-bound content that the hearer understands the intended relationships between the speaker and the utterance, including the time of the utterance and the addressee. Consider again

(10.5) I will finish the paper by tomorrow

and now compare it with

(10.12) Kepa finishes the paper by May 15, 2006.

Both of these utterances could arguably be uttered as commissives, that is, with that intended illocutionary point on the same locutionary content. But (10.12) puts a greater cognitive burden on the listener. To understand (10.12) as a commissive, the hearer has to have at least the information that the speaker is Kepa and the time of utterance is prior to May 15, for one can only commit to future actions, and one can only commit oneself. (10.9), on the other hand, cannot be understood as a commissive. The utterance-bound content of (10.5) imposes the right utterance-relative roles on the finisher of the paper and the time of finishing; the utterance-bound content of (10.12) is consistent with them having the right roles in the utterance, and the utterance-bound content of (10.9) is inconsistent with them playing the appropriate roles; the finishing has to be in the past. Similar remarks apply to (10.6), uttered as a directive.

Searle's theory of speech acts poses two different tasks for the concept of propositional contents. On the one hand, it represents the basic content on which the diverse illocutionary forces operate. On the other hand, it is the content that meets the conditions imposed by certain illocutionary points and forces. But, as we argued for the case of the ordinary concept of what is said, these two tasks cannot be accomplished by a single content. The locutionary or referential content of an utterance can be taken as that basic shared content of different speech acts but, instead of locutionary content, reflexive content is needed to serve as the content fulfilling Searle's 'propositional content conditions.' The theory of speech acts requires a pluralistic view of utterance content, recognizing both locutionary content and various sorts of reflexive content.

10.6   Conclusion

The main focus of this chapter has been the development of the concept of locutionary content, as a theoretical concept that is better suited than the ordinary concept of what is said for some of the theoretical purposes to which the latter has been put, especially that of grounding the concept of the proposition expressed by an utterance.

What does this tell us about how to say things with words? The important lesson, we believe, is that the intentions involved in saying something are not simply a matter of choosing a proposition to serve as locutionary content, and hoping that the uptake circumstances are such that one manages to convey the information one wishes; instead one has to focus on the utterance-bound truth-conditions of the utterance one plans to produce, for only at this level can much of the crucial information necessary to producing the intended cognitive and non-cognitive effects, including the grasping of the intended illocutionary force, be found. Critical Pragmatics allows us to incorporate this point of view into a theory that ties the pragmatics of an utterance closely to the semantics of an utterance, conceived (more or less) traditionally as a matter of its truth-conditions.

11   Reference and implicature

11.1   Introduction

Perhaps the most influential theory in pragmatics is still H. P. Grice's account of conversational implicatures [Grice, 1967a, 1967b], which he first developed in the 1960s. The basic picture behind Grice's theory is this. Speakers say various things, in a more or less strict and literal sense of 'say,' in virtue of the meanings of words and their modes of composition. But they manage to convey in conversation far more (and sometimes less) than what they say. His examples have become familiar classics, such as the recommendation writer, who by confining himself to positive remarks about handwriting and punctuality, conveys that a student has at best mediocre philosophical talents.

The *implicature* that the student is mediocre is generated because the writer's intention to convey this information is part of the most plausible explanation of why he said what he said, and didn't say more, in the way that he said it, in the conversational situation. The letter-reader assumes the writer knows about the student's philosophical abilities, and realizes that handwriting and punctuality are almost completely irrelevant. So he asks himself, "Why is the writer supplying no relevant information?"[1] He assumes that if the writer had positive things to say about philosophical abilities, he would do so, and by saying nothing he conveys that he has only negative things to say, which he doesn't want to say explicitly.

The reader, if he presumes that the writer is being cooperative, and thus following as far as possible the maxims that Grice spells out, can figure out what he intends to implicate. The writer is trying to say everything positive he can, and so be helpful, without saying anything he doesn't believe.

This book has been built on the foundation of Grice's theory of meaning, more or less in the form he presented it. Like most philosophers of language, we also think that there is much that is correct about his theory of implicatures. Implicatures are a real phenomenon. Grice's conversational principle and his maxims are useful in seeing how they work. Still, we are uncertain what their final

---

[1] Or "Why is the writer supplying no more information?" Grice himself takes the example as a case in which the first maxim of quantity is flouted.

role in pragmatic theory should be. We are somewhat inclined to view Grice's principle and maxims as useful heuristic devices, but to suppose that from a theoretical point of view, ordinary ampliative reasoning about the intentions of agents provides an adequate foundation for pragmatics. An intermediate point of view is that of relevance theory, which employs only the maxim of relevance, and gives that a rather special interpretation.

In this chapter we make an important point that we think applies, whatever one ultimately thinks about the status of the conversational principle and the maxims: Grice's theory needs various forms of contents. It is the various contents of an utterance, and not just the referential content, and not just what is said, that are needed as input to the Gricean reasoning.

11.2   Grice and what is said

Grice's remarks suggest that his concept of 'what is said' can be taken as equivalent to 'the proposition expressed' or 'the content' of the utterance. He claims that to know what someone said by uttering a sentence one has to know:

(i)   the conventional meaning of the sentence uttered;
(ii) the disambiguated meaning of the sentence in that particular occasion of use; and
(iii) the referents of referential expressions. [Grice, 1967a / 1989: 25]

It's not clear how much pragmatic 'intrusion' into what is said Grice would allow, but there seems to be a wide consensus that what is said in the Gricean framework roughly corresponds to the proposition expressed or the content of the utterance.

Just limiting our attention to utterances of sentences containing singular terms – that is, proper names, demonstratives, indexicals and (some uses of) definite descriptions – the question is, what kind of proposition is that?

Traditional philosophy of language offers two general, seemingly incompatible, answers: the proposition expressed is either a singular proposition involving an individual referred to by the singular term (the referentialist view) or a general one, involving a mode of presentation of the individual, provided by its linguistic meaning (the descriptivist view). Grice's own remarks are compatible with a referentialist view on what is said. He says:

To work out that a particular conversational implicature is present, the hearer will rely on the following data: (1) the conventional meaning of the words used, together with the identity of any references that may be involved; (2) the Cooperative Principle and its maxims. [Grice, 1967a/1989, p. 31]

Taking item (1) to provide what the hearer needs to determine what is said, Grice seems to suggest a referentialist view or something like it.

Later on, when he discusses the nondetachability of implicatures, he observes that

> Insofar as the calculation that a particular conversational implicature is present requires, besides contextual and background information, only a knowledge of what has been said ... it will not be possible to find another way of saying the same thing, which simply lacks the implicature in question. [Grice, 1967a/1989, p. 39]

Grice's maxims of 'manner' differ from the others, in dealing with the way things are said, rather than what is said, e.g., be brief, avoid ambiguity, and so forth. We discuss this maxim in §11.6 below. Except in the case of conversational implicatures that rely on the maxims of manner, the nondetachability of implicatures implies that it's what is said that matters, and not the way in which it has been said.[2]

Whatever Grice's view about the referentialist or descriptivist account of the proposition expressed by an utterance involving a singular term, our aim is to study a particular demand Grice imposes on the concept of what is said within his theory of implicatures: a demand that seems to be somehow present in all the previous remarks and others like the following, where Grice is reconstructing a bit of a hearer's reasoning:

> He has said that p; there is no reason to suppose that he is not observing the maxims or at least the C[ooperative] P[rinciple]; he could not be doing this unless he thought that q. [Grice 1967a/1989, p. 31]

Among the information required to 'calculate' or infer what the speaker implicated, the hearer must identify, to begin with, what the speaker said. Or, in other words, the proposition expressed by the speaker constitutes, in the Gricean framework, the input for the inference of implicature. We will argue that this input can be taken to be neither just a singular proposition, as the referentialist would claim, nor a general proposition to which the singular term contributes a mode of presentation determined by its linguistic meaning, as the descriptivist would say. Instead, the full panoply of utterance-bound and speaker-bound contents that we have used to explain the speaker's plans with regard to singular terms needs to be brought into the theory of implicatures.

---

[2] To be sure, Grice also makes the following statement: "... the implicature is not carried by what is said, but only by the saying of what is said, or 'by putting it that way'" [Grice, 1967a/1989, p. 39]. This is important. The (propositional) content does not carry any implicature, it is the utterance with that content which carries it. Still, it seems clear that one is supposed to identify what has been said to start the 'calculation' of the implicature.

11.3   Eros' thirst

Situation I

Suppose Kepa is giving a talk at a conference. He notices that the audience, including his friend, the much-admired philosopher Eros Corazza, is getting bored; he's clearly ready to give up philosophy talks for the day in favor of conversation over drinks – a fact that will be equally obvious to his other friends in the audience. Kepa decides to finish his presentation and skip the next talk. Gesturing towards Eros, he utters,

(11.1)   He is thirsty.

Kepa implicates that he intends to hurry up, finish his talk, and, unfortunately, miss the next lecture, because his friend Eros Corazza wants him to join him for a beer. In the imagined circumstances, an utterance of

(11.2)   Eros is thirsty

would have worked as well.

At least at first glance, this seems to fit well with the referentialist picture. Both (11.1) and (11.2), express the same proposition, namely, the singular proposition:

(11.3)   That *Eros* is thirsty.

This proposition is true if and only if Eros is thirsty, even in worlds in which nobody uttered (11.1), or (11.2), or Eros was named 'Thanatos.' (11.1) and (11.2) are just two different ways of saying the same thing in the referentialist view, and as long as the maxims of manner are not involved in the inference of implicatures, that's all that seems to count according to Grice. Since (11.1) and (11.2) express the same proposition, they convey the same implicatures. (11.3) is the proposition that constitutes the input for generating implicatures from (11.1) and (11.2). This gives us a reason to think that input of implicatures coincides with the referentialist notion of what is said, with what we call the *referential* truth-conditions of the utterance. But when we take a second glance, we see that this doesn't seem to work in all cases.

Situation II

Suppose, now, Eros is organizing a get-together at his place – an apartment he keeps free of tobacco smoke – and asks Kepa whether there is anyone from the institute he should invite. Kepa tells him:

(11.4)   Well, maybe what's-his-name ... he is fun, interesting, and a good
          guy ... but he smokes.

Even though Kepa doesn't remember the name right at the moment, so Eros can't really know whom Kepa is talking about, he immediately says "No way." In this case, Kepa's plan doesn't require Eros to have any kind of utterance-independent cognitive fix on the referent "what's-his-name" and "he." The speaker-bound content, that Kepa's candidate is fun, interesting, and a smoker, is enough for Eros to grasp Kepa's implicature, that Eros might not want to invite the fellow since he is a smoker. In this case the relevant input for Eros to calculate the implicatures of (11.4), would be something like

(11.5)   That *the male Kepa has in mind* is fun, interesting, and smokes.

This is the content Eros grasps in virtue of hearing Kepa's utterance and seeing that he is the speaker. He need not understand (and Kepa doesn't plan for him to understand) anything further to infer what Kepa is implicating, and to decide what he thinks of inviting the person in question, whoever it might be. This doesn't mean that (11.4) doesn't *express* a singular proposition. 'What's-his-name' is, at least arguably, a way of referring to someone the speaker has a notion of and some beliefs about, but can't remember the name of. (In many situations, although not as we are envisaging this one, the hearer is able to identify a person referred to in this way, and supply the speaker with the name.) So Kepa expresses a singular proposition, but Eros has no cognitive fix on the person it is about, except his speaker-bound cognitive fix as "the male Kepa has in mind."

One might suppose then, again at first glance, that this sort of case favors the descriptivist theory as an account of the input to implicatures. The proposition that Kepa expressed was a singular proposition about the referent. The utterance-bound content was a proposition about the utterance. The speaker-bound content is a proposition about Kepa. These contents are singular propositions, but they are not singular propositions about the referent. The referent is identified only descriptively, as "the male the speaker of (11.4) has in mind" and "the male Kepa has in mind." Since Eros cannot go further than this, his cognitive fix on the referent is descriptive.

So far, it seems then that both traditional options, the referentialist and the descriptivist, have a role to play in an account of how we grasp implicatures. But they are not enough.

Situation III

Suppose that Eros and Kepa are in a bar late at night. Surprisingly, the bartender serves Kepa his glass of beer, but forgets about Eros. Kepa tells the bartender,

(11.6)   He is thirsty,

implicating that she forgot about Eros' beer and that she should serve it to him. To infer these implicatures and, accordingly, serve the beer to Eros, it does not seem to suffice that the bartender grasp either the singular proposition, that Eros is thirsty, nor even the descriptive one, that the male Kepa has in mind is thirsty. She needs to grasp a proposition such as,

(11.7)   That *the guy in front of me who is not speaking* is thirsty.

Grasping (11.7) will jog her memory that Eros ordered a beer too, and she will get him one. This is not a singular proposition but a general proposition involving a cognitive fix on him. As Bezuidenhout points out [Bezuidenhout, 1996], this general proposition is not determined by the meaning of the words I use, but involves a 'psychological mode of presentation.' This is, of course, in line with our general theory. (11.7) involves the target cognitive fix in Kepa's plan; it involves a mode of presentation that is apt for what he wants the bartender to do: calculate his implicature, remember Eros' order, and serve him his beer. Here the use of the demonstrative is apt, if not quite essential. If Kepa had said merely,

(11.8)   Eros is thirsty

he wouldn't achieve his aim, unless the bartender knows Eros' name and can recognize him as the guy in front of her. Another possibility is that Kepa takes a chance that the bartender is good at implicature detection, and will be able to infer from (11.8) his intent to convey both the name of the person beside him, and that she should get that person a beer.

To sum up, if we are right, we have cases in which the input for the inference of the implicatures of an utterance involves a singular proposition and cases in which it involves a general proposition closely tied to the meaning of the sentence used. But to have a general account, we need to consider the speaker's plan, especially the path and target intentions.

We conclude, then, that Grice was not quite correct in taking what is said to be the input for calculating implicatures. Whether one takes what is said in these cases to be a singular proposition, in line with referentialist thinking, or some descriptive proposition, it is not what is said that, in the general case, serves as the input to implicatures. The appropriate input is the speaker's plan, which will involve grasping a number of propositions, utterance-bound, speaker-bound, and hearer-bound (as the content that involves the target cognitive fix will be).

11.4   Identity, implicature, and cognitive significance

In Grice's theory, hearers try to figure out what a speaker intends to convey, based on what the speaker says (or, sometimes, makes as if to say). But as we have seen, two utterances with the same referential content can have quite different cognitive significance; they may express different beliefs of the speaker, and be understood quite differently by the hearer. These differences correspond to differences in the speaker's plan. It is in speakers' plans that one finds implicatures. Reasoning that takes referential content as the starting point will miss these differences. This idea allows an analysis of some standard problem cases in the semantics of reference – cases that motivated Russell and Frege to adopt descriptivist accounts, but seem to re-emerge as problems on referentialist accounts.

Let's begin with a rather special example of Frege's problem of identity, that Perry discussed at length in *Reference and Reflexivity*. The example involves a photograph by Linda Cicero, of two dogs on the verandah of the Stanford Bookstore.[3] Both dogs are partially obscured by a pillar on the verandah. One sees the head of one dog on one side of the pillar, and the rear-end and tail of the other on the other side. We can pretend that there is just one long dog, which we'll call 'Stretch,' with his head visible on one side of the pillar and his tail on the other.

H has just asked S how many dogs there are on the verandah. S says

(11.9)   That dog is that dog,

pointing first at Stretch's head and then at his tail. Since there are no other candidates for a second dog on the verandah, and the only grounds for thinking there are two dogs would be the supposition that the head and the tail belong to different dogs, S clearly means to convey that there is just one dog, and manages to generate that implicature. If S had uttered (11.9) while pointing twice to Stretch's head, his utterance would have had the same referential content, but would not have generated this implicature. So this example poses a problem for a woodenly referentialist account of cognitive significance, and equally for a Gricean account of what is going on, if it is combined with a referentialist position on what is said.

The natural solution to this difficulty, from our perspective, is to suppose that the inputs to Gricean reasoning are the utterance-bound and speaker-bound contents, rather than the referential proposition. From the utterance-bound content of (11.9), plus the fact that S is the speaker and his demonstrations were to the head and tail, H realizes that (11.9) is true if there is a single dog whose head is the demonstrated head and whose tail is the demonstrated tail. The truth of this proposition generated the implicature, for it undermines any reason one might have for thinking there is more than one dog on the verandah. Supposing that this is what S intends to convey makes (11.9) relevant. So the implicature is generated.

---

[3] The photograph is reproduced on the cover of the paperback edition of *Reference and Reflexivity*.

Gricean reasoning does take off from the proposition expressed, from what is said, in the sense that the Gricean reasoner needs some way of thinking of this proposition to pursue the project of intention discovery. But the description can be, and in general will be, an *utterance-bound* description, which in the situation leads to a relevant speaker-bound description, rather than one that identifies the proposition in terms of its subject matter. In a fairly clear sense, the interpreter need not know *which* proposition is expressed to begin his reasoning. Or, more precisely, the hearer doesn't have to just identify the referential content of the utterance, but a proposition about the targeted hearer's cognitive fix on the object referred to. The speaker's target intention is what he intends the hearer to recognize in order to infer the intended implicatures.

Consider three descriptions of the proposition expressed by (11.9):

(i) what A said;
(ii) the proposition that is true *iff the dog the speaker of* (**11.9**) *is referring to with the first use of 'that dog' is the dog he refers to with the second use of 'that dog'*;
(iii) the proposition that is true *iff* **Stretch** is **Stretch**.

Descriptions (ii) and (iii), unlike (i), identify the proposition in terms of truth-conditions. Description (ii) is 'utterance-bound'; it identifies the dog or dogs in question only vis-à-vis the role it or they play relative to the utterance. Description (iii) is not utterance-bound; it *expresses* the same referential content that the speaker expressed, and doesn't merely identify it. It is (ii) and not (iii) that incorporates links to auxiliary information from the context that is needed to make reasonable inferences about what A intends to say. The hearer sees that the speaker is A (speaker-bound content), and that A is demonstrating a dog's head and a dog's tail – call them **h** and **t** – (by recognition of the speaker's target intention). So he can move from (ii) to

(iv) The proposition that is true *iff the dog with head* **h** *I'm looking at* is *the the dog with tail* **t** *I'm looking at.*

Description (iv) identifies the referents through the hearer's cognitive fix on them, and asserts identity between them. This proposition makes its connection to the reason B has for thinking there might be more than one dog apparent. It thus permits the inference that A is trying to undermine that reason, and so conveying that there is just one dog on the verandah. There is a path from (ii) to (iv), but not from (iii) to (iv).

11.5   The man who has run out of petrol

Let's consider Grice's classic example of the motorist who has run out of gasoline. (It's such a classic that we feel duty bound to use the term 'petrol' as

Grice did.) A is standing by an obviously immobilized car and is approached by B. The following exchange takes place:

A: I am out of petrol
B: There is a garage around the corner. [Grice, 1967a/1989, p. 32]

According to Grice, B *says* that there is a garage around the corner, and *implicates* that it is or at least may be open and selling petrol. Grice provides this formula for understanding such implicatures:

He has said that *p*; there is no reason to suppose that he is not observing the maxims, …he could not be doing this unless he thought that *q*; he knows (and knows that I know that he knows) that I can see that the supposition that he thinks that *q* is required; he has done nothing to stop me thinking that *q*; he intends me to think, or is at least willing to allow me to think, that *q*; and so he has implicated that *q*. [Grice, 1967a/1989, p. 31]

It seems, then, that to understand implicatures, one first must grasp what is said. Then one finds the implicatures, by asking what further communicative intentions a helpful conversational partner would have for saying *that*. But when we look closely, we see that an utterance-bound conception of what is said plays an essential role in the pragmatic reasoning.

Grice is interested in the implicature of B's remark, that the garage around the corner is probably open. But let's think for a minute about B's interpretation of A's opening remark. A's opening remark sets the stage for B's reply, since B is trying to be helpful to A. It is natural to take A's opening remark as implicating that he would like some help in finding petrol for his car.

We can reconstruct B's reasoning about A's utterance as follows:

(1) The utterance I am hearing, *u*, is an utterance by someone of 'I am out of petrol.' [This B knows through hearing *u* and recognizing its basic phonological properties.]
(2) Given that *u* is in English, it is true iff the speaker of *u* is out of petrol at the time of *u*. [B recognizes the language as English, and he knows the meaning of the sentence, and so he understands its utterance-bound content.]
(3) Given all of that, and that the speaker of *u* is the person I am now looking at, *u* is true iff **the person I am looking at** is out of petrol. [B knows that the speaker is the person he has walked up to (as opposed, say, to someone on the car radio) and therefore that the time of the utterance is the present; i.e., he recognizes A's target intention.]

Thoughts (1) and (2) do not contain enough information to motivate B's helpful reply. But thought (2) plus facts available in the context lead to thought (3). It is thought (3) that puts B in a position to ask under what conditions the utterance would be conversationally appropriate. It makes sense to ask why a person would tell someone he is talking to that he, that very person, is out of petrol. At level (3), B can identify the person who is out of gas as the person whom he sees speaking to him. At this level, the roles that the speaker plays vis-à-vis B are available for input into the inquiry as to the intentions with which the utterance is made.

Being conversationally appropriate is a relational concept. The remark is to be relevant to a particular conversation, in this case the one A is initiating with B. The appropriateness of A's remark will not simply depend on what is said, but on further facts about the conversation. Appreciating the relevance may depend on recognizing the various roles the speaker, the hearer, and the person spoken about in the utterance are playing relative to one another. The fact that the speaker is the very person he is speaking about is relevant; hence the use of the word 'I' is crucial. Suppose, for example, that A was Harold Smith. If A had said, "Harold Smith is out of gas," he could not reasonably have expected B to have figured out that the person talking to him was out of gas and might like some advice on where to get some. B's description of what A said will have to interact with the other factors about the conversation, if the desired implicature is to be generated.

In the original example, a reconstruction of B's thinking will go something like this:

> Given that *u* is in English, etc., and that the speaker of *u* is this fellow, then *u* is true iff this fellow is out of petrol now, and *u* makes conversational sense only if this fellow would like me to provide some information about where he can get petrol now.

So, we conclude that, quite generally, it is utterance-bound content that serves as the input to pragmatic reasoning.

11.6   The maxim of manner of reference

Grice indicates that in the cases of different ways of referring to the same thing, his theory can account for differences in implicature because different maxims will be involved. And he allows that in the cases in which the maxim of manner is involved, what is said is not the input to the calculation of the implicature. We need to investigate whether in the cases we have discussed so far, Grice's original theory can be maintained, in the light of these remarks.

In 'Logic and Conversation' Grice remains agnostic about whether proper names and descriptions make the same contribution to what is said by a speaker in making an utterance:

This brief indication of my use of say leaves it open whether a man who says (today) *Harold Wilson is a great man* and another who says (today) *The British Prime Minister is a great man* would, if each knew that the singular terms had the same reference, have said the same thing.

Then he adds:

But whatever decision is made about this question, the apparatus that I am about to provide will be capable of accounting for any implicatures that might depend on the presence of one rather than another of these singular terms in the sentence uttered. Such implicatures would be merely related to different maxims. [Grice, 1967a/1989, p. 25]

It is not clear how we should take this last remark. Let's keep aside definite descriptions for a moment, and stick to proper names and demonstratives. Take the following two utterances in Situation III:

(11.6)   He is thirsty

and

(11.8)   Eros is thirsty.

It seems clear that the name 'Eros' and the demonstrative 'he' make the same contribution to what is said – namely, the individual Eros – as we are happy to assume, with referentialists. But, while (11.8) would be quite an awkward way to convey to the bartender the implicature that she forgot to serve Eros his beer, (11.6) carries the implicature smoothly. This implicature seems to depend on the presence of one singular term rather than another. If this is so, according to Grice, there must be some maxim that is related to (11.6) and its implicature, which is different from the maxim that would be related to (11.8) and its implicature, whatever it is. And that should work whether we take (11.6) and (11.8) as saying the same thing or not. However, if we stick to the referentialist position on what is said and accept that they do say the same thing we don't see how – as Grice claims – the difference in implicatures could be accounted for by appealing to different maxims. If what is said remains constant, the maxims of quantity, quality, and relevance would make no difference. It seems that the only maxims involved here that could account for the difference would be the maxims of manner, that is, the maxims concerning the way in which what is said is said. But the ones presented in 'Logic and Conversation' don't seem helpful:

Manner
- (Supermaxim): Be perspicuous.
- (Maxims):
  - Avoid obscurity of expression.
  - Avoid ambiguity.
  - Be brief (avoid unnecessary prolixity).
  - Be orderly.

The difference between 'Eros' in (11.8) and 'He' in (11.6) does not seem to relate to obscurity, ambiguity, prolixity, or order in any clear sense.

Grice proposed the addition of another maxim of manner in 'Presupposition and Conversational Implicature':

"Frame whatever you say in the form most suitable for any reply that would be regarded as appropriate"; or, "Facilitate in your form of expression the appropriate reply." [Grice, 1981/1989, p. 273]

He introduces the maxim in the context of his theory of generalized conversational implicatures, when discussing the difference between the use of a definite description and its hypothetically semantic equivalent Russellian expansion. We think that, within our approach to reference and implicatures, it is a reasonable 'maxim' to be observed by speakers when using singular terms, and has application to particularized implicatures as well. We could rephrase it as:

Maxim of manner of reference
- Choose your way of referring according to the cognitive fix you want your hearer to get on the reference, to facilitate the inference of implicatures.

This maxim allows us to account for the difference between (11.6) and (11.8). (11.6) complies with the maxim; so long as it is clear to the bartender that I use 'he' to refer to someone on whom I have a perceptual cognitive fix, she will readily have an appropriate cognitive fix on Eros, to understand the relevance of my remark, grasp the implicature, and get him his beer.

Assuming the bartender has no idea who Eros is, (11.8) flouts the maxim. But flouting can generate particularized implicatures. Given that my remark is intended to be relevant and helpful, the bartender may grasp that it is my friend who is thirsty, and infer that he is named 'Eros.' She may infer that I not only intend for her to understand that my friend is thirsty, and to remember that he ordered a beer, but also to figure out that his name is 'Eros,' perhaps because I would like her to interact with him in a more personal way, by saying something like "Oh, you must be Eros! Sorry I forgot your beer."

So we think that Grice's additional maxim of manner, although motivated by his wish to make a rather subtle point about Russell's theory of descriptions, is a good addition to the basic Gricean tool box.

Consider this slightly different version of Grice's original example: A, the British prime minister, Harold Wilson, is standing by an obviously immobilized car and is approached by B. Wilson wants B not merely to tell him where he can obtain some petrol, but also to offer to fetch some for him; he is after all the prime minister, a busy and important man. He might try:

(11.10) A: I am out of petrol.

But television was not so common in the 1960s as it is now. B might not recognize A as Harold Wilson, and so simply reply:

(11.11) B: There is a garage around the corner.

A might try saying:

(11.12) A: Harold Wilson is out of petrol.

His intent would be to flout the new maxim of manner, and thereby induce B
to realize that the speaker must be Harold Wilson. But B may not be so good at
calculating obscure implicatures, and merely reply, perhaps,

(11.13) B: That may be the least of his problems, but anyway, what can I do
         about it?

Wilson's best bet is to say, "I am Harold Wilson, your prime minister. And I
am out of petrol." He explicitly provides both cognitive fixes appropriate to the
responses he wants, and throws in the relevant fact that he is prime minister,
as well. B will almost certainly grasp both implicatures; that A at the very least
needs to know where to get some petrol, and that furthermore he thinks it would
be appropriate, given his high station, for B to fetch it for him. Of course, if B
is a committed Tory, he may choose to be of no help, and just walk away.

Proper names exploit the notion that one has of a person. The use of a proper
name to refer to someone complies with the new maxim of manner, in cases
in which the speaker intends for the hearer's response to be informed by information he has in his notion of the named person. But they do not secure the
link with a perceptual cognitive fix like 'the person in front of me' unless
the hearer's notion incorporates the relevant recognitional information. If B is
a Tory, Wilson might have been better off – like David Israel in the example in which he is interviewed by a rude bureaucrat – to convey his need
for petrol without encouraging B to access all the information he has in his
Wilson-notion.

While our maxim of reference may strengthen Grice's theory, we don't see it
as especially tied to generating and calculating implicatures, but as a part of the
description of the practice of referring to objects, people, or places with communicative intentions, for all sorts of purposes. It is an advantage of our general
account of the pragmatics of reference that it explains why some expressions
are better suited than others to convey various implicatures in various circumstances. Indexicals, demonstratives, proper names, and descriptions provide
different paths for the hearer in understanding the utterance, facilitating some
inferences, and blocking others. These differences are taken into account in the
speaker's plan and they explain the choice of one term rather than another.

We don't see appeal to the maxim of reference as undercutting our main
point in this chapter, that the input to Gricean reasoning on the hearer's part,
and so the focus of the speaker's plan in provoking such reasoning, is not, in the
general case, what is said, or the proposition expressed, but the utterance-bound

content that, in our theory, speakers and hearers always ultimately rely on. The maxim of reference moves the maxims of manner from the periphery to the center of a Gricean theory, and so is basically a way of recognizing our point.

11.7   Conclusion

One might argue that Grice's theory anticipates our pluri-propositionalism, since it recognizes that in addition to what is said there are many other contents, in the form of implicatures, conveyed by an utterance. But of course our view involves a plurality of propositions, the various kinds of reflexive contents, that are involved before one arrives at what is said. Still, in maintaining that the input for reasoning about implicatures is the speaker's plan, rather than what is said, we think we adhere to Grice's original idea, that it is grasping the content of the utterance, a matter closely tied to grasping the meanings of his words, that triggers the hearer's inferences to implicatures, which come into the picture in a quite different way.

However, from the point of view of an utterance-based account of communication, the very production of any utterance whatsoever, or even a noise that might be mistaken for an utterance, triggers a search for an explanation of what the speaker might be doing, and what, if anything, he is trying to convey. Utterances, like any other events we perceive, trigger a process that seeks to set them in the scheme of things and assess their relevance and meaning for our lives. This is an insight of relevance theory, we think, which emphasizes that an utterance is a claim for the hearer's attention, and hence a claim of relevance. While the process of sorting out what is said from what might or might not have been implicated seems to require attention to some level of content, the process of inferring what intentions, if any, might lie behind the noises one perceives begins earlier.

12 Semantics, pragmatics, and Critical Pragmatics

12.1 Introduction

In the second half of the twentieth century, two important developments in the investigation of the meaning and use of natural language pushed the concept of *what is said* to center stage. Kaplan, Kripke, Donnellan, and others developed a theory of reference and truth for semantics that broke with the Frege–Russell descriptivist tradition, based on arguments that the descriptivist theory gave the wrong result about what is said, with sentences involving names, indexicals, and demonstratives, and perhaps even some uses of descriptions themselves. Grice's distinction between what is said and what is meant, and Austin's related distinction between locutionary and illocutionary acts, played an important role in the development of pragmatics. Referential semantics and pragmatics, especially Gricean pragmatics, seemed complementary. Kaplan's version of what is said [Kaplan, 1989a], the concept of the *content* of an utterance (or a sentence in context), seemed to line up pretty closely with Grice's concept of *what is said* by the speaker in uttering a sentence [Grice 1967a/1989]. Speaker meaning, minus Kaplan's content, would leave what is implicated, and between content and implicature would lie the boundary between semantics and pragmatics.

A pretty picture, but it doesn't quite work. One the one hand, Kaplan's contents aren't the right input for Gricean reasoning, as we argued in the last chapter. For another, Gricean reasoning seems to be required in a number of cases of 'semantic indeterminacy' to arrive at what is said, in the intuitive sense that stands behind Kaplan's theory. Gricean reasoning seems involved in resolving indeterminacies of reference, domains of quantification, and many other issues that are involved in arriving at what is said: so-called 'pragmatic intrusion' into semantics. What's worse, such intrusion seems to involve us in a circle, which Levinson dubs 'Grice's circle.'

In this chapter we first state our view rather abstractly. Then we review a range of views that have been put forward as to the nature of semantics, pragmatics, and their relation. Then we develop our own view and compare it in some detail with a selection of alternatives.

12.2   Situating semantics

In our picture, pragmatics and semantics, as well as phonology, syntax, and other disciplines, are subtheories within a more general theory, the theory of utterances. If formalized, the theory would start by quantifying over utterances, and then consider various types of utterances, classed in different ways, and develop more and more detailed generalizations. Semantics deals with utterances classified syntactically, assigning them reflexive conditions of reference and truth. Pragmatics is the theory of communicative intentions and speech acts; that is, of the way speakers use language in communicative situations to plan and execute utterances in the light of semantic properties, and other properties, of the expressions they use; that is, how speakers do things with words. These subtheories come together at the concept of locutionary content, but their relation is not the simple one envisaged by the classic picture. Locutionary contents are jointly determined by the semantics of the expressions used, the intentions of the speaker, and the contextual facts.

Within a theory of utterances, the clauses of semantic theory assign reflexive conditions of reference and truth on the basis of syntactic form. Facts about the intentions of the speaker in uttering the expression, and contextual facts, yield the referential level of content, which in the case of declarative sentences will be the locutionary content of the utterance. So pragmatics, semantics, and other relevant facts about an utterance come together at locutionary content. While everything, in a sense, comes together at locutionary content, the picture is rather different from the classic one. Locutionary content is not the output of the semantic part of the theory, but a joint determination of the semantic part, the pragmatic part, and other facts about the utterance.

How does our proposal compare with other approaches?

François Recanati, in his book *Literal Meaning* [Recanati, 2004] provides an influential scheme for sorting out the issues involved in debates about semantics and pragmatics. He sees the range of positions as having two poles, literalism and contextualism:

[The literalist holds that] we may legitimately ascribe truth-conditional content to natural language sentences, quite independently of what the speaker who utters this sentence means ... [Contextualism] holds that speech acts are the primary bearers of content. Only in the context of a speech act does a sentence express a determinate content. [Recanati, 2004, p. 3]

Both camps call on Grice. Literalists use Grice's ideas about implicatures to create a sort of shock-absorber between our intuitions about what someone says and what their theories deliver as 'semantic content'; these intuitions, they claim, confuse semantic content with conversational implicatures. The contextualists see (broadly) Gricean reasoning about speaker's intentions involved throughout the process of interpretation.

Recanati goes on to distinguish a number of intermediate positions. Cappelen and Lepore, are *minimalists* in *Insensitive Semantics* [Cappelen and Lepore, 2005]. They see the boundary between semantics and pragmatics as *semantic content*, which involves meaning plus resolution of ambiguity, indexicals, and names. Semantic content is a theoretical concept that replaces the imprecise concept of what is said as the point of interface.

Cappelen and Lepore's theory can be seen as an attempt to save as much as possible of the traditional theory; it is clearly inspired by Kaplan's work. Kaplan's contents are determined by the characters of sentences, plus very basic facts about the context: agent or speaker, time, location, and world. Adapting the theory to the vicissitudes of natural language, Cappelen and Lepore add disambiguation and precisification to contextually determined factors. Kaplan takes his contents to explicate the concept of what is said, or the proposition expressed, by an utterance. But Cappelen and Lepore abandon this equation. Their semantic content does not line up with what is said; they take what is said to be a somewhat vague and varying aspect of utterance that belongs to the realm of pragmatics. The semantic content is what is literally expressed, what determines the literal truth-value of an utterance, and is the input to Gricean reasoning.

Emma Borg's theory [Borg, 2004] is even more minimalist. She takes any-thing having to do with the speaker's intentions, including reference, out of semantic content altogether. Then, the concept of what is said lies also at the pragmatic side of the semantics/pragmatics border. Semantic theory should give, according to Borg, a 'formal' account of meaning, explaining the meaning of complex expressions, their semantic content, in terms of the meanings of the simple expressions and their mode of composition, with no appeal to speaker's intentions or any other contextual factor. This makes her semantic minimalism suitable to be incorporated in a modular view of the language faculty.

Recanati and relevance theorists are far over to the contextualist side. They assume that semantics by itself simply does not deliver a truth-evaluable propo-sition in a wide variety of cases, even if we allow resolution of indexical and demonstrative reference, disambiguation, and precisification.

In discussing the first edition of *Reference and Reflexivity*, Recanati sketches an approach that promises to do justice to both literalist and contextualist insights and theoretical ambitions. He is discussing an utterance of the sen-tence 'I am French.' In our view, an utterance *u* of this sentence by Recanati has the singular proposition that Recanati is French as its referential content. Its reflexive or utterance-bound content would be the proposition that *u* is uttered by someone who is French. Recanati says:

[T]he reflexive proposition is determined before the process of saturation takes place. The reflexive proposition can't be determined unless the sentence is tokened, but no substantial knowledge of the context of utterance is required to determine it. Thus an utterance *u* of the sentence 'I am French' expresses the reflexive proposition that the utterer of *u* is French. That it does not presuppose saturation is precisely what makes the reflexive proposition useful, since in most cases saturation proceeds by appeal to speaker's meaning ... The reflexive proposition is admittedly distinct from that which the speaker asserts ... but why is this an objection? [The reflexive proposition] comes as close as one can get to capturing, in propositional format, the information provided by the utterance in virtue solely of the linguistic meaning of the sentence 'I am French.' [Recanati, 2004, pp. 65–66]

This is pretty much the approach we advocate.[1] This also quite close to Borg's minimal view on semantic content.

12.3   Semantic content, raw and refined

We provide two accounts of 'semantic content,' the boundary between semantics and pragmatics. We call the utterance-bound or reflexive content, given only the meanings of the words involved, *without* resolution of ambiguity or reference (i.e., without Recanati's saturation), 'raw semantic content.' Given resolution of ambiguity, we have what we call 'refined semantic content.' It's usually useful for purposes of comparison and dealing with relatively straightforward informative conversation to think of the semantic contribution as refined content. But for a theory of how speakers use ambiguous expressions, and hearers figure out what they mean, raw semantic content is essential.

Grice said, concerning an utterance of 'He was in the grip of a vice':

Given a knowledge of the English language, but no knowledge of the circumstances of the utterance, one would know something about what the speaker had said, on the assumption that he was speaking standard English, and speaking literally. One would know that he had said, about some particular male person or animal *x*, that at the time of utterance (whatever that was), either (1) *x* was unable to rid himself of a certain kind of bad character trait or (2) some part of *x*'s person was caught in a certain kind of tool or instrument (approximate account, of course) [Grice, 1967a/1989, p. 25].

Resolving ambiguity is a matter of near-side pragmatics.[2]

Imagine, for example, that you are a scholar who has found a hitherto unknown diary of an important philosopher, Hume, say, buried in an archive somewhere. For July 3, 1772 you find the lone entry, "He was in the grip of a vice." You assume that the ink you see is a trace of an event of writing by David Hume on that date, an utterance. Of this utterance you know only its

[1] In the terminology we adopt in this book, we do not hold that an utterance *u* of 'I am French' *expresses* the proposition that the utterer of *u* is French.
[2] In American English this is an example of two words, 'vice' and 'vise,' both pronounced /vaɪs/. Parallel considerations would apply. But we follow British English, and Grice, in taking it to be ambiguity.

reflexive, utterance-bound content: Hume's utterance was true iff the person he was referring to with 'he' was either unable to rid himself of a certain bad character trait, or had his hand or some other bodily part caught in a tool that exerts pressure to hold things steady. Looking back in the diary you see that the day before Hume was expecting a visit from his friend and sometime tenant James Boswell. You take it that the use of 'he' refers to Boswell. Knowing a bit about Boswell's difficulties with various forms of temptation, and having never heard that he was much involved with woodworking or carriage repair, you resolve the ambiguity in favor of Grice's first option. This allows you to get to a subject matter description, the referential content of what Hume said: that Boswell was having difficulty shaking a bad habit or character trait.

Does this really involve far-side pragmatics in the service of near-side pragmatics? After all, there is no real conversation; Hume wasn't talking to anyone, merely writing in his own diary. Still, you are making inferences based on a conception of what he was trying to do. You are assuming that he was recording things in his diary that were true accounts of his day's experiences, perhaps to serve as reminders for later. Without that assumption, you can't resolve the ambiguity. Suppose, instead, that he was using the diary to jot down ideas for an amusing one-act play, in which Boswell is uncharacteristically trying to build a birdhouse and clumsily gets both hands caught in a vice, and has to shout for help from his friend Dr. Johnson. Unlikely perhaps – both the imagined situation and the idea that Hume would begin to write a one-act play about it in his diary – but the point is that in excluding alternative explanations and assuming Hume is simply recording the day's events in a truthful way, you are using far-side pragmatics, reasoning about Hume's intentions in using language, in the service of near-side pragmatics, to resolve ambiguity.

In this case, what semantics provided you with was raw content; you used pragmatic reasoning to arrive at refined content. Raw content is also required to understand cases in which the speakers do not intend for the hearer to resolve the ambiguity, but rather intend to exploit the ambiguity, as in poetry, jokes, and many other common situations.

12.4   Minimalism, contextualism, and Critical Pragmatics

So we think our conception should give minimalists all they want, and more. But our position is consistent with a great deal of what contextualists want to say on various issues. To see the differences between literalism, contextualism, and the current approach, consider again the issue of domain restrictions. In our example, Ethel and Fred have been planning a holiday party for the apartment building they manage. Fred asks, looking over the phone-list for the apartment residents, "Did you invite Ricky and Lucy?" Ethel tells Fred:

(12.1)   I've invited everyone.

In the context, it is clear that she intends to convey that she has invited everyone *in the building* to the holiday party. How should we think of what is going on, in terms of pragmatics and semantics?

At a first approximation, here is how the debate shapes up. The contextualist will say that, since Fred and Ethel have been talking about the apartment building, the domain of people in the building is available in the context to serve as an *unarticulated constituent* of what she said. An unarticulated constituent is a constituent of referential content that does not correspond to any explicit phrase in the utterance – as we saw in Chapter 9. She is saying, of that domain, that she has invited everyone in it to the party. So this proposition, what her utterance expresses, what she said, is arrived at through a combination of semantics – the meanings of the words used – and near-side pragmatics, which picks the relevant domain from those that are contextually available for the interpretation of 'everyone.' Near-side pragmatics involves not only saturation, the resolution of reference, but also enrichment, the provision of new content not available from the meanings of the articulated words.

The literalist eschews unarticulated constituents and other forms of enrichment and insists that what Ethel strictly and literally said must be based solely on the semantics of the words in the utterance. So what she strictly and literally said turns out to be that there she invited everyone in the whole world, or perhaps the whole universe. Then far-side pragmatics, that is, Gricean considerations, take over. Fred realizes that she didn't invite everyone in the whole world, and so what she strictly and literally said is obviously false, and violates the maxim of quality. He reasons that she must have intended to convey the more plausible and more relevant proposition, that she invited everyone in the building to their holiday party. The literalist admits that it is somewhat counterintuitive to charge Ethel with saying that she invited everyone in the world, but these intuitions are based on the ease with which we ordinarily employ Gricean reasoning, and need not bind the theorist.

A more subtle literalist position, like Cappelen and Lepore's or Borg's minimalism, abandons the concept of what is said as a serious theoretical notion, in favor of *semantic content*. Semantic content is the output of semantics and the input to Gricean reasoning. What is said is demoted from its favored place as the boundary between semantics and pragmatics; saying is simply one kind of speech act that one can perform by expressing a certain semantic content. Fred understands the semantic content of Ethel's remark, applies Gricean reasoning, and concludes that she said that she invited everyone in the building, and perhaps also that she would like him to quit worrying about the party and get busy washing the windows. So-called unarticulated constituents play no role in semantics, and only come in on the far side when we use Gricean reasoning to figure out why someone produced an utterance with a particular semantic content.

But, the contextualist may counter, does the false proposition that Ethel has invited everyone in the world to the party really play any role in Fred's understanding of Ethel's utterance? Does he really suppose that she said this, or even expressed it? Isn't it more plausible to simply say that, since Fred and Ethel were talking about the people in the apartment building, he simply knew that she was talking about the people in the building, and telling him that she had invited all of them? Moreover, if we admit this rather absurd proposition is the semantic content of Ethel's remark, will Gricean reasoning really get Fred back to a sensible candidate for what Ethel was trying to convey to him?

Here is how it looks from the point of view of Critical Pragmatics. There *is* a proposition that is determined simply by the meanings of the words Ethel uses and the way they are put together, the utterance-bound content of Ethel's utterance,   what we are now calling 'refined semantic content,' roughly:

$\exists X \exists y$ (the speaker of **(12.1)** is talking about X &
the speaker of **(12.1)** is talking about y &
the speaker of **(12.1)** has invited everyone in X to y).

This proposition has the merit, from the minimalist point of view, of being determined simply by the semantics of the words that Ethel used and the way she put them together. But it also has the virtue of being true (assuming Ethel is telling the truth). Had Ethel said,

(12.2)   I've invited everyone in our building to our holiday party

she would have explicitly identified the domain and the party she was talking about. The utterance-bound or reflexive truth-conditions would be, roughly:

$\exists X \exists y(X = \{y|y$ lives in the speaker of **(12.2)**'s building$\}$
& $y =$ the speaker of **(12.2)**'s holiday party
& the speaker of **(12.2)** has invited everyone in X to y).

The difference in content of these two utterances is at the reflexive level; the first relies on context to identify the domain of people invited and to identify the party in question. The second makes these identifications explicitly. Each is true if all the people in the identified domain are invited to the party in question.

So Critical Pragmatics provides candidates for the output of semantics, raw content and refined content, that should please the minimalist, without offending the insights of the contextualist. One gets from semantics, so conceived, to what is said by the usual process of going from reflexive to referential content, without an implausible circuit through false propositions and strained Gricean reasoning.

Kent Bach is often reckoned as occupying a moderate position between literalists and contextualists, although it is unclear that two dimensions suffice to get at all the subtleties of his position [Bach, 2004, 2007]. For example, his account of semantic content is more minimalist than Cappelen and Lepore, in that in Bach's account such contents are often less than full propositions. Our picture of the relation between semantics and pragmatics has much in common with his. He sees the disciplines as having different, if related, subject matters, and dealing with different, if related, properties. Pragmatics concerns utterances and the intentions behind them, while semantics concerns expression types, their conventional meanings, and modes of composition. Pragmatics deals with speaker meaning, semantics with conventional meaning; pragmatics deals with speaker reference, semantics with reference determined by meaning. Something like the traditional picture is maintained, with a threefold distinction between the minimal semantic content, determined by the semantic module, impliciture, determined by the semantic module plus specific pragmatic inputs, and Gricean implicature carving up the area inherited from the twofold distinction of what is said and implicature.

As should be clear by now, regarding the amount of pragmatic 'intrusion' allowed into the semantic content of an utterance, we are minimalist; more radical minimalists than Cappelen and Lepore, and even Borg. With minimalists and contextualists alike we admit that near-side pragmatics has an important role to play in determining what the speaker says in uttering a sentence. That is why our approach might be adequately rendered as radically minimalist – regarding semantics – and moderately contextualist – regarding pragmatics [Korta and Perry, 2007b].

We side with most contextualists in sticking to Grice's divide between what is said and implicatures. Even if what is said is partly determined by pragmatic processes – resulting in implicitures with an 'i' (Bach), explicatures (relevance theory), or an enriched what is said – we think there is a difference between those two elements of utterance meaning.[3] Minimalists like Cappelen and Lepore or Borg think that there is no difference once we step from semantic content to pragmatic territory. On the other hand, we side with minimalists and Bach in accepting that there is room for various propositions with varying degree of minimality in an account of human linguistic communication, besides the

---

[3] Zubeldia [Zubeldia, 2010] argues that the use of the Basque reportative particle 'omen' reflects that distinction: it can be used to report what someone *said* in any of its versions – semantic content, minimal proposition, impliciture, explicature – but it cannot be used to report presuppositions, conversational implicatures, or indirect speech acts.

maximally enriched notion of what is said or the explicature.[4] In fact, a main theme of this book has been the claim that they are needed for an adequate account of human communication.

We don't think that our pluralistic picture of utterance content contradicts relevance theory. Quite the opposite. According to relevance theory, the pragmatic inferences are carried out following what they call the relevance-theoretic comprehension strategy [Carston, 2002, p. 143]:

(a) Consider interpretations (disambiguations, reference assignment, enrichments, contextual assumptions, etc.) in order of accessibility (i.e. follow a path of least effort in computing cognitive effects).
(b) Stop when the expected level of relevance is reached.

Both (a) and (b) seem basically to be compatible with our view, in predicting that the path is not simply from the information conveyed by the linguistic meaning of the referential expression to the referent, but that a particular cognitive fix on the referent is or can be what the hearer should reach. The hearer's comprehension process starts from the utterance-bound truth-conditions of the utterance (our version of their 'logical form'). Then, the reference assignment process would stop when the right target cognitive fix is reached. This is all that is needed for the inference of the implicatures (which can be on-line, and in parallel), and other perlocutionary effects the speaker intends to generate.

12.5   Grice's circle

Like both the minimalist and the contextualist, we see a lot of near-side pragmatics going on; that is, a great deal of pragmatics is often involved in arriving at what is said. But if Gricean reasoning starts with *what is said*, and seeks the best explanation for it, how can it be involved in determining what is said? This is the problem Levinson called 'Grice's circle':

Grice's account makes implicature dependent on a prior determination of 'the said.' The said in turn depends on disambiguation, indexical resolution, reference fixing, not to mention ellipsis unpacking and generality narrowing. But each of these processes, which are prerequisites to determining the proposition expressed, may themselves depend crucially on processes that look indistinguishable from implicatures. Thus what is said seems both to determine and to be determined by implicature. [Levinson, 2000, p. 186]

As we mentioned in §1.3 and §5.5, Grice's circle stems from an assumption about linguistic production and linguistic understanding not always explicit in theories in the philosophy of language, semantics, and pragmatics. They are

---

[4] Recanati argues [Recanati, 2004] that a minimal proposition à la Cappelen and Lepore has no theoretical role to play in an account of human communication; however, a different stance is taken in Recanati, 2007b. See Korta, 2008 for a discussion.

thought of as *linear* processes. As the hearer, one recognizes the language and the words used; then, one selects among the possible meanings based partly on context; and determines the content – what is said, the proposition expressed, the truth-conditions – with further appeals to context; then, one employs Gricean reasoning to figure out why the speaker said what he did – what additional (or alternative) information he intended to convey, and what speech acts he is trying to perform; and finally, perhaps, the hearer figures out what acts he actually performed, perhaps quite unintentionally. Each 'level' determines, typically with the help of appropriate contextual information, the next.

As it is clear by now, we reject this picture, but to reject it does not necessarily amount to rejecting the view that theories of phenomena involved in the planning and reasoning do not form discrete modules. In our view, the semantic facts of utterances are handled by semantic theories of, say, English and Basque. Meanings are assigned to morphemes by the conventions of the language, the subject of lexical semantics. Each language assigns significance to modes of composition, the topic of compositional semantics. Semantics, so conceived, is the study of properties of types. At the key level of sentences, what semantics assigns are utterance-bound conditions of truth – not locutionary content, or what is said.

Pragmatics is the study of how speakers use expressions to convey meaning, often exploiting, but sometimes ignoring, their conventionally determined meanings, and how hearers manage to understand them. We believe that both theories are part of a general theory of utterances. Semantics abstracts from the particular facts of particular utterances; however, it does not abstract by ignoring these factors, but by quantifying over them. Thus in our picture, the 'output' of semantics is a family of reflexive truth-conditions for an utterance, in which the occupants of relevant roles are quantified over, including the utterance-relative roles of speaker, time, and location, and also including many other roles dependent on those, such as the meanings the speaker intends to exploit, the objects he intends to refer to, the domains implicit in his use of quantifiers, the people he is addressing, and so on.

In planning our utterances, and interpreting the utterances of others, we do not apply these theories one after the other, but at the same time. The speaker tries to use expressions that, in virtue of some of the meanings they have, will enable the hearer, given other information available to the hearer, to discover the speaker's intentions.

Our way out of Grice's circle is, briefly, the following one: the hearer need not determine the locutionary content (the proposition expressed, in Levinson's and more traditional terms) for the inference of implicatures to get started. The hearer need not perform disambiguation, indexical resolution, reference fixing, and all the processes needed to determine the locutionary content of the utterance for the inference of implicature to get started. The inference can start from an (possibly ambiguous) utterance-bound content, the speaker-bound content, the network-content, or from an 'intermediate' utterance-independent content about the role the object plays in his life and get to inference implicature; and that can be just what the speaker's communicative intentions are all about.

13 Harnessing information

13.1 Introduction

We close our book by further explaining the view of content and content properties that underlies our approach. We then use these ideas to show how the themes with which we began – language as action, communicative intentions, and content properties – form a coherent whole. We end by returning to the decoding and the intention-discovery models of interpretation.

13.2 Content

In the first chapter, we listed several categories of content properties:

- Cognitive properties, where the contents are usually identified by 'that'-clauses: Believing *that London is pretty*, hoping *that London is pretty*, knowing *that Santa Cruz is east of Berkeley*.
- Properties of linguistic agents: saying *that London is pretty*, implying *that Bush is from Texas*.
- Properties having to do with attitudes and acts where the contents are typically identified by 'to'-clauses or gerunds rather than that-clauses (although near equivalents can usually be formulated in that format): desiring *to own a Bentley*, hoping *to catch a plane*, telling Fido *to quit barking*, asking a waiter *to bring a wine list*, regretting *having gone to the store*, remembering *turning off the oven*.
- Properties whose content clause contains an interrogative rather than a declarative sentence: knowing *who Tony Blair is*, or asking *whether Paris is larger than London*.
- We claim two kinds of content are basic:
    - The informational content of events and states: those tracks show *that a fox has been on the path*, the x-ray shows *that Gretchen has a broken leg*.
    - The success-conditions of acts. By this we do not mean the goal for which the act was done, but rather the conditions under which the act would attain

that goal; more or less, the circumstances assumed to obtain, or hoped to
be obtained, by the agent.

13.2.1   Informational content

The *informational content of an event*, or of a state, is relative to a *constraint*. A
constraint is basically a law, convention, or rule that says if a situation of a certain type occurs, then a situation of another type also occurs. Actual constraints
tell us how the world works; other constraints merely tell us how someone
thinks it works, or hopes it works, or plans to make a part of it work, or how
some governing body has deemed that it should work, or perhaps how the
world mostly worked in some region of space and time in which the traits
of a species, or the habits of an individual, developed. The way the world
works, at least in Palo Alto near the turn of the century, doorbells don't ring
unless there is someone on the front porch pushing the button. Even if that's
not quite right about Palo Alto, it held true almost all the time John developed
his expectations about doorbells. Relative to that constraint, the fact that the
doorbell rings at his house carries the information that there is someone on
the front porch. More precisely, if the doorbell rings, someone pushed the button to which it is connected, and that person is standing on the front porch.
If we unpacked the constraint into more basic ones, they would be about a
heterogeneous variety of things: electricity, the way doorbells are constructed
and connected to buttons, how cats and dogs are ill-equipped and not very
motivated to push those buttons, the sizes and shapes of people and porches,
and so on.

One might complain that this isn't really a factual constraint. Sometimes
doorbells ring because a prankster is poking the button with a stick without
standing on the porch, so he can make a quick getaway. Sometimes they ring
because of short circuits. Sometimes they ring because an electrician is standing
inside the house, touching wires to check that things are wired correctly, before
final installation of the button on the porch. And so on. This is all true and
important. Still, we shape our expectations on non-factual constraints, usually
because they have some status that makes them near-factual. Their instances
may be very probable. They may be exceptionless or virtually so given certain
common conditions – like there being no electrician in the house – that are
hard to list but usually easy to check. The importance of a constraint, for our
purposes, is not that it is factual, but that agents form their expectations and
interpretations on its basis. Since John is attuned to that constraint – that is, he
forms expectations based on it, without having to consciously formulate it in
his mind – he believes there is someone on the front porch, and goes to answer
the door. The informational content of an event or state, relative to a constraint,
is what the rest of the world must be like, for the event or state to have occurred,

given the constraint. If the constraint isn't factual, the informational content of an event, relative to that constraint, may not be information in the strict sense of the term, for it may not be factual.

An illuminating example, mentioned earlier, is the constraint that if one has an unobstructed view of an object, one can travel to it. In the case of birds, this means they can fly to it. Birds evolved at a time when this constraint was exceptionless, or virtually so. They are attuned to it. As a result, millions of birds die each year flying into picture windows, glass doors, and the like. What the world has to be like, given a constraint that is probably hard-wired into their genes, it sometimes doesn't turn out to be like, after all.

13.2.2   Success-conditions

The second basic category of content is the *success-conditions of an act*. This is the one category of content we appeal to, for which there is not a relatively simple natural-language expression. Perhaps that is an indication of how basic it is. Suppose you stand on the front porch, and have the goal of getting someone to answer the door. If, as is often the case, the button is broken, or isn't wired up at all, or isn't wired up properly, or the bell is broken, or the bell is not loud enough for whoever is home to hear it, or they hear it but don't want to bother with it, or there is no one at home, then your act will not succeed. If on the other hand the button works, the bell works and is loud enough, and someone is at home who is inclined to answer the door, your act will succeed. These are the success-conditions of your act.

Success-conditions, like informational contents, are relative to constraints. The wiring has to be right, because electricity makes doorbells work. Someone has to be home, because doors don't answer themselves (at least not most residential doors). That person has to be willing to answer the door, because people who really don't want to answer the door won't do so. So far informational content and success-conditions are on a par; the former is what the world has to be like for an event to happen, given the way the world works; the second is what the world has to be like for an act to succeed, given the way the world works.

But there is a further relativity in the case of success-conditions: the standard of success. In the case of the purposeful activity of humans, the standard is usually the goal of the agent. The door-bell ringer's goal is to get the door opened; the conditions of success we mentioned are relative to that goal. However, as a matter of logic, any goal – any specified end-state – can be used to generate success-conditions for an act. Perhaps I am ringing the doorbell because you told me you would pay me $100 if I could get someone to open the door. But your goal was just to wake up your annoying neighbor during her nap. There are different standards of success, and so different success-conditions. The doorbell and the bell must work, and the bell must be loud, and the neighbor must be home. But your success required her to be asleep, mine does not. Mine requires her to answer the door, yours does not.

Note that roles are already important with these basic categories of content, because they are built into the structure of constraints. Spelled out, the doorbell constraint would be: if the doorbell rings, there is someone who is pushing the button to which it is wired [because of electricity, and the way doorbells are wired, and because dogs and squirrels and cats aren't equipped to press the button] and the person pushing the button will be standing on the porch [because of the location of the button, and the size of the porch, and the length of people's arms]. The button plays a role vis-à-vis the doorbell that rings; the person plays a role vis-à-vis the button, as does the porch.

13.2.3 Harnessing information

Given these two concepts, we can develop a third one, that of using or *harnessing information*. The basic idea is very simple. Events of one kind carry just the information that acts of a certain kind need to succeed. Let events that carry the information *trigger* the acts whose success depends on it. Let the same event that carries the information that P, cause an event whose success-condition is that P.

Consider an automatic door-opener of a simple sort. A mat is placed in front of the door with a pressure switch underneath. When the switch is closed, by a person stepping on the mat, a circuit is completed, and a small electric motor moves an arm attached to the door, opening it. Relative to the constraint, that if the switch is closed, there is someone standing on the mat who wants in, the switch being closed has the informational content that someone is in front of the door and would like to come in. Relative to the goal of letting people in who want to come in and keeping the door shut at other times, this is basically a success-condition for opening the door. The system, we say, harnesses the information provided by the depression of the switch, to guide the action of the subsystem that opens the door.

A person could connect a switch under a mat in front of his front door to an opener attached to his back door. Mechanically, nothing would be wrong with that. But it still wouldn't work, at least not relative to the goal of letting people in the front door. The architecture of the system does not link the crucial roles in the right way. To make the system work, the architecture has to guarantee a key identity:

> In a properly set up automatic door system, the door in front of which lies the mat, under which the switch is placed = the door that is open in virtue of the switch being closed.

The point is, *architectures harness information by linking roles.*

An old-fashioned mousetrap provides a second example. The architecture is simple. Towards one end of a small piece of wood there is a small hinged platform, on which bait – usually cheese or peanut butter – can be placed. At the other end of the piece of wood a rod is attached, which just reaches the platform. In between there is a spring attached to a wired blade that reaches just beyond the platform.

If the spring is opened all the way, so that the blade touches the other end of the piece of wood, the rod can be placed over the blade and then under the platform, where it will be held precariously in place, preventing the spring from closing. If the platform wiggles, the rod will be released, the spring will be released, and the blade will snap down just beyond the platform.

The point of a mousetrap is to kill mice, so the success-condition of the snapping of the blade is that there is a mouse in its path. The event that causes the snapping – the wiggling of the platform – carries just this informational content, given the constraint that the only way the platform will wiggle is if a mouse is eating the bait, which will place it in the path of the platform.

In both cases, the constraints that account for the devices working are not likely to be completely factual. Occasionally the thing that depresses the switch under the rug won't be a person who wants to come in, but someone who wants to look through a window, or is playing hide and seek, or a dog wandering about with no particular purpose. In the case of the mousetrap, it's the job of the would-be mouse-killer to find a place to put the trap where the constraint will hold as true as possible; that is, to put it where dogs and cats and small children and adults looking for midnight snacks are not likely to wiggle the platform.

Simple as they are, both examples illustrate another point: architecture adds content. We have been fudging a bit, when we say that the informational content of the triggering event is the same as the success-conditions of the triggered act. In the case of the mousetrap the success-condition for the blade closing is that there is a mouse in its path. The informational content of the platform wiggling is that there is a mouse in front of it, eating its bait. There is a gap that is closed by the architecture of the mousetrap, which guarantees that two roles will be linked:

> Given the structure of the trap, the place of the mouse that wiggles the platform that releases the rod that releases the blade = the place at the end of the path of the blade.

13.2.4   Information games

Talk of automatic door-openers and mousetraps may give the impression our goal here is some unduly reductive account of language use that bypasses reason, consciousness, and the other interesting manifestations of the mentality that door-openers and mousetraps do not share with humans. That is not our purpose, however. It is rather to highlight, in these simple cases, the relations between information and action, and the job of the structure that links the pick-up of information to the performance of action, in securing links between roles. It is this structure that we think survives all the additions that the complexity of the human mind brings to a basic problem of intelligent action, how to harness information to guide action.

The automatic door and the mousetrap illustrate a feature that we think is at the core of any system of harnessing information: a linkage between the roles involved in picking up information and those involved in acting; the roles are linked so that the objects whose information was picked up are the very ones to which it is applied. In simple systems, this job is handled automatically by architecture; with more complex intelligent systems, memory, recognition, and reasoning are involved to make the links. In the case of communicating information, it is up to the speaker's planning and the hearer's understanding to make them.

What we call an *information game* involves one person (or other sort of system) gathering information at one time, and that person or another person, at the same time or a different time, using the information to guide action. In the 'straight-through' information game one person picks up information perceptually about the situation he is in, and then immediately puts it to use to guide action. You perceive a cup of coffee in front of you, and you use that information to guide your hand in grabbing the cup and picking it up, with the goal of getting a sip of coffee.

Coffee goes together with consciousness, at least for many of us. Perceiving a cup of coffee and drinking it is usually a conscious act undertaken in pursuit of improving or maintaining one's level of consciousness. Still, the basic need for role-linking is the same as in the case of the door or the trap. The coffee cup plays two important roles in your life. It is the cup you see, and it is the cup you will grasp if you move your arm and hand in a certain way. What you directly perceive is that the cup plays the first role; that is, it is the cup that has a certain effect on your eyes and visual system, characteristic of a cup located in a certain direction at a certain distance from your eyes. What you learn, the information you put to use, is that it occupies a certain position relative to your arm and hand, in a direction and at a distance so that a certain movement of arm and hand will grasp it. That an object that plays the first role also plays the second one is a contingent fact that depends on the basic architecture of human beings, and particular facts about you and your arms and hands and eyes, just as the fact that the person who comes through the door is the person who steps on the entry-rug is due to the architecture of the automatic door, and the fact that the mouse nibbling is the mouse killed is due to the architecture of the mousetrap. You are attuned to these facts, and infer effortlessly from perception the information that is needed to guide action.

The importance of the role-linking is easily missed, because we are attuned to the basic architecture of many natural and artifactual objects. When you drive, you pick up information visually about the car whose windshield you are looking through. The information you pick up is used to guide your action in steering and braking. Turning the wheel has an effect on the car whose front wheels are connected with the steering mechanism; stepping on the brake has an effect on the car whose wheels are connected to the braking system the pedal is connected to. Three roles are involved in the transaction: being the car whose windshield you are looking through, being the car whose wheels you are steering, and being the car whose wheels you are braking. Thanks to the intelligent architecture of automobiles, all three roles are occupied by the same car, and you as driver don't need to think about it.

In these cases, we can distinguish between the system information and the triggering information. The fact that the same person who smells the coffee and sees the cup is the one whose arms move towards the cup and whose hand grasps the cup, and the same person who will taste the coffee, is system information. As long as we are not in the laboratories of mad scientists or in the imaginations of clever philosophers, these architectural relations will be intact and can be taken for granted. Information about the location of the cup, the fact that it has coffee in it, and the like are not built into the system, but are the responsibility of our perceptual systems to register.

Now consider a more complicated information game, what we call the 'detach and recognize' game. You go to the kitchenette adjacent to the office in which you work, and fix yourself a cup of coffee just the way you like it, perhaps a rich espresso made from expensive beans, perhaps a cup of weak American coffee with the right amount of sugar and cream. You use your favorite cup, the one with the picture of Nietzsche on it. Then your phone rings and you need to return to your office quickly, and you leave the cup behind. A bit later you return, pick up the cup and drink from it, fully expecting just the coffee experience you most enjoy.

Here you pick up information about a certain object, a cup, at one time. You put that information to use at a later time. At the time you picked up the information, the cup played a certain role in your life; it was the one you held in your left hand while you poured coffee from the pot in your right hand; perhaps it was the one into which you poured some sugar and cream. Now it plays a somewhat different role your life; it is the one you see on the counter as you re-enter the kitchenette. The fact that the *same* cup plays these two different roles is crucial. In this case, however, its doing so is not just an automatic consequence of the architecture of human beings, coffee cups, and kitchenettes. The fact that you have your own favorite cup, with a picture of Nietzsche on it, allows you to *recognize* the cup as the same one that played the earlier role in your life. You perceived the cup as you poured your coffee; then the perceptual link was broken. Still, you retained information about the cup in a detached way. Even as you spoke on the phone, you remembered the cup with the picture of Nietzsche on it waiting for you. Then, upon re-entering the kitchenette, you perceived the cup again and were able to recognize it because you remembered this distinctive fact.

To detach and recognize is basic to human existence, as Peter Strawson pointed out in *Individuals* [Strawson, 1959]. In the detach and recognize information game, the distinction between system and triggering information re-emerges as a distinction between *identifying information* and *treatment-relevant-features*. The architecture of human beings and the world no longer guarantees that the objects about which we pick up information are the ones we apply it to when we act. States of the system are involved in both picking up information about objects that is relevant to what actions are appropriate towards them, and identifying those objects about which we have such information, that is recognizing them after perception has been broken off.

You left the kitchenette knowing two things about a certain cup. It had a picture of Nietzsche on the side. This has no effect on how it tastes, and whether you would like to drink it or not; it is information for identification, not a treatment-relevant feature. And you know that the coffee in it was prepared for you, just the way you like it. This won't help you identify it, but it has everything to do with how much you will enjoy drinking from it. It is a treatment-relevant feature, not helpful for identification.

The distinction permeates our methods for dealing with things, people in particular. When a student applies to a graduate department, the forms will have a place for name, address, telephone number, email, and the like. These are basically information for identification, in a somewhat generalized sense. They permit the admission department to interact in various ways with the same person who filed the application, the same person whose credentials they have assessed. Information for identification, in this general sense, is basically role-linking information: the person who filled out this form you are reading, is the person you will contact if you call this number, or send a letter to this name and street address, or a message to this email address.

Language is too flexible for many exceptionless generalizations, but at least in simple cases the subject–predicate structure of sentences tends to mirror the information versus treatment distinction. The subject terms, in all the ways we have looked at in this book, provide information for identification: role-linking information. The predicate tells what the person or place or thing identified is like, which is relevant to how you may want to treat him or her or it. "That man is a bore"; that is, the fellow you can see by following my gaze and could interact with by going over where he is, is a bore, that is, you probably don't want to interact with him.

Communication is an extension of the detach and recognize information game, where the information picked up by one person at one time, in one situation, is used by another person, at another time, in a different situation. I have met Dikran; I know what he looks like, what his passions are, and what topics to avoid. You are going to meet him for the first time, so I share this information with you. Information I picked up in interactions with Dikran over the years, you will put to use when you meet him. If things go right the very same person I picked up information about will be the one with respect to which you use it, namely Dikran. But then how do we make sure that this is so? How do we make sure that the person who played a certain role in our life, when we picked up the information, is the same person who plays another role in someone else's life, when they put that information to use? It is this problem of role-management that, in our theory, the meanings of singular terms help us to solve.

13.3   Propositions and the structure of action

We cited three central ideas in Chapter 1, as the keys to our approach: the idea that language is action, Grice's theory of communicative intentions, and the reflexive–referential account of meaning. The first two ideas fit naturally together; language is intentional action, and Grice's theory tells us of the characteristic structure of those intentions. But how does the third idea fit in?

Theories of the content of language and propositional attitudes are usually 'mono-propositional.' That is, there is a single proposition that is thought to capture the content of a belief, desire, or what is said by an assertion. In contrast, theories in the philosophy of action have long recognized the multi-level structure of action. Even the simplest of actions have a structure. An agent moves in certain circumstances, and the combination of the nature of the movement and the nature of the circumstances produces certain results, given the way the world works. I move my arm in a certain way unthinkingly, and because of the circumstances I'm in, I knock a cup to the floor. By knocking the cup to the floor, I cause it to break. By causing it to break, I make its owner angry. And so forth.

We can classify actions in terms of the changes they bring about in the pre-existing circumstances, using that-clauses: he brought it about *that his arm moved*; by doing that in the circumstance in which there was a cup on a table in front of him he brought it about *that the cup was knocked from the table*; by doing that in the circumstance in which the cup was owned by Miranda, and was one she cared about, he brought it about *that Miranda was angry*. It would be rather perverse, however, to suppose that action was basically a relation to propositions, and only indirectly, through the propositions, to arms, cups, tables, and people. The role of the propositions, vis-à-vis the descriptions of action, is not to get at an element of the act but to characterize or classify the act, by the difference it makes in what the world is like.

Such characterization is naturally hierarchical. If we take different things as given, or characterize what is given in various ways, we get different characterizations of the results. The agent brought it about that the cup in front of him broke; the agent brought it about that Miranda's cup broke; the agent brought it about that the owner of the cup was angry; the agent brought it about that Miranda was angry. We classify things differently, for different purposes, involving different methods of projecting general truths onto the specific situation. If we say that the agent moved his arm, knocked the cup off the table, broke the cup he knocked off, broke Miranda's cup, broke Miranda's favorite antique, and angered Miranda, our descriptions are consistent descriptions of what the agent did, but descriptions that describe these results relative to different circumstances, based on various relations the agent and his arm had to various objects – the cup, the table, Miranda – and various properties of and relations among these objects.

A key function of cognition is to motivate intelligent action; that is, to motivate action that will contribute to the agent's goals, given what he knows, or has reason to believe. To simplify, a belief and a desire should motivate actions whose result will promote the satisfaction of the desire, given the truth of the belief. Given this relation between cognition and action, we should expect beliefs, desires, and other cognitive states to be classifiable in the same sort of hierarchical way that the results of action and the success conditions of action are. That this is so, that cognitions have multiple contents, is a main idea of the reflexive–referential theory.

Let's return to our example involving the coffee cup. You return to the kitchenette. You have a belief you would express with, "That cup has good coffee in it." We would ordinarily think of the content of the statement, and of the belief it expressed, as simply a singular proposition with the cup as a constituent. But according to the reflexive–referential approach, your belief also has a reflexive or perception-bound content: that the cup which the perception associated with the belief is of, has good coffee in it.

The belief you express is one that is not based simply on present perception, for you can't perceive the quality of the coffee in the cup. It is based in part on memory, the memory of filling a certain cup with good coffee a couple of minutes before. You might express that belief by saying, "I remember filling that cup with good coffee, only a couple of minutes ago." But this fudges a bit. What you remember is filling the cup you were perceiving and holding at the time with good coffee. Given that the cup you remember filling is the cup you now see, your memory is true only if the cup you now see has good coffee in it. But that is not given in memory, but by the process of recognition. The whole story, or something close to it, goes like this. You have a memory, the memory-bound content of which is that you filled the cup that your memory is a memory of a perception of, with good coffee, and it had a Nietzsche picture on it; you have a perception, the perception-bound content of which is that the cup it is a perception of has a Nietzsche picture on it and coffee in it; based on these contents, and some auxiliary beliefs – that there are not many other Nietzsche cups in the office, and that your officemates are not prone to pranks like pouring Sanka or Diet Pepsi in freshly brewed cups of coffee while their owners' attention is diverted, for example – you believe that the cup your present perception is of is the cup your present memory of a perception is of, and that since the latter had good coffee in it a couple of minutes ago, the former has good coffee in it now.

Looking forward, your belief motivates your reaching out, grabbing the cup in front of you, and drinking from it. But we can't get at the content that motivates that act simply in terms of the singular proposition that the cup has good coffee in it. The perception that you have of the cup is veridical only if there is a cup a certain distance in a certain direction from the person who has the perception, and that distance and direction will dictate what sort of movement is required to reach the cup and pick it up. Both in terms of the memories that justify it and the action it motivates, we need to consider not simply the referential but also the reflexive content of the belief. A mono-propositional account of cognition cannot explain the connection between the pick-up of information through perception, cognition, and the application of information in action.

We said above that the idea of action as fundamentally a relation to propositions was bizarre; the role of propositions is classificatory, not constitutional. We believe the same applies to cognition. The picture of a 'propositional attitude' suggested by the phrase is not correct. Having a propositional attitude does not consist in having a certain relation or attitude towards an abstract object. It consists in being in a state that in virtue of the circumstances of its acquisition and its causal and informational role can be assigned conditions of truth (or other conditions of satisfaction). The role of propositions is to indirectly characterize the state in virtue of its truth-conditions, given various combinations of circumstances.

13.4   Coding and classification

The dominant paradigm of communication, at least outside the realm of pragmatics, is probably still the code model of communication, aka the 'message,' 'tube,' 'channel,' 'transmission' model, etc., namely the model that goes back as far as, at least, Aristotle, is explicit in Locke, and gets successfully mathematized by Shannon and Weaver [Shannon and Weaver, 1949]. The basic idea when applied to the case of human linguistic communication would be basically this:

> The speaker (or sender) has a thought (or message) that he wants to communicate to the hearer (or receiver). To do that, the speaker has to utter (send via the channel) a linguistic expression – typically a sentence – that encodes his thought. Perceiving the utterance, given that she shares the language (the code) with the speaker, the hearer decodes the sentence uttered back into a thought.

According to this picture, communication is successful if and only if the thought encoded by the speaker is the same as the thought decoded by the hearer. If speaker and hearer share a language, and there is no 'noise' in the channel, there is not much room for error in this model of communication.

There is, we think, a basic ambiguity in the picture, depending on what one takes the *thought* to be shared to be. In one interpretation, the thought is a mental representation, or a type thereof. If S tells H, "two plus two equals four," he wants the thought that H thinks to be of the very same type as the thought he thinks; if they are both English speakers, who think in English, the thought in question will be a thinking of the same sentence S speaks. A rather different picture is more Fregean. What is passed on is not a form of words, or even of ideas, but a proposition, in this case, the proposition that two plus two equals four.

The insufficiencies of this model, interpreted in either way, when it comes to account for human linguistic communication have been widely noticed. Common linguistic phenomena present problems. In the case of indexicality, for example, the first model doesn't seem to get the success-conditions correct. Suppose S expressed a thought by saying, "I am getting hungry." H's understanding will not consist of thinking, "I am getting hungry" but, "You are getting hungry" or "He is getting hungry." The second, propositional, model can only be evaluated relative to an account of what proposition is expressed. If, in this case, it is the singular proposition that S is getting hungry, the account seems incomplete, for H needs to think of S in a certain way. And of course the model does not deal with traditional pragmatic phenomena such as illocutionary force and implicatures.

Should we adapt the code model to deal with features such as indexicality, ambiguity, and the like, and then add an account of intention-recognition to deal with pragmatic phenomena? Or should we adopt the intention-recognition model as basic, dealing not simply with pragmatics but with basic semantic phenomena, and treat coding as a rather peripheral phenomenon? Sperber and Wilson [Sperber and Wilson, 1986] rightly claim that Grice's picture of meaning and communication can be interpreted either way. But we basically agree with them that the right option is the second.

However, we should keep in mind Wittgenstein's point, in his *Investigations*, that language is a congeries of activities and structures, and the plausibility of one approach or another can depend on which part of it one has in mind. For the purpose of stating and communicating results in mathematics and science, the part of language that was perhaps of most interest to Frege, Russell, and the logicians and philosophers of language in the logical empiricist movement, the code model has considerable plausibility. In an inviting picture of how such discourse *should* be conducted, ambiguity, indexicality, underspecification, metaphor, irony, implicature, and other such things should be eliminated or held to a minimum. Although the speaker's intentions are involved, there should be little need for discovery; someone who makes a statement in a scientific meeting, or publishes a result in a scientific journal, should be assumed to have the intention of producing a sentence that captures what she has in mind and will enable the hearer to think the same thought.

But from the point of view of the ordinary use of natural language in conversation and literature, the code model will not get us very far. Consider our example from above. S says, "I am getting hungry." H, we may assume, hears the words with no problem. Assume that it is clear that S is not being ironic. Knowing the code, that is, understanding English, what can he infer? He can infer that the utterance he hears has a speaker, and was made at a certain time, and the speaker at the time intended to express the belief that he was becoming hungry – whether for food, or knowledge, or carnal pleasures, the code model will not tell him. The code will not tell him which time and which speaker these are; assuming it is face-to-face communication, he will need to rely on perception to figure this out.

Assume that S is H's guest, so that H has some responsibility for feeding S, and S is hungry for food. Then the thought that S wants H to think is not, as we observed, "I am getting hungry." Nor is it the thought that mere decoding can provide: "There is some time and some person, such that the person made this utterance at the time, and the person was getting hungry (for something or other) at the time." It is something like "My guest is getting hungry for food." What this thought shares with S's original motivating thought is referential content: that S is getting hungry for food. But while referential content should be preserved in a communicative transaction like this, H's grasping the same referential content that S expressed is clearly not adequate for understanding. S intends for H to grasp it *in a certain way*, one that will motivate further action. It won't do for H merely to think, "This man is getting hungry," without recognizing that the man in question is his guest, so that he has a responsibility to do something. It is part of S's plan that H will think of him this way, and part of what he assumes is that H will recognize him as his guest, and H needs to understand all of this.

From our point of view, what the code – that is the rules connecting sounds and meaning – provides is a structure of constraints on the contents, which the speaker can exploit the hearer's knowledge of, as an aid to recognition of his intentions. This structure will not deliver a single proposition, rather a family of propositions, depending on what is taken as given, known, or fixed, and what is allowed to vary. While coding is ubiquitous, the code model seems to pertain only to rather special cases as in the straightforward communication of information within a fixed context by ideally dispassionate and articulate communicators. Only in such cases can the complex of constraints be thought of as the *message* that is being conveyed.

We agree with Sperber and Wilson, and many other theorists inspired by the views of Austin and Grice, that coding/decoding is just a small part of the processes involved in human linguistic communication. And we agree with them that the main task on the part of the hearer is to infer the speaker's communicative intentions, using various sources of evidence, including the meaning of the sentence uttered. Where the theory developed in this book differs from Sperber and Wilson, and many other theories inspired by the Austin–Grice view, is our focus on the speaker's plan, and our claim that a family of truth-conditions or propositions is required to properly track the causal, inferential, and content relations between the elements of this plan and the hearer's understanding of it.

13.5   Back to Hondarribia

Take again our initial example, in which John utters the Basque sentence

(1.2)   Ni naiz John.

If this book is not a complete failure, the critical role that John's communicative (and referential) intentions and their recognition by his audience play in John's utterance and its comprehension should be beyond doubt by now, as well as the limitations of the code model of communication as an account of what was going on there. Even if we supplemented it with some contextual parameters, fixing the referent of the first-person singular pronoun 'Ni,' that would give us a trivial statement of John's identity with himself.

In our view, that would be just one content of John's utterance of (1.2), the locutionary content, determined by the linguistic conventions of the sentence, John's directing intentions, and the fact that John is the occupant filling the roles exploited by those directing intentions, namely, being the speaker of the utterance, and being the origin of the notion-network exploited by his use of 'John.' The locutionary content, however, cannot offer by itself an account of John's cognitive motivation – why he uses (1.2) rather than 'ni naiz ni' or 'John da John' – or the utterance's cognitive impact on his audience – why Larraitz understands it correctly while Joana doesn't.

Our theory, however, offers a variety of contents that help us in understanding it naturally, taking utterances as a sort of action. Which action is taken as basic is a matter of theoretical or, as in this case, practical interest. Joana's comprehension route is diverted at the pre-syntactic level. She takes the sounds '/ninaizdjon/' to correspond to the English sentence 'Nina is John' and cannot go beyond what would correspond to its network-bound truth-conditions, namely,

Given that **/ninaizdjon/** is English, has the syntax it does, 'is' means identity in English, John is the speaker of **/ninaizdjon/** and N_{Nina} is the network John exploits with 'Nina' and N_{John} is the network John exploits with 'John', **/ninaizdjon/** is true *iff*

$\exists x, y$ such that x is the origin of N_{Nina}, y is the origin of N_{John}, and $x = y$.

She can guess that y might be John himself, the guest they were supposed to pick up at the airport, but cannot make sense of the joke he was intending to make. Appealing to the code model you can argue that she just failed to choose the right code, the right language, Basque, that John was using in the exchange. However, it seems clear that the fact that the sounds '/ninaizdjon/' correspond to Basque and not to English is not itself coded. Given that the grammars of Basque and English allow those sounds to be a sentence in either language, once again, it's John's intentions that are determinative. In monolingual settings, the intention to speak a certain language is usually taken for granted. You don't have to form the intention to speak English if it's the only language you speak and you assume is the only one that your addressee speaks. The language used is built into the situation. But in plurilingual environments it is often the case that one intends to speak a certain language and one's addressee's first task is to recognize that intention. Joana didn't recognize John's intention to speak Basque. Larraitz did. And she recognized his referential plan, too:

(a) His *grammatical intention* to express the identity relation between the individuals designated by 'Ni' and 'John' according to Basque syntax (even if somewhat clumsily reproducing the SVO order of English).
(b) His *directing intention* of exploiting the roles corresponding to the speaker of the utterance and the origin of a certain notion-network N_{John}.
(c) His *path intention* that goes, first, from her cognitive fix on him as speaker of the utterance to her cognitive fix as the person in front of them (*target intention*); and, second, from his detached notion of himself to her detached notion of John (*target*).

Merging these two notions – the perceptual buffer of the person she sees in front of her and the nominal notion of 'John' – is the crucial step in John's plan and Larraitz's understanding. This is how she is able to recognize John's intended implicatures and perlocutionary effects. The critical content of (1.2) is not the trivial referential truth-conditions of John's self-identity. The critical truth-conditions of (1.2) for his communicative plan to succeed involves the self-identity of the object Larraitz has two cognitive fixes on: John. Something like:

The person in front of me is *the origin of my John-notion.*

This might seem like an extraordinarily complicated account for such ordinary and simple phenomena as introducing oneself or referring to other people, object, places, etc. About that, we will only repeat Russell's words about his theory of descriptions, at least as apt for our case as they were for his over a hundred years ago.

> I will only beg the reader not to make up his mind against the view – as he might be tempted to do, on account of its apparently excessive complication – until he has attempted to construct a theory of his own on the subject ... This attempt, I believe, will convince him that, whatever the true theory may be, it cannot have such a simplicity as one might have expected beforehand. [Russell, 1905, p. 493]

14   Examples

(1.1)   Nina is John.

(1.2)   Ni naiz John.

(1.3)   Ni Larraitz naiz [I-Larraitz-am].

(1.4)   **F** shows that the person of whose arm it was taken has a broken arm.

(1.5)   **F** shows that Elwood has a broken arm.

(1.6)   If an x-ray *y* of a human arm exhibits pattern ψ, then *the person of whose arm y was taken* has a broken arm.

(1.7)   Elwood is the person of whose arm **F** was taken.

(1.8)   That the person of whose arm **F** was taken has a broken arm.

(1.9)   That Elwood has a broken arm.

(1.10)   I have a broken arm.

(1.11)   Any English utterance **u** of the form 'I have a broken arm' is true if and only if the speaker of **u** has a broken arm.

(1.12)   That the speaker of **u** has a broken arm.

(1.13)   Elwood is the speaker of **u**.

(2.1)   The present king of France is a Catholic.

(2.2)   The senator from Utah is a Mormon.

(2.3)   Hesperus is Hesperus.

(2.4)   Hesperus is Phosphorus.

(2.5)   Nessie lives in Loch Ness.

(2.6)   Cicero was bald.

(3.1)   I'd like some salt, please.

(3.2)   She'd like the salt.

(3.3)   Julia Roberts would like the salt.

(3.4)   Bob Dole would like some salt.

(4.1)   Your train leaves from Union Station.

(4.2)   Your train leaves from that station.

(4.3)   Mr. Muggs is wanted on the phone – would you tell him?

(5.1)   That's a painting of the greatest philosopher of the twentieth century.

(5.2)   That building houses the ILCLI.

(5.3)   That is the same building as that.

(5.4)   That monster can really stir things up.

(6.1)   I am in charge.

(6.2)   I am Larraitz.

(6.3)   I am I.

(6.4)   Larraitz is Larraitz.

(6.5)   This is Kepa. Please fax me the colloquium schedule.

(6.6)   Please fax me the colloquium schedule.

(6.7)   I am a computer scientist.

(6.8)   David Israel is a computer scientist.

(7.1)   If John would quiet down, John could hear what John is saying.

(7.2)   Robert lost his job.

(7.3)   He must be very worried.

(7.4)   Robert must be very angry.

(8.1)   Fred: Have you invited Lucy and Ricky?
          Ethel: Every adult has been invited to the party.

(8.2)   H: I told him that he was wanted on the phone.
          S: Thanks.
          H: He wasn't drinking a martini, it was a gimlet with an olive.
          S: I know.

(9.1)   On the top shelf.

(10.1)   He is a fine friend.

(10.2)   John is turning red.

(10.3)   Flying planes can be dangerous.

(10.4)   Will I finish the paper by tomorrow?

(10.5)   I will finish the paper by tomorrow.

(10.6)   Kepa, finish the paper by tomorrow!

(10.7)   [I hope] to finish the paper by tomorrow.

(10.8)   If I finish the paper by tomorrow, [John will be pleased].

(10.x1)   That the speaker of (10.x) finish the paper referred to by the speaker of (10.x) before the day after (10.x) is uttered.

(10.x2)   That Kepa finishes the paper by May 15, 2006.

(10.9)   I finished the paper yesterday.

(10.10)   You finished the paper yesterday [as you promised].

(10.11)   I promise to finish the paper by tomorrow.

(10.x3)   That Kepa promises at the time of (10.11) to bring it about that Kepa finishes the paper before the day after the time of (10.11).

(10.12)   Kepa finishes the paper by May 15, 2006.

(11.1)   He is thirsty.

(11.2)   Eros is thirsty.

(11.3)   That *Eros* is thirsty.

(11.4)   Well, maybe what's-his-name ... he is fun, interesting, and a good guy ... but he smokes.

(11.5)   That *the male Kepa has in mind* is fun, interesting, and smokes.

(11.6)   He is thirsty.

(11.7)   That *the guy in front of me who is not speaking* is thirsty.

(11.8)   Eros is thirsty.

(11.9)   That dog is that dog.

(11.10)   A: I am out of petrol.

(11.11)   B: There is a garage around the corner.

(11.12)   A: Harold Wilson is out of petrol.

(11.13)   B: That may be the least of his problems, but anyway, what can I do about it?

(12.1)   I've invited everyone.

(12.2)   I've invited everyone in our building to our holiday party.

Bibliography

Almog, Joseph, John Perry, and Howard Wettstein (eds.), 1989. *Themes from Kaplan*. New York: Oxford University Press.

Austin, John L., 1961. *How to Do Things with Words*. Oxford University Press.

Bach, Kent, 2004. Minding the Gap. In Claudia Bianchi (ed.) *The Semantics/Pragmatics Distinction*. Stanford: CSLI Publications, pp. 27–43.

2007. The Excluded Middle: Semantic Minimalism without Minimal Propositions. *Philosophy and Phenomenological Research* 73(2): 435–42.

Barwise, Jon and John Perry, 1983. *Situations and Attitudes*. Cambridge, MA: Bradford/ MIT. Reprinted 1999, Stanford: CSLI Publications.

Bezuidenhout, Anne, 1996. Pragmatics and Singular Reference. *Mind and Language* 11(2): 133–59.

Borg, Emma, 2004. *Minimalist Semantics*. Oxford University Press.

Burks, Arthur, 1949. Icon, Index and Symbol. *Philosophical and Phenomenological Research* 9: 673–89.

Cappelen, Herman and Ernie Lepore, 2005. *Insensitive Semantics*. Oxford: Blackwell.

2007. The Myth of Unarticulated Constituents. In O'Rourke and Washington, 2007, pp. 199–214.

Carnap, Rudolf, 1950. *Logical Foundations of Probability*. University of Chicago Press.

1956. *Meaning and Necessity*, 2nd edn. University of Chicago Press.

Carston, Robyn, 2002. *Thought and Utterances. The Pragmatics of Explicit Communication*. Oxford: Blackwell.

Chastain, Charles, 1975. Reference and Context. In Keith Gunderson (ed.), *Minnesota Studies in the Philosophy of Science*, vol. VII, *Language, Mind and Knowledge*, pp. 194–269.

Clark, Herbert H., 1992. *Arenas of Language Use*. University of Chicago Press.

1996. *Using Language*. Cambridge University Press.

Clark, Herbert and R. Gerrig, 1984. On the Pretense Theory of Irony. *Journal of Experimental Psychology* 113: 121–26.

Corazza, Eros and Jérôme Dokic, 2007. Sense and Insensitivity: Or Where Minimalism Meets Contextualism. In G. Preyer and G. Peter (eds.), *Context-Sensitivity and Semantic Minimalism: Essays in Semantics and Pragmatics*. Oxford University Press, pp. 169–93.

Corazza, Eros and Kepa Korta, 2010. Two Dogmas of Philosophical Linguistics. Unpublished manuscript.

Crimmins, Mark, 1992. *Talk about Beliefs.* Cambridge, MA: Bradford/MIT.

Crimmins, Mark and John Perry, 1989. The Prince and the Phone Booth: Reporting Puzzling Beliefs. *Journal of Philosophy* 86: 685–711. Reprinted in Perry, 2000, Chapter 12.

Donnellan, Keith, 1966. Reference and Definite Descriptions. *Philosophical Review* 75: 281–304.

1970. Proper Names and Identifying Descriptions. *Synthese* 21: 335–58.

1974. Speaking of Nothing. *Philosophical Review* 83: 3–31.

Dretske, Fred, 1981. *Knowledge and the Flow of Information.* Cambridge, MA: Bradford/MIT. Reprinted, Stanford: CSLI Publications, 2000.

Elugardo, Reinaldo and Robert Stainton, 2004. Shorthand, Syntactic Ellipsis and the Pragmatics Determinants of What Is Said. *Mind and Language* 194: 442–71.

Feigl, Herbert and Wilfrid Sellars, 1949. *Readings in Philosophical Analysis.* New York: Appleton-Century-Crofts.

Føllesdal, Dagfinn, 2004. *Referential Opacity and Modal Logic.* New York: Routledge.

Forguson, L. W., 1973. Locutionary and Illocutionary Acts. In I. Berlin *et al.* (1973), *Essays on J. L. Austin.* Oxford University Press, pp. 160–85.

Frege, Gottlob, 1892. Über Sinn und Bedeutung. *Zeitschrift für Philosophische Kritik* n.s. 100: 25–30. Reprinted in Frege, 1962, pp. 40–65.

1918. Der Gedanke. Eine logische Untersuchung. *Beiträge zur Philosophie des deutschen Idealismus* I: 58–77.

1949. On Sense and Nominatum, trans. of Frege, 1892 by Herbert Feigl. In Feigl and Sellars, 1949, pp. 85–102.

1960a. On Sense and Reference, trans. of Frege, 1892. In Frege, 1960b, pp. 56–78.

1960b. *Translations from the Philosophical Writings of Gottlob Frege,* ed. and trans. Peter Geach and Max Black. Oxford: Basil Blackwell.

1962. *Funktion, Begriff, Bedeutung: Fünf logische Studien,* collected and ed. Günther Patzig. Göttingen: Vandenhoeck and Ruprecht.

1967. The Thought: A Logical Inquiry, trans. of Frege, 1918. In *Philosophical Logic,* ed. P. F. Strawson. Oxford University Press, pp. 17–38. This translation, by A. M. and Marcelle Quinton, originally appeared in *Mind* 65 (1956): 289–311.

French, Peter A., Theodore E. Uehuling, Jr., and Howard K. Wettstein, (eds.), 1979. *Contemporary Perspectives in the Philosophy of Language.* Minneapolis: University of Minnesota Press.

Garmendia, Joana, 2007. A Critical Pragmatic Theory for Irony: What an Ironic Utterance Means, and How it Does So. PhD dissertation, University of the Basque Country.

2010. Irony is Critical. *Pragmatics and Cognition* 18(2): 397–421.

Geach, Peter T., 1965. Assertion. *Philosophical Review* 74: 449–65.

1969. The Perils of Pauline. *Review of Metaphysics* 23: 287–300.

Ginzburg, Jonathan and Ivan A. Sag, 2001. *Interrogative Investigations: The Form, Meaning and Use of English Interrogatives.* Stanford: CSLI Publications.

Grice, H. Paul, 1967a. Logic and Conversation. In D. Davison and G. Harman (eds.), 1975, *The Logic of Grammar.* Encino: Dickenson, pp. 64–75. Also in P. Cole and J. L. Morgan (eds.), 1975, *Syntax and Semantics 3: Speech Acts*. New York: Academic Press, pp. 41–58. Reprinted in Grice, 1989: pp. 22–40.

1967b. Further Notes on Logic and Conversation. In P. Cole (ed.), 1978, *Syntax and Semantics 9: Pragmatics*. New York: Academic Press. Reprinted in Grice, 1989, pp. 41–57.

1969a. Utterer's Meaning and Intentions. *Philosophical Review* 78: 147–77. Reprinted in Grice, 1989, pp. 86–116.

1969b. Vacuous Names. In D. Davidson and J. Hintikka (eds.), *Words and Objections*. Dordrecht: Reidel, pp. 118–45.

1981. Presupposition and Conversational Implicature. In P. Cole (ed.), 1981, *Radical Pragmatics*. New York: Academic Press, pp. 183–97. Reprinted in Grice, 1989, pp. 269–82.

1989. *Studies in the Way of Words*. Cambridge, MA: Harvard University Press.

Hume, David, 1748. *An Enquiry Concerning Human Understanding*.

Israel, David and John Perry, 1990. What is Information? In Philip Hanson (ed.) *Information, Language and Cognition*. Vancouver: University of British Columbia Press, pp. 1–19.

1991. Information and Architecture. In Jean Mark Gawron, Gordon Plotkin, and Syun Tutiya (eds.), *Situation Theory and Its Applications*, vol. II. Stanford: CSLI, pp. 147–60.

Israel, David, John Perry, and Syun Tutiya, 1993. Executions, Motivations and Accomplishments. *Philosophical Review* 102: 515–40.

Kaplan, David, 1969. Quantifying In. In D. Davidson and J. Hintikka (eds.), *Words and Objections*. Dordrecht: Reidel, pp. 206–42.

1970. What is Russell's Theory of Descriptions? In Wolfgang Yourgrau and Allen D. Breck (eds.), *Physics, Logic, and History*. New York: Plenum, pp. 277–88. Reprinted in David F. Pears (ed.), 1972, *Bertrand Russell: A Collection of Critical Essays*. Garden City, NY: Anchor Books, pp. 227–44.

1979. *On the Logic of Demonstratives*. In French *et al.* 1979, pp. 401–12. Reprinted in Youngrau, 1990, pp. 11–33.

1989a. Demonstratives. In Almog *et al.*, 1989, pp. 481–563.

1989b. Afterthoughts. In Almog *et al.*, 1989, pp. 565–14.

1990. Words. *Proceedings of the Aristotelian Society Supplementary Volumes* 64: 93–119.

Korta, Kepa, 2008. Review of F. Recanati, *Perspectival Thought: A Plea for (Moderate) Relativism. Notre Dame Philosophical Reviews*, http://ndpr.edu/reviews.cfm.

Korta, Kepa and John Perry, 2006a. Three Demonstrations and a Funeral. *Mind and Language* 21 (2): 166–86.

2006b. Pragmatics. In *The Stanford Encyclopedia of Philosophy* (Winter 2006 ed.), Edward N. Zalta. http://plato.stanford.edu/archives/win2006/entries/pragmatics/.

2007a. How to Say Things with Words. In Savas L. Tsohatzidis (ed.), *John Searle's Philosophy of Language: Force, Meaning, and Thought*. Cambridge University Press, pp. 169–89.

2007b. Radical Minimalism, Moderate Contextualism. In Gerhard Preyer and Georg Peter (eds.), *Context-Sensitivity and Semantic Minimalism. Essays on Semantics and Pragmatics.* Oxford University Press, pp. 94–111.

2007c. Varieties of Minimalist Semantics. *Philosophy and Phenomenological Research* 73(2): 451–59.

2008. The Pragmatic Circle. *Synthese* 165(3): 347–57.

2009. Reference: A New Paradigm. In Jesus M. Larrazabal and Larraitz Zubeldia (eds.), *Meaning, Content and Argument.* Bilbao: UPV-EHU, pp. 73–88.

Kripke, Saul, 1963. Semantical Considerations on Modal Logic. *Acta Philosophica Fennica* 16: 83–94.

1977. Speaker's Reference and Semantic Reference. In P. French *et al.* (eds.), *Contemporary Perspectives in the Philosophy of Language.* Minneapolis: University of Minnesota Press, pp. 6–27.

1980. *Naming and Necessity.* Cambridge, MA: Harvard University Press.

Levinson, Stephen, 2000. *Presumptive Meanings.* Cambridge, MA: Bradford/MIT.

Lewis, David, 1976. Survival and Identity. In A. Rorty (ed.), *The Identities of Persons.* Berkeley: California. Reprinted in his *Philosophical Papers*, vol. I. Oxford University Press, 1983, pp. 55–78.

Marcus, Ruth Barcan, 1946. A Functional Calculus of the First Order Based on Strict Implication. *Journal of Symbolic Logic* 11: 1–16.

1961. Modalities and Intensional Languages. *Synthese* 13: 303–22.

Martí, Genoveva, 1995. The Essence of Genuine Reference. *Journal of Philosophical Logic* 24: 275–89.

O'Rourke, Michael, 1994. Understanding Descriptions. PhD dissertation, Stanford University.

O'Rourke, Michael and Corey Washington (eds.), 2007. *Situating Semantics. Essays on the Philosophy of John Perry.* Cambridge, MA: MIT Press.

Parfit, Derek, 1971. Personal Identity. *Philosophical Review* 80: 3–27. Reprinted in Perry, 1975, pp. 199–223.

Peirce, Charles Sanders, 1931–36. *The Collected Papers, vol. I–VI*, ed. Charles Hartshorne and Paul Weiss. Cambridge, MA: Harvard University Press.

1958. *The Collected Papers, volumes VII and VIII*, ed. Arthur Burks. Cambridge, MA: Harvard University Press.

Perry, John, ed., 1975. *Personal Identity.* Berkeley: University of California Press. Reprinted 2008.

Perry, John, 1986. Thought without Representation. *Proceedings of the Aristotelian Society Supplementary Volumes* 60: 263–83. Reprinted in Perry, 2000, Chapter 3.

1994. Davidson's Sentences and Wittgenstein's Builders. Presidential Address. *Proceedings and Addresses of the American Philosophical Association* 68: 23–37. Reprinted in Perry, 2000, pp. 271–85.

2000. *The Problem of the Essential Indexical*, expanded ed. Stanford: CSLI Publications.

2001a. *Identity, Personal Identity and the Self.* Indianapolis: Hackett Publications.

2001b. *Reference and Reflexivity*. Stanford: CSLI Publications.

Peters, Stanley and Dag Westerståhl, 2006. *Quantifiers in Language and Logic*. Oxford University Press.

Quine, Willard van Orman, 1953. *From a Logical Point of View*. Cambridge, MA: Harvard University Press. Revised ed., 1980.

Recanati, François, 2004. *Literal Meaning*. Cambridge University Press.

2007a. It Is Raining (Somewhere). *Linguistics and Philosophy* 30(1): 123–46.

2007b. *Perspectival Thought: A Plea for (Moderate) Relativism*. Oxford University Press.

Russell, Bertrand, 1905. On Denoting. *Mind* 14: 479–93.

1912. *The Problems of Philosophy*. London: Williams and Norgate. Reprinted 1997, Oxford University Press.

1957. Mr Strawson on Referring. *Mind* 66 (263): 385–89.

Searle, John R., 1968. Austin on Locutionary and Illocutionary Acts. *Philosophical Review* 57(4): 1405–24. Reprinted in I. Berlin *et al.* (eds.), 1973, *Essays on J. L. Austin*. Oxford University Press, pp. 141–59.

1969. *Speech Acts: An Essay in the Philosophy of Language*. Cambridge University Press.

1989. How Performatives Work. *Linguistics and Philosophy* 12: 535–58.

Shannon, Claude E. and Warren Weaver, 1949. *The Mathematical Theory of Communication*. Urbana: University of Illinois Press.

Sider, Ted, 2001. *Four Dimensionalism*. Oxford University Press.

Sperber, Dan and Deirdre Wilson, 1986. *Relevance. Communication and Cognition*. Oxford: Blackwell. Second expanded and revised edn., 1995.

Stainton, Robert, 2006. *Words and Thoughts: Subsentences, Ellipsis, and the Philosophy of Language*. Oxford University Press

Stanley, Jason, 2000. Context and Logical Form. *Linguistics and Philosophy* 23: 391–434.

Strawson, Galen, 2009. *Selves*. New York: Oxford University Press.

Strawson, Peter F., 1950. On Referring. *Mind* 59: 320–44.

1959. *Individuals*. London: Methuen.

1964. Identifying Reference and Truth-Values. *Theoria* 30: 96–118.

1973. Austin and Locutionary Meaning. In I. Berlin *et al.* (eds.), 1973, *Essays on J. L. Austin*, Oxford University Press, pp. 46–68.

Taylor, Kenneth A., 2007. Misplaced Modification and the Illusion of Opacity. In O'Rourke and Washington, 2007, pp. 215–50.

Van Heijenoort, Jean, 1967. *From Frege to Gödel: A Source Book in Mathematical Logic, 1879–1931*. Cambridge, MA: Harvard University Press.

Wettstein, Howard, 1991. *Has Semantics Rested on a Mistake?* Stanford University Press.

Yourgrau, Palle, ed., 1990. *Demonstratives*. Oxford University Press.

Zubeldia, Larraitz, 2010. 'Omen' partikularen azterketa semantikoa eta pragmatikoa. PhD dissertation, University of the Basque Country.

Index

act
  illocutionary, 4, 10, 115, 117, 139
  locutionary, 4, 9, 10, 12, 50, 114–16, 120,
    121, 139
  perlocutionary, 4, 10, 51, 114, 117
action, 2–5, 8, 14, 25, 27, 31, 34, 40–42, 84,
  102, 116, 120, 123, 150, 153, 155, 156,
  158–60, 162
Alaska, 90
ambiguity, 5, 37, 60, 75, 135, 141–43, 161, 162
Angus, 29, 57, 58
Aristotle, 17, 81, 160
Augustine, Saint, 76, 77
Austin, John L., 3–5, 8–10, 17, 50, 114, 116,
  120, 121, 139, 163

Bach, Kent, 146
Barwise, Jon, 5, 6, 75
belief, 2, 3, 5, 10, 12, 22, 32, 34, 39, 42, 43,
  50, 51, 53, 56, 58, 59, 64, 68, 69, 78, 83,
  85, 98, 103, 117, 158–60, 162
  motivating, 40–42, 44, 47, 57, 58, 64, 66,
    78, 84, 95, 105, 108
Biden, Joe, 63
Borg, Emma, 141, 142, 144, 146
Boswell, James, 143
Boxer, Barbara, 90
Burks, Arthur, 19
Bush, George W., 68, 150
  and Cheney in the Oval Office, 64–66

Cappelen, Herman, 108, 110–13, 141, 144,
  146
Carnap, Rudolf, 18, 20, 46
  and the portrait, 47–51
character, 20, 21, 63, 115, 141

Chastain, Charles, 76
Cheney, Dick
  and Bush in the Oval Office, 64–66
  and the portrait, 47–51
Cicero, 13, 19, 22, 43, 56, 86, 88
Cicero, Linda, 131
Clark, Herb, 32, 33, 41, 104, 118
co-reference, 21, 55–75, 76, 77, 80
coco-reference, 58, 76–83, 87, 88
  anaphoric, 77, 78
  convergent, 78
  same name, 75, 77, 78
cognitive fix, 30, 33–35, 39, 40, 42–44, 47, 52,
  56, 64, 66, 70, 84, 88, 96–98, 100, 102,
  106, 129, 130, 132, 136, 137, 147, 164,
  165
Conan Doyle, Arthur, 89
constraint, 6, 7, 12, 28, 31, 151–54, 163
content, 4, 5, 7, 10–12, 20, 21, 23, 40, 57, 58,
  64, 115, 126, 127, 129, 139, 140, 145,
  150, 158, 159, 165
  designational, 95, 96, 100
  informational, 6, 32, 151–54
  locutionary, 59, 114, 115, 117–20, 140, 148,
    163
  locutionary versus propositional, 120–24
  network-bound, 115, 149
  notion-bound, 58
  perception-bound, 160
  referential, 7, 56, 58, 96, 100, 114, 115, 117,
    121, 123, 126, 130–32, 141, 143, 144,
    146, 162
  reflexive, 115, 123, 138, 141–43, 146, 160
  semantic, 112, 113, 141, 142, 144, 146
  speaker-bound, 57, 115, 118, 127, 129, 131,
    132, 149

content (*cont.*)
  utterance-bound, 58, 115, 117, 118, 121–23,
      127, 131, 133, 134, 138, 141–43, 145, 149
contextualism, 108, 109, 140, 141, 143–47
Coolidge, Calvin, 97
Corazza, Eros, 128
Crimmins, Mark, 102
CSLI, 117

demonstrative, 7, 12–14, 20, 30, 36, 44,
      46–58, 60, 62, 71, 72, 75, 83, 84, 86, 100,
      102, 115, 117, 126, 130, 135, 137,
      139, 141
denotation, 16, 19, 21, 90, 93–95, 100
description, 13, 14, 16–23, 30, 36, 37, 45, 46,
      74, 82, 83, 88, 90–102, 117, 126, 132,
      134–37, 139
designation, 90, 92, 94–97, 99, 100, 107, 164
Dole, Bob, 35, 36
Donnellan, Keith, 17–19, 21, 24, 37–39, 76,
      80, 88, 91, 92, 94–97, 101, 139
Donostia, 1, 51, 62
Dretske, Fred, 32
Dupré, John, 75

Elba, 62
Elizabeth, Queen, 108, 109
Elugardo, Reinaldo, 105
Elwood, 5, 6, 61
Etchemendy, John, 75
Ethel, 93, 104, 108, 109, 143–45
execution, 25

Føllesdal, Dagfinn, 18
Feinstein, Dianne, 90
Fiona, 57, 58
Fred, 68, 69, 79, 86–88, 93, 104, 108, 109,
      143–45
  and John Searle, 68–69
Frege, Gottlob, 13–17, 20–22, 55, 119, 131,
      139, 162
Fritchey, Alice, 80
Fritchey, Christopher, 42
Fritchey, Elwood, 42

GDTPA structure, 41–43
Geach, Peter, 18, 119
Ginzburg, Jonathan, 111

Grice's circle, 11, 53, 54, 139, 147–49
Grice, H. Paul, 4, 5, 10, 11, 14, 18, 31, 32, 68,
      108, 115, 116, 118, 125–40, 142, 146,
      147, 158, 161, 163

Holmes, Sherlock, 89, 95
Homer, 77
Hondarribia Airport
  conversation at, 1–4, 8–9, 11, 163
Hume, David, 5, 6, 109
  imagined diary of, 142–43

ILCLI, 51–55, 67, 83, 98, 99
Illinois Politicians' Prison, 44
implicature, 4, 5, 10, 11, 14, 15, 22, 115, 118,
      125, 127–33, 135, 136, 165
index, 29, 30
indexical, 2, 11, 13, 14, 19–23, 30, 36, 46, 55,
      59–73, 75, 84, 85, 100, 102, 114, 117,
      122, 126, 137, 139, 141, 147, 148
information game, 154–58
intention, 2–5, 8–12, 15, 18, 24, 29, 32, 37, 40,
      47, 48, 55, 57–62, 76, 77, 79, 85, 99, 102,
      110, 116, 117, 119, 124, 125, 132, 140,
      141, 143, 146, 148, 162, 163
  auxiliary, 41, 52, 53
  communicative, 4, 10, 13, 31, 66, 92, 95,
      133, 137, 140, 149, 150, 158, 163
  directing, 40–44, 46–48, 50, 52, 59, 64–66,
      68, 78, 102, 164
  grammatical, 40, 41, 164
  Gricean, 23, 92, 97
  implicative directing, 99
  path, 41, 43, 48, 52, 66, 69, 96, 164
  referential, 40, 41, 44, 47, 52, 64, 84
  target, 41, 42, 44, 47, 64, 84, 96, 132, 133,
      164
Israel, David, 5, 6, 32, 67, 68, 137

Joana, 1, 2, 4, 8, 9, 11, 12, 23, 60, 116, 122, 164
Johnson, Samuel, 143
Juno, 88, 89
Jupiter, 88, 89, 112

Kaplan, David, 14, 15, 18, 20–23, 46–48, 60,
      63, 72, 74, 75, 82, 83, 114, 115, 139,
      141
Kaplan, Jordan, 74
Kaplan, Valerie, 74, 82
Karagueuzian, Dikran, 105, 158

Kringle, Kris, 78
Kripke, Saul, 14, 18, 19, 21, 38, 76, 139

Larraitz, 1, 2, 4, 8, 11, 12, 60, 66, 67, 75,
    164–65
Larrazabal Hall, 51, 52, 54, 55, 83, 98
Lepore, Ernie, 108, 110–13, 141, 144, 146
Levinson, Stephen, 11, 139, 147, 148
Lewis, David, 61, 107, 108
Lewis, Galen, 61
Lincoln, Abraham, 62
literalism, 140, 141, 143, 144, 146
Loch Ness, 56–58
Locke, John, 160
logical form, 111, 147
Lucy, 93, 108, 109, 143

Marcus, Ruth B., 18
Martí, Genoveva, 19
Mercury, 89
Mill, John S., 17, 18
minimalism, 108, 109, 141, 143–47
mode of presentation, 30, 88, 126, 127, 130
mono-propositionalism, 158, 160
Muggs, Mr., 44

nambiguity, 37, 60, 74, 77, 83, 117
name, 1–3, 7, 12–14, 16–24, 29, 30, 35–40,
    43–46, 55, 58, 66–68, 74–89, 91, 100,
    102, 114, 116, 117, 126, 130, 134–37,
    139, 141, 157
Napoleon, 61, 62
Nessie, 17, 56, 58
network, 58, 76–82, 86–89, 94, 102, 115, 117,
    122
Nietzsche, Friedrich, 156, 160
notion, 27, 34, 35, 38, 43, 58, 63, 69, 83–85,
    88, 102, 137
    buffer, 27, 28, 31, 39, 51, 52, 63, 65, 69–71,
        84, 102
    detached, 39, 40, 44, 47, 63, 70
    self-, 63, 64, 66, 69

Obama, Barack, 13, 21, 61–63, 76, 108
Obama, Michelle, 13, 21, 108
Oslo, 21
Oswald, Lee Harvey, 41
Oxford, England, 78
Oxford, Nebraska, 78

Palo Alto, 102, 104, 107, 113, 151
Peirce, Charles S., 19
Perry, Frenchie, 104
Perry, Jamaica, 106, 108, 110
Philip, Prince, 108, 109
Philip Morris (commercial), 82
Plato, 76, 77
Plotinus, 77
pluri-propositionalism, 92, 94, 138
pragmatics, 125
Predelli, Stefano, 72
pronoun, 12, 13, 23, 36, 45, 71, 77, 86, 98
Putnam, Hilary, 60

Quine, Willard V. O., 18

Recanati, François, 76, 77, 85, 108, 110, 111,
    140–42
referential plan, 34, 40–45
relevance theory, 126, 138, 141, 146, 147
Ricky, 93, 108, 109, 143
Roberts, Julia, 34, 83–85
role, 6, 25, 26, 28–31, 33, 37, 43, 59, 61–63,
    67, 68, 70, 75, 82, 83, 117, 123, 132, 134,
    149, 153, 156
    epistemic, 28, 30, 38, 39, 42, 47, 50, 51, 60,
        63, 82, 84, 88, 102, 114
    exploited, 40
    linking, 31, 39, 51, 65, 66, 72, 73, 85,
        154–57
    management, 14, 34, 36, 38, 65, 74, 83, 85,
        158
    nesting, 27, 28, 31, 39, 65
    pragmatic, 26, 28, 30, 38, 39, 42, 47, 50, 60,
        88, 102, 114
    target, 40, 41, 64
    transfer, 44, 57, 69, 84
    utterance-relative, 22–24, 28, 60, 64, 75, 84,
        123, 148
Ruby, Jack, 41
Russell, Bertrand, 13, 15–17, 19–22, 46, 55,
    88, 90–93, 131, 136, 139, 162

Sag, Ivan, 103, 111
Santa Claus, 78
Saudi Arabia, 103
Searle, John, 120–23
Shannon, Claude E., 160
Sider, Ted, 61
Sinn, 22, 46, 88

situation, 5, 6, 8, 9, 12, 13, 17, 29, 30, 33, 43,
    44, 49, 51, 59, 64, 70, 73, 75, 77, 83, 84,
    92, 99, 103, 105, 109, 110, 122, 125, 128,
    129, 132, 135, 140, 143, 151, 155, 158,
    159, 164
Smith, Elwood, 71
Socrates, 61
speech act, 9–11, 15, 114, 115, 122–24, 140,
    144, 146, 148
  illocutionary point, 122
  propositional content conditions, 122
Sperber, Dan, 5, 118, 161, 163
SRI, 67
Stainton, Robert, 105
Stanley, Jason, 111
Stotts, Megan, 81
Strawson, Peter F., 17, 20, 93, 157
Stretch, the dog, 131–32
success-conditions, 150, 152–54, 161

Taylor, Ken, 109–10
token, 4, 16, 23, 25, 59, 71, 72, 79, 119
truth-conditions, 7, 13, 15, 22, 38, 53–56, 86,
    89, 93, 104, 105, 112, 132, 148, 160, 163
  designational, 94, 95, 100
  network-bound, 86, 89, 94, 164
  notion-bound, 58
  referential, 5, 7, 55, 57, 86, 89, 94, 102, 105,
    106, 117, 128, 165

reflexive, 5, 7, 54, 121, 145, 148
  speaker-bound, 54–56, 86, 94, 105
  utterance-bound, 7, 54, 55, 86, 94, 117, 122,
    124, 147
Tully, 13, 22, 56, 86–88
Tutiya, Syun, 5

unarticulated constituent, 14, 93, 102–12, 144
Union Station, 43, 44, 47, 56
Urmson, James O., 17
utterance, 8–10, 12–15, 22–25, 28, 33, 34, 36,
    37, 40, 41, 43, 44, 48, 51–60, 62–66, 68,
    69, 71–74, 76–81, 84, 86–89, 91, 93–95,
    97, 100, 102, 104, 105, 108, 109, 112,
    115–18, 120–24, 126–31, 133–35,
    137–42, 144–48, 162–64

Washington, D.C., 13
Watson, Dr. John H., 95
Weaver, Warren, 160
Wettstein, Howard, 17, 30, 39
Wilson, Deirdre, 5, 118, 161, 163
Wilson, Harold, 134, 136, 137
Winkle, Rip Van, 21
Wittgenstein, Ludwig, 162

yeti, 58

www.ingramcontent.com/pod-product-compliance
Ingram Content Group UK Ltd.
Pitfield, Milton Keynes, MK11 3LW, UK
UKHW020326140625
459647UK00018B/2028